Chris Chester

$\mathcal{P}$ROVIDENCE OF A $\mathcal{S}$PARROW

Chris Chester is an electronics
technician and writer. He lives in
Portland, Oregon.

$\mathcal{P}$ROVIDENCE OF A $\mathcal{S}$PARROW

LESSONS FROM A LIFE
GONE TO THE BIRDS

≡ *Chris Chester*

Anchor Books

A DIVISON OF RANDOM HOUSE, INC.

NEW YORK

FIRST ANCHOR BOOKS EDITION, APRIL 2004

Copyright © 2002 by Chris Chester

All rights reserved under International and Pan-American Copyright
Conventions. Published in the United States by Anchor Books, a division
of Random House, Inc., New York. Originally published in hardcover by
The University of Utah Press, Salt Lake City, in 2002.

Anchor Books and colophon are registered trademarks of Random
House, Inc.

The Library of Congress Cataloging-in-Publication Data
Chester, Chris, 1952–
Providence of a sparrow: lessons from a life gone to the birds /
Chris Chester.
      p.   cm.
Originally published: Salt Lake City : University of Utah Press, c2002.
1. English sparrow—Anecdotes.   I. Title.
ISBN: 978-1-4000-3385-0
QL696P264C48 2004
639.9'78887—dc22
2003062988

Author photograph © Amy Ouellette

www.anchorbooks.com

FOR MY PARENTS,
George and Ann

Not a whit, we defy augury; there's a special
providence in the fall of a sparrow.
　　—William Shakespeare, *Hamlet*

Let no one say I love until aware
What huge resources it will take to nurse
One ruining speck, one tiny hair
That casts a shadow through the universe . . .
　　—W. H. Auden

I need only begin with a subject that I fancy, for all subjects are
linked together.
　　—Michel de Montaigne

CONTENTS

ACKNOWLEDGMENTS

SCOTT AND LINDA CHISHOLM—OUR FRIENDSHIP, NOW IN ITS FOURTH decade, has helped sustain me in more than this. I also owe a debt of gratitude to the University of Utah Press and to my friend and editor, the incomparable Dawn Marano. Her early and steadfast interest in this story was instrumental in making it a book. Thanks are due, as well, to my editor at Anchor Books, Alice van Straalen.

And to Rebecca—without whom, nothing.

Providence of a Sparrow

OVER THE YEARS I'VE HAD A RECURRING DREAM REMARKABLE FOR ITS CLARITY and detail. Until recently, it produced no affect other than a pleasant sense upon waking of having spent time in a past more interesting to me now than it was at the time: I'm eight or nine years old and drifting around my Aunt Stella's kitchen, trying not to get in the way. It's Shrove Tuesday, and Stella and my grandmother, both closemouthed women, are quietly rolling out dough, making doughnuts. I like doughnuts, so I'm eager for the first batch to be ready. But closemouthed women prefer closemouthed children—I remain, therefore, seen and not heard. I know that in a few hours I'll walk the twelve blocks home with a couple of doughnut-filled bags, grease turning the brown paper glassy. In the meantime, I watch the canary. And he, from his perch in his small cage by a south-facing window, watches me. He never sings in my presence.

1

B

The kingdom of ornithology is divided into two departments—
birds and English sparrows. English sparrows are not real birds,
they are little beasts.
    —Henry van Dyke, *American Ornithology for the
    Home and School*

I did wonder, if English sparrows were such bad birds, how they
had gotten to America in the first place. To hear my father talk, the
sparrows might have been delivered to the new world by the devil
himself.
    —Calvin Simonds, *Private Lives of Garden Birds*

". . . a whole room to a bird. My, my."
    —Avis

MORNINGS BEGIN WITH "WAR BIRD." USUALLY. SOMETIMES
he's not in the mood or I can't deal with it, drugged as I am from
too little sleep, trying to reacquaint myself with the rigors of consciousness, confused by sunlight flouncing through the windows. But
B's desperate when it's spring and swoops the room, turning, as Yeats
would have it, in a widening gyre. Up to the mirror, tail flicking he
checks, I think, his look. I move to the bed and he to the top of the

towel-draped television. That tail: flick, flick, flick. Wings akimbo, beak parted a little, he assesses my opening gambit in a game that is our first rite of the day. "Bad, messy bird," I say, sweeping my hand back and forth across the bed. "Toss him outside; that's where he belongs. Just *look* at this room; germs, poop, and seed everywhere. To hell with birds, especially house sparrows." More flicks, a quick evacuation to lighten his load, and down he bears in a rush of wings, chirping, nipping my fingers, following quickly and precisely whatever reversals and arcs I make with my hand. I surrender at last, chastened for my slander. B struts atop my lifeless fingers, savoring his win. He dances and bows, chirps and pants. "Fierce, brave bird," I say, "you've slain your enemy, you've bested the foe."

He flies to his water dish to drink, and I sit on the little couch by the window. He'll join me presently and preen, working wing feathers first and then his black bib. Every few seconds he raises his head, scanning for cats and hawks that will never come. Small creatures are cautious, the burden of being prey seldom laid down. During his first year he would flinch when light, glinting from a passing car, moved across the ceiling stirring racial memories of death from above. He has since learned to ignore it. He stretches his wings and combs them with his toes, wing and leg extending completely—a movement that has about it a sense of tai chi forms perfectly rendered. Often he sits on my shoulder to do this, just as often in the palm of my hand or perched on a finger. I can see his tongue, a pointed, triangular affair, working the plumes into the svelte vanes that form each contour feather. His beak reseals the barbules by zipping them together.

His grooming habits are as fascinating to me now as when I first became privy to them. Since his arrival as a naked blob of flesh in my flower beds, he's claimed my attention in a way that few other things ever have. I may be adrift in a limitless universe, but this bird on my shoulder drifts with me. At least once a day I catch him looking at his feet as if he's noticed them for the first time. Three toes in front, one in back, they seem (measured in human terms) large for his body. He looks at his feet, and I look at him, a circumstance more remarkable to my here-and-now than a billion galaxies spiraling outward to some unfathomable denouement. Two citizens of a shared reality eyeing one another's improbable fortune.

A reality my friends find puzzling and my relatives, what's left of them, an eccentric aberration from doting on quadrupeds. My family was always firmly rooted in the feline camp. We were "cat people" spanning four generations, at least. My grandmother's canary and one or two preliminary parakeets she owned were, aside from an occasional dog, the only deviations from our love affair with cats. The first I remember was Elizabeth, a gray ill-tempered menace given to ambushing ankles, shredding expensive draperies, and biting everyone but my father. She disappeared (in answer to my mother's prayers, I suspect) the spring I turned four. The last was sleek, black epileptic Barney whom I discovered in our yard one summer while I was home from college. He was about seven weeks old and using our hedge as a fort from which he'd now and then debouch. Too fey to beg for food, he floated out of reach on the periphery of our vision until I made a contorted leap from a lawn chair and nabbed him skirting by. A few elastic ounces of fur and bone, he squirmed hissing from my hands and fell head first to the paving stones below. We always wondered if his infrequent grand mal seizures were a result of that no doubt painful blow to the skull. He became a good friend and a great favorite of my mother. When she was dying, he spent most days by her side, curled on her bed like a narcoleptic sentinel. He lived another eight years until, his kidneys failing, my father held him in a towel and wept as the vet rang the curtain down.

Prufrock might have been better served measuring out his life in the lives of his pets rather than with coffee spoons. Or, maybe not. I've lost eating utensils and remained unshattered. It is clear to me that a great dividing line runs through my time: Before B and after B.

≡

I WASN'T EXPECTING A LIFE-ALTERING EVENT TO COME MY WAY, A deus ex machina to drop from the stage rafters and resolve issues of meaning and direction in a world I've frequently thought in need of less wrenching plots. Nor is this what B represents. In fact, to the extent I view him metaphorically, it is as a model of self-possession unblemished by artifice or facade. Like the Old Testament God he might with perfect justice say, "I am that I am." Deities and beasts inhabit themselves free from the heartache of coveting a plausible alternative; humans mostly work on their masks. Having finagled our way to the top of the food chain, we find the view from the summit soothing and assume mastery for ourselves of all things seen and unseen. B reminds me gently I'm more or less an idiot. When he brings a toy, drops it in my hand, and nudges around asking for a game, I think of Thoreau's words on being affected by a mosquito's faint hum, "There was something cosmical about it; a standing advertisement, till forbidden, of the everlasting vigor and fertility of the world." Once in a while the tent flap falls open. If these glimpses are fraudulent, our spiritual leg pulled by renegade neurons, they're delusions worth cultivating when they point the way, however briefly, past dishes in the sink and beyond all the quotidian fretting that gobbles up so much of our lives. I may be misinformed, but I believe my time with B is filled with such glimpses. I hate to describe these moments as "transcendent" or "numinous," so let's just say they've been tranquil enough to hint at the divine. Very different from an underwear-staining encounter with a twitchy god in a flaming bush (an image of which I formed from the benign Episcopalianism in which I was raised) or from the exhilarating but frightening suspicion that creation itself is too unlikely to be true. As a child, I'd lie in bed and sense in the filigree of lapsing consciousness that comes with approaching sleep an unsettling enormousness stationed forever beyond reach or comprehension, a barrier, I now realize, of metaphysical imponderables welded together to form an overwhelming composite of everything I will never know. Many of my concerns fell into the "expanding universe" category like those plaguing Woody Allen's prepubescent alter ego in *Radio Days.* I was a depressed kid.

When B arrived, I was forty-one years old, engaged to Rebecca, and hoping to rise finally above the low-level angst I'd been living with all my life. I avoided taking antidepressants (viewing their use as vaguely unsportsmanlike), as if failing to overcome depression without chemical assistance were tantamount to cheating, an admission of failure on the part of my psyche to configure itself into something healthier. Better, it seemed, to endure a known quantity than to muck about inducing change on that little island of awareness I take to be myself. After all, depression can be as much a defining characteristic as any other mental state. When it came to taking pills, the old philosophical chestnut seemed to apply: "If I were someone else, would I still be me?" I knew all this to be nonsense, but early conditioning dies hard. My father said to me when I was eleven or twelve, "What have you got to be depressed about?" I had loving parents, a roof over my head, and food in my stomach. The logic of his question seemed unassailable. I don't think either of my parents ever considered or were even aware of the distinction between situational depression (Granny just died in a silo explosion) versus the free-floating variety (this beautiful, sunny day appears to me a dark emblem of what, exactly, I cannot say).

Baseline for me had always been slightly below sea level. Too modest a depth in which to drown but deep enough to suggest what life must be like for those truly debilitated by anxiety and sadness that doesn't go away. I suspect my mother and I had this in common and that her rather nonspecific complaints of "not feeling well" I recall from childhood were tendrils snaking out from that buried root. She died of cancer when I was twenty-three, long before I developed enough compassion and insight to know her better. A pity, it's likely we'd have found lots to discuss.

B, for example. The joy I take in him mingled with undercurrents of foreboding over that inevitable time when I shall lose him. If nothing else, depression teaches understanding of brevity as an ironic constant—that what endures also flits by, that if we bear the mark of Cain it is in our awareness of temporary gain followed by eternal loss. The trick is to largely ignore this fact along with the fear of losing who and what we love, even those things likely to outlast us. Goethe's Faust has it about right when he says:

> Though nothing happens, dread you always feel,
> What you never lose, you mourn throughout your life.

THE AVERAGE AMERICAN SEES THOUSANDS OF B'S KIND EVERY YEAR: house sparrows, English sparrows, or, as the Audubon people refer to them, "Pesky Brown Jobs." (Native sparrows such as Vesper sparrows, chipping sparrows, lark sparrows, etc., merit the less pejorative appellation "Little Brown Jobs") *Passer domesticus:* small, drab birds chattering in bushes. Inexorable hordes of bird-feeder plunderers. Gamins, tramps, hoodlums. Dirty, ubiquitous beggars, sidewalk-fouling avian thugs that push out "desirable birds" and steal when they can the souls of children. In league with starlings and pigeons, the other winged felons flapping through our cities, they work fast-food parking lots and city parks. They infest every neighborhood and build in every cranny their inelegant nests. Bane, pariah, miscreant. Disease-carrying vermin, parasite-ridden destroyers of crops and the American way of life. Antichrist with a beak. This from *Birds of America* published in 1936 and edited by T. Gilbert Pearson: "The English Sparrow among birds, like the rat among mammals, is cunning, destructive and filthy." In a used bookstore some years ago, I ran across the beguiling title *Befriending Backyard Animals*. Checking the index for *sparrow, house,* I was led to a four-page entry devoted to killing them.

B and I move together well. From long association, I've developed what Rebecca and I refer to as "B Consciousness," a state of being (pun intended) formed around the principle of never shifting my weight unless I know exactly where the bird is—an ethic that can be difficult to impress upon visitors: No casual sitting down, standing up, or rearranging your ass on the sofa. No heedless sallying forth. From B's point of view our physical construction must seem more than a little freakish: Great lumbering things thousands of times his mass. No wings, knees inverted wrongly, the agility of boulders. He, on the other hand, is less than six inches long, weighs twenty-five grams, and trusts me completely. That I've clocked him moving near the speed of light introduces a troublesome variable. At rest he can be invisible, seemingly able to blend into *any* background. Time and again I've looked right at him and been unaware of the fact.

Eager to hop onto my hand or up to my shoulder, B is generally waiting on the screen door frame as I enter his room. If not, I direct my gaze to the hilt of the sword that hangs on the wall to the left, or to the ceramic gremlin on the side of the bookcase, or to the plastic container where Cheerios are kept. But never to either of the ficus trees that form the primary sources of flora in his room. In contradiction of Robert Louis Stevenson's assertion that "trees are the most civil society," B avoids them consistently, as if landing in one would violate a sacred oath or point of honor. We thought he would like trees, that they would make a nice counterpoint to the human conventionality of the room it-self, cater to the avian imperative to perch aloft and be hidden. A simi-lar thing happened with the tray I filled with organic topsoil and pre-sented thinking he'd use it for the kind of dust bathing that wild sparrows enjoy. No sale. Nor did he approve of a planter of sprouts I furnished in the mistaken belief that he'd enjoy having fresh greens to nibble. This, like the trees, affronted his urbanity. I apologized eventu-ally and removed it.

B lies drowsing in my hand. He opens and shuts his eyelids slowly and yawns in bird time (avian yawns happen quickly, unlike our protracted, toothy gapes), his head droops and nods as if he's fighting the effect of a long-winded sermon. He eases into his nap, scapular feathers fluffed and forming a mantilla into which he may decide to tuck his beak. Even in the weak winter light seeping into the room, his colors astonish me. Russet brown and tan, silver, black, white, and gray. Other hues resistant to naming. No ruby of the hummingbird's throat nor blue jay iridescence, no rioting with the spectrum as some parrots do. His are the shades of subtle intimation, the perfection of understated tones. I've held him to my ear as he sleeps and heard his heart's tarantella try to outpace the same eternity overtaking us all. It is difficult for me to understand the vehemence with which these birds are detested. Since my association with B began, I find it increasingly difficult to hate much of anything.

ALTHOUGH SOME AUTHORITIES NOW PLACE THEM IN A SEPARATE category, house sparrows belong to the family Ploceidae and are actu-ally weaverbirds native to Eurasia and North Africa. The term "spar-row," however, pertained originally to any small bird. When European settlers arrived in North America and began naming wildlife, it's likely they applied the term to those birds that reminded them of the house sparrow. Given the similar morphology and coloration (native spar-rows tend, overall, to be more uniformly brown), such taxonomic im-precision is understandable and, to the average person, unimportant.

House sparrows, by most accounts, made their North American debut in the early 1850s with Brooklyn, New York, serving as the site where they were first released. Assigning blame is more difficult for what must, to the inveterate house sparrow hater, seem a cataclysmic event. One report has a homesick Englishman, Nicholas Pike, liberating fifty birds he'd brought back from England. Other sources fault Spanish immigrants who liked to sit in parks but were dainty about caterpillars dropping into their laps from trees as they did so. Accordingly, they had eight pairs of house sparrows trapped in London and shipped posthaste to Brooklyn. How quickly these eight pairs and their offspring were expected to solve the caterpillar problem is unknown. A variation of the tale has it that house sparrows were imported to control the fruit- and foliage-eating cankerworm. In other renditions, anonymous persons released, for reasons unspecified, an indeterminate number of birds in 1850, 1851, or 1852 in, of course, Brooklyn. In truth, there were multiple releases of imported house sparrows during the latter half of the nineteenth century that, in the aggregate, resulted in the established population we have today. Were it possible to determine the precise location where the first release took place, I'd make it my business to pilgrimage there.

None of these stories have the wacky romanticism behind the starling's introduction into America by a group calling itself the American Acclimatization Society whose stated goal was to bring into the United States every species of bird mentioned in Shakespeare's plays. Thus, the line from *Henry IV*, "Nay, I'll have a starling be taught to speak nothing but Mortimer" became, as it were, the starling's passage to these shores and an 1890 release in New York's Central Park. Still, I like Nicholas Pike and his sparrows best. Were I to expend the effort, it might be possible to track down a picture of Mr. Pike. Probably a daguerreotype of a man wary of the technology about to capture his image. I expect his face would stare out with that expression of grim bemusement worn by most nineteenth-century photographic subjects, an image of monochromatic inscrutability that the passage of time seems to confer on the long dead. For reasons known only to the vagaries of my imagination, I think of him in life as rich, tubercular, and lonely—all irrelevant to whatever essence in the man drove him to his odd solution to the problem of homesickness. Whim, perhaps, or the bottle, but I prefer to think he chose something that represented for him not only an essential part of life in England but also a link between human life and the rest of creation. Alone among birds, the house sparrow has forsaken a "natural habitat." And, having cast its lot with ours, lives where we live and nowhere else. Thus, if the owl, as Athena's familiar, is the bird of wisdom and the bluebird the harbinger of happiness, and if crows are raucous, jays saucy, and magpies thieving, then surely the house sparrow is the people's bird.

But it would be unfair not to acknowledge complaints against the house sparrow. The basic indictment involves a syllogism: Only native species belong here. House sparrows aren't native. Therefore, house sparrows don't belong here. And its corollary: Exotic species upset the balance of nature. House sparrows in North America are an exotic species. Therefore, house sparrows upset the balance of nature. There's some truth in these assertions.

Let's try another syllogism: Only native species belong here. European settlers (including those who imported and released Old World birds) are not native. Therefore, European settlers (and their descendants) don't belong here. Nor, for that matter, do "Native Americans" who simply traipsed onto the continent before that convenient land bridge from Asia was swamped by the sea. The corollary to this is also disturbing: Exotic species upset the balance of nature. Settlers are an exotic species. Therefore, *we* upset the balance of nature. Turns out there is plenty of truth to go around, but as T. S. Eliot put it, "Go, go, go said the bird: human kind cannot bear very much reality."

Fortunately, it's now generally recognized as dangerously foolish to introduce a species into a niche it wasn't meant to inhabit or, more to the point, introduce a life form into an ecosystem that hasn't evolved defenses against it: English rabbits denuding large swaths of Australian outback; Nile perch destroying the ecological balance of Lake Victoria and resulting in the eradication of the much smaller tilapia upon which native fishermen depended for their livelihood; an Asian fungus, Endothia parasitica, that arrived in North America in the first decade of the twentieth century and began killing off the American chestnut tree with an eventual mortality rate of 100 percent—to name but three examples. The theory of unintended consequences is a harsh taskmaster. Of course, species migrate without direct human intervention. Killer bees heading north from South America are a famous example. Sometimes humans provide the means without conscious intent. Brown rats carrying fleas that were vectors for the bubonic plague bacillus are a case in point. The rats hitched rides on trading ships, and millions of people died as a result. Interestingly, recent scholarship has questioned whether the disease that devastated medieval Europe was, in fact, bubonic plague. Historians point to a scarcity of contemporary accounts from the period describing epizootic rats dying from the disease. They are also troubled by how quickly the contagion appears to have spread compared to modern transmission rates of bubonic plague— often by rats and their fleas. This, despite much slower methods of transportation in the fourteenth century than what's available now. Nevertheless, something uncommonly lethal followed the trade routes, as did diseases such as smallpox that later accompanied New World settlers and annihilated native populations whose immune systems hadn't evolved an effective defense.

With our unsurpassed ability to manipulate the environment and hasten by orders of magnitude processes that might have played out anyway but at a much more leisurely pace, human beings are a force of nature that tends to produce unnatural results. Excluding, let's say, the impact of an asteroid, nothing leads more quickly to extinction than people extending their range. And even though such shopworn observations have been in vogue for some time, the lessons involved have not, I fear, significantly minimized the impact of humanity's collective gluttony—or of my own when it comes down to it. That I drive cars, buy a lot of overpackaged crap, and continue to eat meat are good examples of behavior failing to conform to belief.

Of course, most living things are busy and destructive when it suits their perceived or immediate interest. I have two maple trees alongside the house intent upon prying up my sidewalk with their roots. I don't believe their vandalism is conscious, but I do believe it serves their need to make a living from the soil. These trees exploit their niche and have, if not the "right" to do so, then certainly the excuse of life blindly seeking to maintain itself. Without descent into farce, I doubt a similar dispensation can be applied to human activities such as razing a copse to make way for a strip mall. Aside from whatever antiraping-of-the-environment arguments can be brought to bear in support of this assertion, it seems to me a poor aesthetic bargain to give up trees (and nesting sites) as a method of meeting our pressing shortage of ear-piercing salons and venues specializing in driftwood clocks.

B stands high on my chest as I laze on the sofa. He's evaluating hairs in my nose and thinking of pulling one. We've been down this road before. He's aware, of course, of my policy against having anything stolen from my nostrils. But under the circumstances, the thing that concerns me is his ability to bide his time in pursuit of a goal. He can be as patient as a cat waiting for a mouse to emerge from a hole and has been known to wait an hour or more for my vigilance to wane. Also to be considered is his apparent belief that what I want and what I shall have are two entirely different things. His tactical sense is sophisticated, as is his love of sport for its own sake. The question now is whether or not I'll be losing a nose hair in this game he invented and drafts me into playing at least once a week. Experience suggests that I will.

House sparrows—sturdy, numerous, and highly intelligent—have probably made life more difficult for some native birds. These competitive advantages, so valued in ourselves, are viewed by house sparrow detractors as profound character flaws. Many backyard birders hoping to attract a variety of species to their feeders are driven to distraction by the preponderance of house sparrows showing up for a handout. They resent the tendency of the house sparrow to dominate the housing market they share with other cavity-nesting birds such as the purple martin. A male house sparrow can be aggressive and very persistent in securing a nesting site. He's not above evicting existing tenants—unlike those bashful Europeans who showed such remarkable tact when relieving Native Americans of the drudgery of looking after two large continents. To quote once again from *Birds of America:* "Not infrequently he [the house sparrow] attacks Robins, Song Sparrows, Chickadees, Flycatchers, Thrushes, Tanagers, and other birds, while they are feeding and [I love this] annoys them by repeated calls at their homes." Doesn't that conjure up an irresistible image of house sparrows in bad suits selling encyclopedias door to door?

I mean Mr. Pearson no disrespect; by his lights, he called 'em as he saw 'em and was certainly far more knowledgeable about birds than I can ever hope to be. He served at one time as president of the National Association of Audubon Societies. I'm confident that he genuinely loved birds, and to his credit included in an article on American sparrows, towhees, and longspurs appearing in the March 1939 issue of *National Geographic* a picture of a New York City policeman giving a sip of water to a prostrate house sparrow overcome by heat. But I do wonder how much time Pearson spent actually observing house sparrows. In the years I've been putting seed outside for neighborhood birds, I have yet to see a house sparrow harass another species. They behave with unfailing politeness at the feeder, sharing items on the menu with wrens, junkos, and whatever else happens to show up. Rows, when they occur, are limited to internecine squabbling and lovers' spats. Now and then there's an ownership dispute over a piece of bread I've tossed out. Blue jays descending like Thor's hammer are the ones that prove to be a trifle overbearing. Maybe those who swear they've seen house sparrows armed with crossbows and axes driving off everything from emus to eagles are dealing with a subspecies mysteriously descended from Visigoths. On the other hand, perhaps I get only well-bred birds whose ids are kept in check by the surfeit of food with which I stock my feeder. Pearson, it seems to me, took a received body of wisdom—the idea that house sparrows are sociopathic pests—and did his part to enshrine it as fact. Things haven't changed a great deal in the sixty-plus years since publication of *Birds of America.*

Checking the Internet for information on house sparrows leads to dozens of sites hostile to this bird. One, maintained by "Dead Sparrow Productions," uses as its logo a cartoon bird that has, not to put too fine a point on it, fallen off the twig. These friendly folks sell starling and house sparrow traps. While they don't explicitly recommend a "final solution," the implication is obvious. The less said the better about a half-wit in the Midwest with a .22-caliber rifle and an interest in cyberspace. Judging from the website he maintains as a vehicle for recording his exploits, it appears that his life revolves around assassinating house sparrows when they land at his feeder. I suppose it's too much to hope that he'll thin the herd one day by accidentally shooting himself. Most people who have a problem with house sparrows try to enforce a policy of exclusion. Putting up birdhouses with entrances too small for a house sparrow to enter is one strategy. Not putting food outside in winter is another. Individual house sparrows maintain small territories and avoid nesting in areas that don't provide year-round support. Only one web site, "Backyard Birds of Winter in Nova Scotia," was refreshingly benign. It does, however, mention the house sparrow's reputed role in the decline of the eastern bluebird.

To the extent that house sparrows have contributed to diminishing numbers of other species, I am truly sorry. But human activity (hunting, power lines, automobiles, farming, pollution, direct destruction of habitat, etc.) and predation by domestic cats result in the deaths of millions of birds every year. These menaces are far more potent than anything house sparrows bring to bear. Even the charge that house sparrows are agricultural pests seems to me tenuous. Ironic too, if, as mentioned above, people imported them to help control crop-destroying insects. As a largely urban bird, it prefers cities to fields. Adult house sparrows are vegetarian and eat primarily seeds and grain, some, undoubtedly, stolen from farmers by those birds living in rural communities. But there is a quid pro quo: baby house sparrows are fed mostly on insect larvae, often of species that eventually attack maturing crops.

When I walk out onto my porch in the morning, house sparrows swoop down. They land in the rhododendron bush, in the tree out front, on the fence around my yard. There seems to be a core group of thirty to thirty-five birds, a loose confederation of tribes. Sometimes they all show up, some days only a few. I say "Morning, ladies," and "Howdy, boys." We regard one another for a minute or two before they rematerialize at the feeding area and begin eating. I've noticed they frequently delay breakfast until after I show up. They've seen me run cats from the yard, fill up the bath, and scatter seed. Maybe I symbolize the good things in life. Maybe their sense of decorum requires the simple courtesy of acknowledging their host. When the feeder is empty, two or three delegates stand on the porch rails looking in the windows. It wouldn't surprise me if they ring the doorbell one day. I think this circumstance suggests interesting possibilities for those waiting in sorrow and anger for bluebirds to arrive.

≈

MY WIFE'S PATERNAL GRANDMOTHER WENT AWAY DUMBFOUNDED. She'd come with her daughter for a visit a few months before my marriage to Rebecca. It was the first time she'd been to the house. After a tour of the downstairs she opted to sit with me in the living room while Rebecca and her aunt went upstairs to work at the computer. Avis (for those who remember a smattering of Latin, I'm not kidding about her name) and I made polite conversation. She talked about a set of lace curtains she might be prepared to part with as a wedding gift, but "Somebody would have to be real nice to me," she said. "Real nice." Eventually, she asked about the bird. "What kind is it?" "Where did you find it?" "Real tame, you say?"

She listened, but seemed dubious, as I gave her the abbreviated version of the story I recite for guests. It's well rehearsed and amusing enough to arouse most people's interest, and with a little cajoling I was able to persuade Avis to go upstairs and see B for herself. A slender woman with a round face and dark eyes that fought the slyness of her smile for prominence, she stood just inside the bird-room door, tentative, the way people act who believe bats are about to become tangled in their hair. Wilbur, her first husband and an abusive alcoholic, nearly burned their house to the ground one evening many years before. Tired of him blustering around drunk, Avis snatched his bottle of Jack Daniels from the sideboard and hurled it into the street before legging it, a couple of daughters in tow, downhill to the comparative safety of the neighborhood market. In a fit of dipsomaniacal pique, Wilbur then carted Avis's clothing from bedroom to basement—piled dresses, skirts, blouses, and underwear on the floor and doused them with gasoline. Before he got around to applying a match, hesitant perhaps because it occurred to him he now lacked an audience, the water heater's pilot light ignited the fumes and a conflagration ensued that sent him scurrying from the house and into his car. As he drove down the hill (oblivious, I imagine, to the idiocy reflected in the flames he was leaving behind) he passed his loved ones hightailing it back up, inspired to go home by the sound of sirens and by reports from Rebecca's father, a teenager at the time, who had tried reasoning with Wilbur until the old man introduced the gas motif. Wilbur did, however, rally around eventually with the trenchant observation, "I guess we'll have to rebuild the house," uttered as the reunited family watched the fire department hosing down the remains. I never met Wilbur, but based on his legend in the existing oral tradition, it is my belief he would, even when sober, have considered his behavior a prudent, conservative means of dealing with marital strife and an acceptable method of self-expression. Rebecca appears to have weathered the strands of her grandfather's DNA careening around inside her, and so far we've been relatively blaze free.

Because it sounds like a poorly crafted dramatic contrivance tacked on for effect, I hesitate to mention that a mixed colony of between thirty and forty canaries and parakeets perished in Wilbur's Folly. Left in the basement where many of them had been born and raised, they came with the house, the original owner either unable or unwilling to move them when he vacated. Wilbur and Avis kept the birds as curiosities, as entertainment for their kids. Perhaps becoming "tentative" is how Avis coped with an unpredictable world.

B, wary of a newcomer, flew reconnaissance loops, then landed on my shoulder. Bird and guest studied one another. I prattled. Like the singing frog in the old Warner Brothers cartoon, B refused not only to sing an aria but also to do much more than stare at Avis while bristling his crown (an indication he viewed the situation as potentially danger-ous) and flicking his tail. He declined the bits of cookie I placed in her hand as a bribe. He's like that. Moody.

Avis turned to me as we left the room and said in her pleasant West Virginia drawl while slowly shaking her head, "You gave a whole room to a bird. My, my."

2

FOUNDLING

I think I could turn and live awhile with the animals . . .
    they are so placid and self-contained.
I stand and look at them sometimes half the day long.
They do not sweat and whine about their condition,
They do not lie in the dark and weep for their sins,
They do not make me sick discussing their duty to God,
Not one is dissatisfied . . . not one is demented with the
    mania of owning things,
Not one kneels to another nor to his kind that lived
    thousands of years ago,
Not one is respectable or industrious over the whole earth.
    —Walt Whitman, "Song of Myself"

I WONDER WHAT HE THOUGHT AS HE FELL. IT WAS A LONG DROP FOR a small bird, for most things other than windblown seeds. Twenty-five feet or more from the eaves of my house. I wonder if his naked wings flapped, his will to fly failing the instinct. Then the abrupt earth and cold wait in the dying irises. It was a rainy Sunday in Portland, Oregon, June 1993.

Birds, as far as their young are concerned, come in two varieties. Ducks and chickens, for example, are precocial species, able at birth to more or less fend for themselves. As soon as the downy feathers they're hatched with dry out, the chicks are able to follow their mothers and feed on their own. House sparrows, on the other hand, are altricial. They are born, like us, helpless and bare.

My compassion having been hobbled by childhood memories of failed bird rescues, I almost decided to let B meet his fate without assistance from me. I remembered shoe boxes with plucked-up grass as padding, inappropriate offerings of bread and worms. The tiny, inevitable corpse come morning. Most of them we buried by our mulberry tree.

Because I'm averse to lice and all manner of pathogens and parasites with which wild birds are rumored to teem, I was really quite hesitant about picking B up. I believed for about a week at the age of six that I had parrot fever, a disease my father had mentioned in some forgotten context shortly before an encounter I had with a baby robin. My parents cleared up my misapprehension by pointing out that robins aren't parrots and that by my own admission I felt perfectly fine.

I remember my indecision clearly, am troubled by it. I could have chosen wrongly, and my life would have tacked in a different direction. I'd be unaware that a remarkable mind had died in my yard.

WE'D NO IDEA WHAT TO DO FOR A BABY BIRD, BUT REBECCA AND I took him inside. His eyes were unopened, his body bulbous and pink with only a few incipient quills along his wings to suggest what would soon be primary flight feathers. He looked like a testicle with a beak attached.

Because mammals instinctively believe milk to be the great panacea for all infant nutritional needs, Rebecca warmed some in the microwave while I searched for an eyedropper. After prying open B's mouth, we squirted a few drops down the hatch(ling), but he sputtered and turned his head away; most of the milk dribbled from his beak.

Next we tried canned cat food. We buy an expensive brand composed, if my analysis is accurate, of fish rectums packed in some sort of urine. It appalls the eye and bludgeons the nose. A pinkish dollop of reeking putrefaction, it's the jewel of the food processing industry's blackest art. Our cats wish to be buried in it. B, however, more or less gagged. Certainly what I'd have done in his place.

"Don't try milk or cat food, they can't handle it," Craig informed us when we got him on the phone and explained the situation. Craig, a veterinary technician and friend of a friend, was knowledgeable and gracious. He's a compact man with thinning hair, and I enjoy watching his hands as he speaks, his fingers moving with the patient dexterity of the jewelry maker his family's business trained him to be. Over the years, often while living in tiny apartments, he has nursed a large number of birds back to health, mostly pigeons. "What you need to do is get yourself a can of puppy food, something pretty mealy and smooth. If you can get him to eat that, your bird might have a chance. And you need to keep it warm. I'd rig up a box with a heating pad set on low. Other than that, there's not a lot you can do right now. Don't be surprised if he doesn't make it."

I ended up buying Blue Mountain Puppy Food. Compared with the glop we serve our cats, its bouquet is divine. Its texture reminds me of the extruded ham loaves that put in appearances at family picnics when I was a child. A delicacy that now strikes me as an indeterminate, protomolecular form of matter, more a precursor to food than something edible in the classical sense. I consumed it with gusto, which, to our relief, is what B eventually did with the puppy food.

Rebecca found a shallow cardboard box in the basement while I was at the store and outfitted it with a heating pad covered by a towel. It's a funny thing about birds; they're warm blooded (homeothermic) exactly like mammals, but altricial species are born cold blooded (poikilothermic) and for the first few days of their lives need to be brooded. Parental body heat keeps them warm until their chemical engines turn over and the ability to regulate their own temperature begins. Failure to provide the necessary warmth is a primary reason why amateurs have scant success keeping nestlings alive.

By the time I returned from the store, Rebecca had placed B in his new quarters. She arranged the towel in a way that afforded privacy beneath an overhanging flap, an important detail to a bird at a stage of life when eating and hiding are its principal concerns. Squatting in his corner, he looked like an over-the-hill boxer waiting for the next weary round to begin. I can't say whether his composure was bred of fear (If I don't move maybe they won't eat me), resignation (Why struggle? Fate has spoken), or denial (I only dreamt falling from the nest, I'm still bunged in with the rest of my clan). I suspect that instinct told him to keep still so as not to draw attention to himself. I imagine also he was close to death.

To no immediate effect, I fetched a round toothpick from the cupboard, nipped off one of the pointed ends and gobbed it up with a dab of puppy food. Whereas human infants grope for the teat, baby birds gape—as we all know from watching nature programs on television. In addition to the sometimes luminous colors inside their throats, the bills of the young in many species are bright yellow and make a striking target at which the caterers aim. Their beaks are also unnaturally wide, the sides stretched laterally in order to form a larger pocket for collecting whatever the parents have gathered on their latest foraging trip. In the case of house sparrows, it's often an insect. Studies indicate that as much as two-thirds of a baby house sparrow's diet consists of bugs or bug larvae. One day last spring I spotted what turned out to be a female house sparrow flying erratically a couple of hundred feet in front of my car. I thought she was injured, judging from the way she gained and lost altitude and flapped madly like a shotgunned pheasant. Before she turned left onto a side street, however, I got close enough to see that she was pursuing a large moth as it made a good show of fleeing for its life. It likely began its long slog into eternity as a dinner guest back at the nest.

It's interesting to note that small passerines such as sparrows make *hundreds* of feeding visits to their nests each day and typically lose a significant percentage of their body weight by the time breeding season is over. For some migratory birds that shortly after summer's end must fly thousands of miles to reach their winter quarters, the need to recover strength and body mass before departure is critical. It can mean the difference between making landfall and dying at sea. "Zugdisposition" is the term for this gorging process that builds up fat reserves before these birds begin their journey. Every autumn I listen for Canada geese honking their way south and on clear nights sometimes watch the sacred vee piercing moonlight—a journey more important to the sanity of the world than any possible destination, a vision of which the least rural among us still carry in our bones. I always wish them well, and mouth a prayer to the god of anonymous lives on behalf of all small, less glamorous birds entering their own vast stretches of darkness.

House sparrows never bought into the migration concept, are year-round residents preferring the rigors of winter to the inconvenience and danger of moving twice a year. When, in midwinter, I see them huddling wet and dejected in our arbor vitae, I wonder if they regret their species' policy of staying put for the winter. If they wish they'd taken wing and followed the sun.

We dangled puppy food in B's face for a minute or two without getting a response. I began to think he was too far gone, neither strong enough nor scrappy enough to fight for his life. Rebecca and I were discussing the pros and cons of trying to force-feed him, and debating whether or not to get Craig back on the phone when, in a sudden eagerness to eat, B came to life and took half the toothpick down his throat. I can't imagine why organs weren't pierced. It was like watching someone make a spontaneous decision to embark on a sword-swallowing career. Lunging upward to meet the food rather than sit, mouth open, waiting for the food to come to him, B ate seven or eight large portions, cheeping madly between each one. He finally subsided with a satisfied wheeze and sat nodding in his corner, bloated and somnolent, with a hint of feather fuzz sticking up on his head. We arranged the overhanging towel into a makeshift tent, placed the box on a high shelf, and left him alone to sleep off his meal.

Thus began a series of feedings we were obliged to deliver at twenty- to thirty-minute intervals during daylight hours. This continued for a week or so in a predictable pattern of B gorging himself and then lapsing into silence. But his incredibly efficient digestive system soon nudged him back into consciousness and an acute awareness of returning hunger. He'd announce his needs with tentative chirps that were quickly superseded by full-throated shrieks. We'd come running, toss back his towel, and top him off. Once in a while he'd sleep for half an hour or more after feeding, a worrisome departure from routine that always frightened me into thinking he'd died. It took days until I stopped being surprised by his persistence in living from one moment to the next. I'd tiptoe to his box, lift the flap gently, and inevitably trigger another vigorous plea for food. I was so fascinated by him, though, I couldn't stop myself. Perhaps helpless things are compelling because we're all vulnerable, our faith in strength, vigor, and immortality a kind of pocket change that's quickly spent.

B sits on my shoulder as I type. In my absence, the constructions "zxg" and "wqe" appeared on the screen. The keyboard attracts him. He enjoys pecking the keys, is fond of composing sentences in an unpronounceable, consonant-cluttered language. Anyone who's ever tried sounding out Welsh place-names understands the difficulty I have in trying to parse these statements of his. He glances at the monitor as he works, aware of cause and effect between changes on the screen and what he does with his beak. If I could decipher his orthography, I'd present the world with an interspecies Rosetta stone. He has entered prosperous middle age, a recognition that ignites in me a frisson of despair. He is no longer positively young.

Their voices raised in lamentation, our cats began throwing themselves against the basement door. "I called thy name, O Lord, out of the low dungeon," they seemed to wail. We'd locked all three of them down there when we brought B into the kitchen after finding him in the yard. They'd begun to eddy about the way cats do (that felines lack prominent dorsal fins has always struck me as an unfortunate oversight), the scent of something easily killed and eaten coaxing them out of their housebound lethargy. All had lengthy conviction records involving unauthorized food removal from counters and tables.

We released the cats but moved B upstairs into the front bedroom, which served at that time as Rebecca's study. We placed his box on her desk and plugged in the heating pad. It was getting on toward dusk, and objects in the room were deconstructing into toe-stubbing blobs that wait in the gloaming. I remember standing there fearful of night's ability to part body and soul. It was hard to resist lifting the flap one more time, to look again for the rise and fall of B's tiny chest. Since I'm not above taking refuge in aphorisms, to this day I often slip into B's room at night to check his vital signs. If water in the watched pot never boils, the watched bird might never die.

B awoke at first light. A barely audible murmuring came from his room, the overture to a pathetic cheeping that segued into an apoplectic tantrum when I turned over in bed and caused our box springs to squeak. I was truly surprised he was still alive, said as much to Rebecca. What she and I hadn't discussed (probably because we didn't think it would be an issue) was how we'd provide for a baby bird during weekdays while both of us worked.

When we shambled into his room that first morning and lifted the flap, it seemed to me that B's feathers were slightly more prominent than when we put him to bed. A nude bird is an oddity, and one tends to notice any change. We didn't realize how rapidly house sparrows fledge and begin flirting with the concept of flight. The time line is remarkable: chicks hatch, open their eyes four or five days later, leave the nest in just over two weeks.

Small birds such as house sparrows increase their body weight tenfold during their first two weeks of life and expend enormous energy manufacturing keratin, the same protein from which our fingernails and hair are made and that birds alchemize into feathers. In human terms, this would be the equivalent of a person's body converting keratin into weapons-grade fingernails or a full head of hair in slightly less time than it takes to get a Jehovah's Witness off one's porch. Rapid development requires a lot of fuel and explains why baby birds fixate on eating and why their parents spend most of their time procuring meals. My sympathies are with them. Whereas we had only one mouth to feed, a pair of mated house sparrows have several insistent maws to provide for—two or three times a season.

Curious about what an infant bird did during those intervals between eating and sleeping, I didn't cover B again as soon as he'd eaten. Good light angling in our north-facing windows cut a swath across his corner of the box and afforded me a nicely illuminated view of the tenant. From a worn-down boxer the day before, he looked that morning like a sumo wrestler who had just consumed a side of beef, four dozen eggs, and a couple of gallons of orange juice, needing only a gigantic diaper to complete the effect. He embodied contentment, as if the luxury of a full stomach allowed his mind to dwell on a higher plane. Light, however, made him uncomfortable, and he tried to hide, flailing his poorly coordinated legs behind him until he worked his head once again beneath the safety of the towel.

I slid Rebecca's desk chair over and sat down next to B, uncertain what it was I hoped to learn from an underdone bird. I was unsure what I found so interesting about a creature my intellect regarded as little more than a reptile with wings. Birds were but one of nature's lovely flourishes. Useful too in the scheme of things but as alien and inscrutable to me as a coral reef. I pitied him, sensing intimations in his small form that were different from anything dreamt of in my philosophy. I have no idea what, if anything, governs creation, but as I sat and watched the beginning of all that has followed, two lines from Milton's *Paradise Lost* drifted through my mind:

> In contemplation of created things
> By steps we may ascend to God.

B flinched a little as, lost in musings about nature's ingenuity, I pulled over a chair and sat down to watch. "Good stimulus response," I thought —a thing already evident, of course, in his reaction to approaching food and to the groaning of our elderly bedsprings. He dislodged himself from the folds of his towel and with a certain sheepish urgency, turned 180 degrees, backed himself to the box's center and fired off an impressive turd—the kind of thing a neighbor's dog wouldn't be ashamed to leave on your lawn. I was surprised he possessed the manufacturing capability to produce such a thing. It seemed to be gift wrapped.

As it turns out, the excreta of many species of baby birds come swaddled in a gelatinous membrane designed to facilitate its removal from the nest—or towel-covered box, as the case may be. Parent birds pick up the waste and toss it overboard or roll it like a water-filled balloon to a similar fate. Gilbert White describes this circumstance with fine delicacy in *The Natural History of Selbourne,* his justly revered book of observations on the plants and animals in and around his tiny eighteenth-century English village. "But in birds there seems to be a particular provision, that the dung of nestlings is enveloped into a tough kind of jelly, and therefore is the easier conveyed off without soiling or daubing." This "tough kind of jelly" is the fecal sac—a term I remembered from high school biology. For months after our teacher introduced the concept, my friends and I found it absolutely riotous to call one another "fecal sacs" in lieu of the more traditional but less refined "sacks of shit" we'd been using since grade school. This was around the time I discovered Noel Coward's work and memorized his immortal lyrics about the midday sun, mad dogs, and Englishmen. I imagined Noel remarking in a bitchy snit: "Well, old thing, isn't Lord Broadbottom quite the fecal sac since leaving that frowsty pile he infests in Hampshire and coming down to London for the season?"

WE ENDED UP TAKING B TO WORK. REBECCA THE FIRST DAY, I THE
second, and so on in an alternating pattern throughout the next ten
days. She packed him up like a piece of offbeat office equipment, set his
box on the front seat of her car, and drove away. Twenty minutes later
she arrived at her desk and plugged him in. He remained silent while
she drove, hunkered down waiting, I suppose, for the Four Horsemen
to appear. If he retains memories of those days (notwithstanding the
fact that his eyes had barely begun to slit open), how haunting those visions must be: synaptic collage of traffic, bridges, exit ramps, and Rebecca swearing at other drivers. God knows what he thought of her office, typical of corporate America's passion for function over form in
workplace design. Right down to an anesthetizing rabbit warren of
cubes hewn from neutral-toned room dividers. Windows, accessible by
exiting the maze, looked out over a patch of diminishing green space
that's now all but gone. There was a little stand of trees in which a murder of crows often gathered. That's gone too.

Rebecca works with programmers and with others who, like herself, write software documentation. Any intrusion of novelty into this
world of mole people is usually welcome. Misinterpreting the "cheeps"
coming from Rebecca's cubicle, her fellow troglodytes emerged from
their burrows convinced, literally, that a computer or some other piece
of electronic paraphernalia was singing its death song. People arrived
as she uncapped the food container. "What's that," asked one, "some
kind of bird?" Another diagnosed "starling" and B, therefore, a creature
best drowned. I like to think that Mozart would have objected to this
suggestion. He reportedly kept a pet starling and found in its chirping
the melodic basis for the third movement of his seventeenth piano
concerto.

But an interesting question had been raised. If I'd paid attention to
what was going on in our eaves, I might have been able to deduce B's
lineage, but determining he was a bird had seemed at the outset sufficiently precise. During her lunch hour, Rebecca drove to the Audubon
Society where the volunteer on duty identified B as a house sparrow.
She explained the society's laissez faire philosophy regarding nonna-
tive species, gesturing as she spoke to a row of glass cases containing a

menagerie of stuffed specimens (bobcats snarling, beavers gnawing, that sort of thing), some of which at least might have been happier had a hands-off policy applied to them. "House sparrows are pests," the volunteer opined, "far too many of them as it is." Rebecca's moue of disappointment at finding we possessed an avian pariah seemed, however, to soften the woman. "Forgive me," she said. "It's just that at this time of year people call up every day wanting to drop off house sparrow young. We're stretched thin caring for the native birds we get, not to mention squirrels and raccoons and everything else that comes in. But you've got a healthy-looking bird there. You're doing a good job. It'll probably survive." She gave Rebecca a handout that contained tips on raising baby birds and that told you what to do when it came time to release them. "If you'd like," she added as Rebecca packaged B for the return trip to her office, "we'll put your name on a list of volunteers who are willing to raise house sparrows and other nonnatives." Rebecca and I didn't sign up, but we try to give Audubon a donation every year.

B spent the rest of the workday parked in the office of Rebecca's boss, an ex-zoo employee who volunteered her space in order to preserve the peace. Noise complaints from Bunny (not her real name), the resident harpy, occasioned this. I've seen drawings of Aello, the hag of ancient myth, and believe me, these two could have been separated at birth. (Please note: No sexist or antifeminist construction should be placed on my use of "hag" in this context. I'm simply using the term generally applied to this, until now, mythical creature. In any event, Bunny is female in only a strictly academic sense.) As a visual assist, one could do worse than to picture the essence of Margaret Hamilton's facial expression as she pedals her bike, Toto stowed in a basket behind her, into the gathering cyclone that soon transports Dorothy to Oz.

To my knowledge, Bunny did not say to Rebecca, "I'll get you, my pretty, and your little bird too," but I wouldn't have been surprised if she had. My guess is that Bunny emerged from the womb middle-aged and dyspeptic. She advertises herself as a great lover of animals, her rabid vegetarianism based upon this evidently shaky foundation. On occasions before and since the incident with B, she's gone out of her way to be petty, intractable, and mean. Booby-trapping her office chair with a latticework of dental floss in an attempt to expose the incursions of trespassers is but one of many examples. Though crude, the adage "There's an asshole in every group" does seem to reflect a fundamental social condition. But, as is often the way with difficult people, Bunny can be extraordinarily pleasant. This creates a sort of intermittent reinforcement dynamic that eventually makes you seethe with frustration.

It was the vehemence and predictability of Bunny's response that I found galling, more so than the complaint itself—everyone's entitled, after all, to be comfortable at work. I'd wager that Bunny's girlhood was spent whining and snitching, the intervening years hardening this behavior into unbreakable habit, robbing her in the process of a sense of proportion. From the shrillness of her protest, "Birds do not belong in the office. We do not bring our pets to work," one might have thought she'd been strip-searched with a vacuum cleaner. Since the old notion of buying someone's way out of hell implies, to my mind, the sensible notion of being able to buy someone else's way in, I'll pay the requisite fees to any religious organization willing to book Bunny's passage. A kind of reverse indulgence. In this case, expenses should be nominal.

B has just bathed and is flapping around the room flinging water on me, my books, and everything else I'd prefer remained dry. I gather from his exuberance that this is the best part of the process. Because he's drenched, he sputters and flies like a small plane with engine trouble, seeming at times to stall midflight. His course is erratic, takeoffs and landings are slapstick masterpieces. He usually bathes once a day, typically in the morning, but afternoons will do, as will evenings shortly before bed. He begins by landing on the edge of his large plastic water dish and circumnavigating the miniature lake it contains. There's a sort of droll poise in the way he dithers, stalling for time while he searches for the optimum entry point as divined through the principles of avian hydrology. I imagine him evaluating currents and tides that are obvious to him but invisible to me. Or maybe he just thinks the water might be cold. These are times when I'd like to dress him in an 1890s-style full-length bathing suit.

He wades to the center of the dish, stands a moment before dipping first his head, then his whole body. He spreads every feather, immerses himself three or four times, flaps vigorously to complete the drenching. Wings down, tips touching the water, he toddles about like a penguin on an ice floe. He turns when I chuckle, fixes me with an eloquent stare, "You know the rules, no laughing at the bird." I do know the rules and try to obey them—honored that B permits me now to witness his ablutions. He was nearly three years old before he'd take a bath in my presence. Rebecca says he was "too modest" to undress in front of me. She, for some reason, was never excluded.

I looked forward to seeing Rebecca that evening, more so than I normally do. She'd called with bird updates several times during the day, but I was eager to get a thorough face-to-face debriefing. Especially since B was slated to go with me to my office the following morning. "I've taken a bird to work, kept it alive, and didn't get fired" is how, I believe, Rebecca began her tale. She's good at recounting workday minutia, spins interesting yarns even when she has next to no actual material to work with. My narrative gifts are feeble in this regard. I viewed days in the office as a Work was OK–Work sucked dialectic not susceptible to much elaboration. Of course, Rebecca toils on the broader canvas of a large company with all the attendant corporate absurdities. Plus, an inordinately high percentage of her office chums seem to lead lives that convert easily into gossip. My coworkers were cadavers by comparison. They were, however, nice to my bird.

This may have been because I was their boss, but I doubt it. They all wanted to take turns feeding B, expressed disappointment on days when he went to work with Rebecca. Most people haven't seen a baby bird surviving in a box eating dog food off a toothpick. I worked for a company that serviced computers, computer terminals, and printers, spent my days repairing failed circuit boards and supervising other technicians. Electronics is precise work and appeals to a compulsive side of me that craves definitive answers. Even when (frequently) I failed to solve a particular problem, it was comforting to know that a solution existed in theory—electricity obeying laws as elegant and reliable as those formulated by Newton to describe gravity and motion.

Many years ago, however, I worked with a guy who didn't appreciate this aspect of the craft, probably didn't realize it existed. A hulking man in his late forties, he always dressed in blue coveralls with his name stitched over the breast pocket—a fashion statement picked up during his years as a diesel mechanic. I assume the bolt that must have run through his neck had been removed for cosmetic reasons. He was in the process of changing careers due to injury and was fresh from a state-subsidized retraining program in electronics when we hired him as an entry-level technician. His approach to troubleshooting was unorthodox: avoiding oscilloscopes, volt-ohm meters, and any other diagnostic tool he found intimidating (the occupational equivalent of a plumber afraid of a plunger), he'd pick up a circuit board and gaze at it like someone sizing up a box of assorted chocolates hoping to distinguish, via some sixth sense, between pieces having caramel centers and those filled with jellied beets. Eventually, he'd make a decision, remove a part, and replace it. If this didn't fix the problem, and it never did, he'd put a red self-adhesive paper dot on the component he'd just installed and then desolder and exchange some other equally blameless transistor or chip. One day I asked, "What's with the red dots, Lucas?" "I use them," he said, "because red means stop. Then I won't replace *that* part again."

Our minds make odd connections, disparate memories and events toiling toward one another since, for all I know, the beginning of time. On my way to work that morning, I wondered how it was that B had fallen from his nest. Had he been jettisoned by parents obeying a Darwinian imperative to not waste resources on the weakest member of their brood? Later that day I thought of Lucas and hoped that he, too, would find his niche. I thought of red dots and the religious tracts he read at noon every day while eating his inevitable fruit cup and egg salad sandwich, a black lunch bucket open on his lap. If ever a working man needed divine guidance, it was Lucas, more so if somewhere in Scripture Ohm's Law is revealed. The company fired him after a few weeks, and another lost soul drifted away to an uncertain future. As B murmured in his box, dreaming, perhaps, of huge beings with featherless faces, I found it easy to imagine Lucas, outcast to outcast, guiding a toothpick to B's gaping mouth.

B's eyes were open a few days later, and he'd become adept at maneuvering in his box. He was still unsteady on his pins but seemed less likely to get tangled in his own legs as they splayed out in ways that made them seem either broken or unhinged. Tail feathers began emerging just above the exit point for the food we shoveled in, the quills fletched enough to make them look like miniature versions of English pub darts or, given how fast they were developing, like petals unfurling in time-lapse photography. A few days later, he started sitting outside his fortress for several minutes instead of ducking inside immediately after eating. I inferred from the way he wobbled on the gnarled twig we put in his box that he was teaching himself how to perch in anticipation of gaining enough strength to do it properly. By the middle of the second week, he was beetling around the perimeter of his box, scaling the uneven terrain of his bunched-up towel, exercising his incomplete wings by standing in place and fluttering them—a calisthenic that many young birds continue to practice even after they're flying well. House sparrow juveniles capable of feeding themselves incorporate the movement into the food-begging routines they persist in directing at their exasperated parents.

B wasn't keen on being held. Still, I'd pick him up after one of our toothpick sessions and let him range over my chest as I lay half-recumbent in a chair, careful not to let him tumble off as he tried to escape. Rebecca said I was becoming "too attached," but I'd catch her doing the same thing every chance she got. I have photographs to prove it. I told her she looked like Koko the gorilla holding a kitten, that I'd be happy to provide her with a tire on a rope if she'd use it. Our mammalian tactile urges were hard to suppress when it came to B. We'd found him, fed him, cleaned up after him, and kept him warm. Now that he was mobile and alert (he followed my moving finger well enough with his eyes that, had he been a concussion patient, the neurologist would have discharged him), clinical detachment was impossible to maintain. I swear I could see his mind forming.

HAVING ALTERED THE NATURAL COURSE OF EVENTS BY SAVING B, WE could even things out by letting him go. It was our chance to be high-minded and noble. I imagined inspiring music swelling in the background as we held firm to our selfless resolve. The rationalist in me favored releasing him, but my emotional side called the shots. I became evasive in my dealings with Rebecca over the issue of where, when, and how we'd act on our convictions. The few serious talks we had on the subject broke down over our failure to agree on specifics. These discussions left me depressed and Rebecca angry.

"Setting the bird free appeals to my unshakable faith in the medieval Chain of Being as the principal organizing force in the universe,"

I declaimed one day while watching Rebecca clean out B's box. She'd become tiresome on the release topic, prompting me to meander off into pseudointellectual palaver as a means of throwing her off her stride.

"I thought you had a thing for the eighteenth century," she said.

"No, the thirteenth," I replied. "Definitely the thirteenth."

"Since when? And what the hell is a medieval Chain of Being, and what has it got to do with our bird?" She was using swatches of toilet paper to pick up excrement from B's box and dropping them into a plastic bag.

"Since deciding the eighteenth century isn't as funny as the thirteenth. It's an unattractive century difficult to love, but I think it needs champions other than dusty little men who make it the focus of their scholarly attention. The science of the day was wrong about most things, and there was a great deal of mud. By the way, have I mentioned my theory that each succeeding century has less mud than the one before it? No? Well, doesn't matter, I'm probably mistaken. Given the current rate of deforestation, the reverse is probably true. Anyway, the Chain of Being worldview is tidy, and I like it."

Rebecca finds me irritating when I get like this, and so I continued.

"The Chain of Being was the belief that all things are linked and arranged hierarchically from heaven down to hell. Objects like stones possess mere existence up through God who embodies pure actuality. If anything slipped out of place, nature reacted violently to show its displeasure—earthquakes, thunderstorms, comets, whatever was necessary until the problem got fixed. This concept of linkage and order also applied to human affairs. Killing a king, for example, resulted in more than a dead monarch. The structure of society, which mirrored the design implicit in creation itself, was rent. Kill a king and you ran the risk of golf ball–size hail falling suddenly from a cloudless sky. The belief persisted well into the Renaissance. Shakespeare used it to dramatic effect, confident that his audience understood the paradigm. If we don't let the bird go our house might collapse, both of us could become afflicted with boils. The cosmological assumptions of the doctrine point— I don't doubt its adherents would be nonplused by this assertion—the way toward human development of an ecological awareness."

"But what has any of this got to do with the bird?" Rebecca per-

sisted, while holding a squirming B in her palm. "We'll set him free because he's a wild creature, and it wouldn't be fair to keep him caged."

One day followed the next, and the release never took place. I was
in conflict over this for months until B's first trip to Pet Samaritan Clinic
the following February. I came away from visiting Dr. Huff with two
specific pieces of information. I learned how they weigh small birds (in
a bag) and that the life expectancy of house sparrows in the wild is
about two years. I reflect on this statistic whenever I fret over the immorality of denying B the benefits of a "natural" life. Having dragged
all three cats to the vet for one thing or another, I felt right at home in
the examination room with its stainless steel table and glass jars filled
with cotton swabs. One memorable visit had been to X-ray our cat Winnie after she'd eaten, for some obscure reason, most of a dish sponge.
Fortunately, it later passed harmlessly through her intestines by imper-
sonating a turd. When I opened B's cage he flew to my shoulder and
sidestepped in close to my neck and huddled. Dr. Huff smiled the smile
of one who has seen it all and said, more to herself than to me, "Yep,
right to the shoulder."

THE VET'S "SHOULDER" COMMENT TOUCHED OBLIQUELY UPON AN
aspect of human-avian relationships I had just begun to appreciate. An
extremely close bond can result when a person raises a bird by hand.
This is why wildlife specialists feeding chicks destined for release go to
a great deal of trouble to prevent their charges from forming attach-
ments to them or even becoming the slightest bit tame. They don't talk
to the birds, they don't handle the birds, and they sure as hell don't
cuddle the birds and whisper endearments. Surrogate caregivers will
sometimes hide behind screens, doling out food while wearing puppets
on their hands that resemble adult birds of the appropriate species.

Many people are familiar with the concept of "imprinting," as the
term applies to newborn precocial birds such as ducks and geese. This
very sensible mechanism, referred to technically as "filial imprinting,"
ensures that newborn chicks follow the first large moving object they
see upon hatching, which, in most cases, is their mother, the one best
suited to lead them to food and protect them from predators. Because

this arrangement results now and then in comic, if not tragic, consequences—a gaggle of baby geese, for example, toiling under the misapprehension that a recently parked bulldozer is their *Stabat Mater*—it's easy to regard birds as unthinking automatons. In a word, stupid. But instinct-driven behavior works reliably because of its rigidity, because it requires no thought.

Humans pride themselves on their status as thinking beings and find it unflattering to accept the instinctual basis of many of their own actions. Unless it's a case of "I didn't even stop to think when my house exploded, I plunged right in and retrieved my stock portfolio," we tend to downplay how capable we are of acting out of motives based on something other than calm deliberation. We appreciate the usefulness of instinct, but its power to control us makes us uncomfortable.

"Filial imprinting" is not the type of bond I've forged with B. Nor is our connection related to the "sexual imprinting" some birds use to ensure that their genetic line remains free of hybridization—the young are taught to recognize only members of their own species as potential mates. In a display filled with puffing and bowing that we call "Love Bird," B makes sexual overtures to Rebecca, who always makes it clear to him that she just wants to be friends. Or so she tells me. B accepts this platonic limitation but enjoys practicing his moves. I thought at one time that he'd cut a dashing figure through a bevy of house sparrow debutantes, and would know what to do with them. As Rebecca said, "He'd have them tossing their panties and swooning off branches." Reminds me of Daisy Duck wearing lipstick, high heels, and a tight-fitting dress while she waited at her house for Donald to show up for their date. I found it maddening that he always dissipated the sexual tension smoldering between them by obsessing over some idiotic thing such as opening a window.

Our vet's prediction that B would either ignore a prospective mate or assume an offensive posture if he viewed her as a threat turned out to be correct. B verified her insight some years later when we introduced him to our third sparrow—a female he treats with polite reserve. Remember, B is a bird that won't sit in trees.

I was well aware of how sensitive cats and dogs are to the schedules of their human partners, but I hadn't expected to find the same tendency, let alone capacity, in birds. But back when I worked a nine-hour day, B would fly to his window perch promptly at 6:00 P.M. and wait for my car to appear. According to Rebecca, he'd grow anxious on days I ran late and flit from window to door calling for me, listening at the heating grate for my reply. He discovered early on that our ductwork acts as an efficient intercom that funnels sound to and from all areas of the house. Our version, I guess, of tin cans and a string. I can be in the basement and converse with B in his room on the second floor. His calls echo through the sheet metal like coins dropped down a chute.

I've often walked up our front steps and seen B looking down at me from his window perch. He calls my name in sparrow as I unlock the door. When I walk into the house late, his hail is peremptory. I'm being ordered to his room, not invited. He has a way of staring at me from across the room when I haven't adhered to his schedule that makes me feel petty for having taken a pee before heading upstairs for twenty minutes of groveling. If I've been gone a very long time, overnight, for example, he flies to me immediately, relieved I'm not dead—killed and gutted by a skulking cat. He dances in my hand, nips my nose when I lift him to my face. He cheeps with excitement as if to say, "Is it really you? You were away so long I thought you'd died or gone off with another bird. I thought I'd never perch on your finger again, and I couldn't imagine what that would be like."

I apologize for nauseating those for whom the commandment "Thou shalt not anthropomorphize" is an ironclad law. It's difficult to refrain from putting words in B's mouth. People who have close relationships with animals do this kind of thing. They accept with a shrug the futility of trying to document, in a scientifically acceptable way, every interaction they have with their pets. *I* know B misses me when I'm gone, but I have no wish to argue the point with the behaviorists and reductionists among us.

Usually involving the dispensing of food bribes, the laboratory system of controlled experimentation is fine as far as it goes. If I were hungry enough, I dare say I'd try my best to pull whichever lever netted me a peanut, but at least one or two of the people who know me well might be willing to testify that I'm capable of behavior that is somewhat more subtle. While I understand how fascinating it is to see if a test subject can figure out how to get a peanut, and while I appreciate the relative value of making the inquiry, this approach seems to me as limited as the supposedly inferior intellects it attempts to quantify. In a foreword to Konrad Lorenz's *King Solomon's Ring* (a tender yet scientifically important book about Lorenz's life with an array of animals he kept in his home), Julian Huxley writes the following: "I will conclude by expressing my fullest agreement with him when he [Lorenz] repudiates the unimaginative and blinkered outlook of those who think it is `scientific' to pretend that something rich and complex is merely its jejune and simple elements and in particular that the brains of higher organisms, such as birds, those complex body-minds with their elaborate emotional behavior, are `really' nothing but reflex machines."

The "stimulus-response" crowd is naturally made nuts by people prattling on about how remarkably human their animals are. "My schnauzer, Humper, is just a whiz at differential equations and writes the most amusing limericks you've ever heard in your life—`there once was a dog from Nantucket. . . .'" I share their revulsion, but refuse to sacrifice on Pavlov's altar my belief that some animals have traits and abilities similar to those we traditionally reserve for ourselves alone. Although it can be a reflection of emotional need (or wishful thinking or vanity or bad science), the habit of casting animals in our own image is, at its best, an attempt to find common ground with another species by appealing to features of our own consciousness, the only frame of reference with which any of us are remotely familiar. I'm a poor flyer, and can't peck worth a damn, but perhaps B sees in me something recognizably avian.

≈

"DO YOU THINK HE'S GETTING SICK OF THIS?" REBECCA ASKED, palpating B's puppy food. "What do you think these gooey white specks are?"

"Gristle."

"Does he need gristle?"

"Who doesn't?" I said. "Maybe it builds strong beaks and feathers."

"No, seriously, I think we should try him on something else. He's been eating this crap for almost two weeks now. Let's get him some baby food."

I hadn't realized how many decisions are required when buying baby food. "First Year," "Second Year," "Third Year," "Lil' Glutton" are the basic categories. There are also many flavors: Chicken, Chicken with Rice, Chicken with Applesauce, Beef, Veal, Turkey, Turkey with Vegetables, Green Beans, Peas, Mixed Vegetables, Spinach, Carrots, Potatoes, Potatoes and Wieners, Pear, Plum, Banana, Pineapple, Blueberry Cheesecake, Opium Poppy. More expensive varieties claiming to be "All Natural," "Organic," and "Preservative Free" can be found next to the unnatural brands that have the advantage of lasting six months or more after the container's been opened and left in the sun. All of them develop a crust on the underside of their lids that looks as if it has a plan.

Figuring the "Second Year" stuff would have the right consistency, we bought jars of Green Beans, Chicken, and Chicken with Applesauce. The olfactory lobes in avian brains are relatively small. As a result, most birds are thought to have a poor sense of taste and smell, choosing or rejecting foods based for the most part on visual inspection. Experiments designed to test this supposition have found that many birds will continue to select and eat favored foods that have been made bitter with additives. B, however, appeared to delight in the new tastes, showing marked enthusiasm for Chicken with Applesauce and, to a lesser extent, Green Beans. Birds don't have lips to smack, but he made a fair approximation of the gesture with his beak and tongue. His enthusiasm spelled an abrupt ending to his cordial relationship with puppy food. We offered it another time or two, but he behaved like Emily Post confronting toenails in her salad.

He looked more like a proper bird as the days passed and his feathers filled in. His beak narrowed into a surgically precise tool capable of picking up a seed, husking it, and ejecting the chaff in less time than it takes me to register the anguish I feel as he removes from my finger another piece of cuticle I'd been planning to keep. We decided to name him.

The psychological significance of this decision didn't dawn on us at the time. We'd been calling him "The bird" or "The sparrow" or "She's" as in "She's shrieking again, your turn to feed her." For reasons entirely arbitrary, we thought B was female, used pronouns accordingly up until he acquired adult plumage in early autumn. Gender in some bird species is distinguishable by differences in feather coloration between the sexes, in some it isn't. The fancy term for this characteristic is "sexual dimorphism," and adult house sparrows have it. Males sport black beaks and bibs, gray cheek patches, russet crowns, and white wing bars. They are altogether more variegated than the females.

Prejudices have a way of working themselves to the surface, and "Birdbrain," which seemed an amusing choice for naming a silly creature, is a good example of how this tendency works. I viewed a bird's brain as a nonstarter, a device so absurdly small and intellectually impoverished as to make it an apt metaphor for describing the mentally negligible as it has been doing since the 1920s when the term entered the language as slang for a foolish or idiotic person, a nitwit. "Birdbrain," however, we soon shortened to "BB," which in turn became "The B," which we've long since finalized simply and affectionately as "B." "The B" (his full name) is still in use, but as a title more than anything else. Rebecca and I now refer to all birds as b's. An evolution in usage similar to the way in which some brand names eventually become generic: Kleenex, kleenex. But, of course, there's only one B.

Mid-September, unseasonably warm and desert dry. Two days of brisk wind burnishing the light have done nothing to reshape the sky, and the concept of rain may as well be some vanished culture's preposterous myth. As if the weather itself were a lens, every house, tree, person, and leaf seems uncoiled and distinct, and I am moved to laughter by how beautiful it is. P. G. Wodehouse knew something of this feeling when he said, "It was one of those jolly, peaceful mornings that make a chappie wish he'd got a soul or something." I wonder if we've sinned against B by giving him a comfortable life without the freedom to fly off into such fine weather. I'll feel different when the first winter storms swagger in off the Pacific, moving inland, and Portland is wet again forever.

B has problems. He's molting, has been since August when tiny breast feathers began to fall out. At the height of this yearly process, which is now, he looks like a chemo patient, his head and nape almost bald, his eyes appearing abnormally large in the absence of so many of the minute black feathers that surround them like the mask of Zorro. I am struck by how fragile he looks, pink flesh and tendons visible on his neck as he tucks his head and sleeps in the cave I've made with one hand held beneath my chin. He relaxes into my palm as if lowering himself into a mound of leaves.

It's hard to imagine how uncomfortable molting must be for B. I thought he'd tried a Tabasco Brand Enema the way he exploded off my shoulder ten minutes ago and bounced all over the place pulling at a tail feather. The damn things must poke him as the old ones fall out and new ones come in. He's much hungrier than usual, eats huge amounts of seed, spinach, and apple along with a concoction we buy from the vet called Harrison's Adult Lifetime Mash that we mix with water and refer to as "goop."

All birds replace their worn feathers at least once a year, many species doing so in late summer or early autumn while food is still plentiful and the rigor of raising their young is behind them. Large birds such as eagles or cranes can take two years to complete a molt; most small birds do so in two months or less. In some species, males and females molt at different times; some birds molt twice a year. There are many species-specific molting peculiarities with specialized names. Terms such as "basic plumage," "supplementary plumage," "alternate plumage," and "prealternate molt" describe cosmetic changes in the feathers of some birds (gulls, for example) that relate to the bird's maturity or to the time of year. The process with B is easily summarized: beginning every August, B's old feathers drop out; new ones grow in.

He hates when I leave the room, clings to me as I go. It's curious that he no longer protests audibly after I've gone, doesn't call me back the way he ordinarily would. Of course, with so many feathers missing, flight is compromised. He sounds off-kilter when he flies. I think he's laconic because instinct makes him unusually cautious about betraying his position to predators at a time of year when he's relatively slow off the mark. The outside house sparrows are scarce, look dilapidated, and are far less vocal than they are as a rule. I find their feathers in the feeding area, just as I find B's on the floor and collected by morning beneath the perch where he sleeps. Rebecca and I have saved feathers from each of his molts, keeping some in a small wooden box, some in a blue sugar container. She says we have enough to build several new birds; but still we collect, unwilling to throw these talismans away.

A couple of days short of the two-week mark, we moved B into a deeper box and covered it with an adjustable window screen that, being slightly too narrow for the box, left a two- or three-inch gap along one side. He'd been getting pretty rambunctious by that time, had started to spill out of his original accommodation by half-climbing, half-fluttering his way over the side. Since we didn't want him falling or in some other way harming himself in our absence, his increasing mobility was an obvious concern. Besides, imprisoning a bird is what one does as naturally as saddling a horse, tethering a goat, declawing a cat, rubbing a dog's nose in the pile it left on your rug. For that matter, training bears to ride bikes and chimps to wear pants.

Rebecca and I discussed buying a cage. Pursuant to that conversation we obtained a small twenty-dollar job from Newberry's. Our reasoning was that, whether we kept B or not, he'd need to be confined in the interim—just couldn't imagine a bird flitting about loose. We eventually moved from viewing a closed cage as a necessity to recognizing it as a dispensable evil. As it affected B, our evolution on this issue was rapid and to his advantage but not quick enough to benefit the first zebra finches we got him as companions. They lived relatively brief, unhappy lives locked in a cage (albeit a large one) because of our slowness in giving them the same privileges we extended to B. By most standards they were well cared for, certainly never lacked an adequate supply of food and water. But in my reading of poor, mad William Cowper's poem, "On a Goldfinch Starved to Death in His Cage," I see, despite the title, loss of freedom described as a privation more brutal than any other. Coming from a man whose periodically unhinged mind generated enough demons to keep itself trapped (and the poet in and out of mental institutions), his words interest me:

> Time was when I was free as air,
> The thistle's downy seed my fare,
>   My drink the morning dew;
> I perch'd at will on ev'ry spray,
> My form genteel, my plumage gay,
>   My strains for ever new.
> But gaudy plumage, sprightly strain,
> And form genteel, were all in vain,
>   And of a transient date;
> For, caught and cag'd, and starv'd to death,
> In dying sighs my little breath
>   Soon pass'd the wiry gate.
> Thanks, gentle swain, for all my woes,
> And thanks for this effectual close

And cure of ev'ry ill!
More cruelty could none express;
And I, if you had shown me less,
    Had been your pris'ner still.

For years now, B's cage has consisted of a large room with high ceilings. We've offered him access to the rest of the upstairs, but he prefers the familiarity of his room and usually demurs. The cage we bought from Newberry's sits on a table by a window, the door held open by a safety pin. A cloth draped over one side forms a canopy under which he sleeps at night. Trips to the vet are the only times the door is closed. If he ever has a feeling of being trapped, I think it must be akin to the sense any of us have sometimes had of finding ourselves indefinably hemmed in. If not by our lot in life, then by the limits of the universe itself, the largest cage of all. In the belief that every creature with an inner life is entitled to some level of dissatisfaction, I respect B's right to a share of existential dread.

Since a morning several years ago when B stood in my palm eating a Cheerio and, having finished that, reached up to touch my lips in a kind of kiss, and I caught (literally) a blast of Cheerio breath, and he made a high "E-e-eeing" sound that expresses affection, I've known beyond doubt there's more good in this arrangement than otherwise.

"IT'S LIKE HE'S DOWN A WELL," REBECCA SAID, LOOKING AT B INSIDE his new box as he fluttered his wings and propelled himself in grounded circles like someone rowing a boat with only one oar in the water. She lifted him out and placed him in the center of a large blue cushion. When the music started and Rebecca began to move, B stared at her the way my high school chemistry teacher gaped at a classmate friend of mine he'd caught lighting farts with a Bunsen burner. Pressed for an explanation, Ed claimed it was a valid scientific experiment that demonstrated the flammable properties of methane.

Rebecca undulated her hips, her coin-laden belt jingling in time to a drum solo on one of her recordings of Middle Eastern dance music. Typical titles in the genre are "Rhythms of the Nile" and "Let's All Belly

Dance!" B took an interest in these practice sessions and sometimes clung to Rebecca as she shimmied through a routine—provided she wore mufti and didn't in the least rattle or clang. He seemed as impressed as I am by her ability to move individual muscles in isolation from the rest. Saying, "He doesn't like crowds, and he hates all my costumes," Rebecca dismissed my facetious suggestion that she incorporate B into her routine. She's afraid he'd upstage her. There used to be a dancer in town who rendered herself more or less superfluous whenever she performed with a six-foot python draped around her neck, a lesson not lost on Rebecca.

I must have been about seven years old the first time I found myself startled by noticing something intensely. In this case, a cabinet in our basement where my mother stored laundry detergent and bleach along with surplus clothespins and an unopened can of paste wax left behind by the previous owners of the house. I'd passed that cabinet a million times, usually on my way to play in our coal bin since it had a pretty firm grip on my sensibilities at that point in my life, containing as it did spiders that terrified me and big chunks of coal I used for drawing on sidewalks or for hurling against walls where they'd shatter into dust. I'd thoroughly investigated this cabinet, rifling through its uninteresting contents after gaining access by climbing up and standing on our old Kenmore washing machine. And yet, on my way to the coal bin one day, there it was. As if it hadn't existed until, my back being turned, mysterious carpenters cobbled it in using wood and hinges from another dimension. Amazement turned to anxiety as I experienced how malleable and fickle reality can be when perception is filtered through puckish senses and matched against memories impossible to verify—at least on the spot. I later asked my mother, "Has that shelf thing above the washing machine always been there?" No telling where I'd be today if "Of course not, dear," had been her reply.

Nothing existed for a few seconds more intensely real than that cabinet with its chipped off-white paint and chrome handles. But the spell soon evaporated and cellar, cabinet, and brain settled whatever feud they'd been having and agreed on the old interpretation of how things should appear. I've had similar experiences over the years with objects, both animate and inanimate, stepping out from the chorus line and making spectacles of themselves. Usually these events are trivial, interesting only because of whatever mental legerdemain occurs to produce them, giving me briefly an artist's ability to see something significant (I can never explain afterward what it was) in a splash of mud or a Styrofoam cup crushed in the gutter. Then it passes, and my old, dull faculties are pressed back into service.

Seeing B on that blue cushion was one of those times of heightened awareness when even the dullest intellect can be said, for once, to understand the punch line, to see the lay of the land in a flash of lightning. The present seemed to me a hazy brochure of things to come, the future's outline momentarily drifting on Rebecca's music and in the rhythmic clanging of her finger cymbals; patterns coalescing around a center that has held.

Our life would proceed with a small bird at its center. We'd order our schedules, priorities, and beliefs to accommodate. I couldn't see specifics, of course. Neither the good nor the bad approaching the horizon—my father's death, my sister's death, my mother-in-law's death all within a period of less than a year. I couldn't see that Rebecca and I would acquire finches and canaries and raise three more house sparrows, that our entire upstairs would soon be an aviary.

B'S TINY CLAWS SLIDING DOWN THE CARDBOARD WALLS OF HIS GULAG made a distinctive scraping sound as he jumped and fluttered inside it. I don't know if he was more interested in breaking out of prison or in flight for its own sake, but he made a lot of noise doing it. I'd lift him up and hold him in my open palm a couple of feet over the bed where, unable to work up the courage to launch out, he'd teeter for a while in fearful indecision. I wondered how adult birds knew when their nestlings were ready to fly. Did they administer a test of some kind? B looked reasonably complete in his fluffy coat of juvenile feathers, Rebecca terming his appearance "dewy," whereas I thought he looked fluffy. I have a picture of him from about this time that supports the accuracy of both observations. He was at once fluffy *and* dewy, a seeming contradiction since dewy implies moist and moist tends to deflate fluff. But like Dickens's description of Jacob Marley's ghost, B seemed to carry with him a private and inexplicable atmosphere of his own that I came to believe would either ground him until it dissipated or increase in measure until it finally lifted him into the air. As it turned out, that "two- or three-inch gap" left by the ill-fitting window screen proved to be his escape hatch.

B's first food that didn't come from a jar or can was a ripe strawberry sliced into bits. The season's first good crop had arrived (fresh Oregon berries rather than the desiccated impostors trucked in from California) and with it, the yearly madness of eating more than our fill that results in stained hands and little puddles of red juice congealing on 90 percent of the surfaces in the house. B's beak had nearly assumed its adult proportion and shape, but he hadn't yet tumbled to the idea that nature had designed it for picking up food. We taught him how to peck a few days later by tapping a chicken and applesauce-laden toothpick on the surface in front of him. Even a pampered child should learn how to work for a living.

I believe house sparrows are such a successful species, in part, because they are deeply suspicious of unfamiliar things. They are careful observers and insatiably curious. B notices if the least item in his room is out of place and, depending on how much significance he attaches to said item, will flit around chattering until I make it right. If I walk in with one of my hands clenched, he'll sit on my fist poking his beak between my fingers until I show him what, if anything, I'm concealing. And it's not food he's looking for; he's got a constant supply he grazes on at leisure. He'll *stop* eating to come and investigate. When he's playing hard to get, I'll occasionally pretend I'm hiding something from him, act suspiciously secretive in an outsized, silent movie–gesturing sort of way. Unless he's nettled or involved in some project, the importance of which isn't always obvious to me, this strategy will sucker him into coming over for a look. He can't stand thinking I know something he doesn't. Nothing gets past him.

One afternoon several weeks ago, we had a power outage while I sat reading in B's room. He half-dozed on my shoulder but jerked his head around to glance pointedly at the wall switch when the overhead light went out. When, a minute later, power was restored and the light came back on, B flew to the switch, hovered a few seconds, and stared at it as if he were thinking, "Now isn't that the damnedest thing?"

Because strawberry fell into the "unfamiliar" category, B turned his head upside down and scrutinized my offering before agreeing to try it. There is something almost digitally efficient about this mannerism of his when evaluating objects he finds particularly interesting—new foods, changing numbers on the clock's LED display, the inside of my nostrils. As I doled out berry, pieces of it devolved into stringy mucus draped over his beak, an uncomfortable situation for a creature I've come to regard as priggishly fastidious about his appearance and personal hygiene. "Foppish" is an apt description. I visualize him in satin breeches, think he'd be happy dressed like Louis XIV and living at Versailles. He shook his head back and forth until most of what clung to his beak flew off onto my T-shirt—the first of many red stains on my clothing that never washed out. Beak wiping was followed by beak flicking, which is a quick back-and-forth movement across whatever's available that B uses to clean, hone, and polish his bill. A utilitarian mannerism that's developed into a gesture expressive of anticipation and desire. "Cookie?" elicits an affirmative series of swipes against my finger. He'll sit on the center brace of the screen door that opens into his room, looking when I call out, "B, I'm coming in," like he's an old-time barber stropping a razor.

I made numerous trips to B's room with strawberry that day. By late afternoon, I thought it unlikely he'd ever lose what I took to be an inborn fear and distrust of humans. All for the best, of course, if we ended up releasing him. He shied away from my touch and seemed constitutionally opposed to anything other than a formal, distanced, businesslike relationship. I picked him up from time to time but mostly sat watching him alternately exercise his wings and nap beneath his towel. I kept in mind that learning to fly was a stressful time in a bird's life and that B had little reason to be convivial. The likelihood of dying after a crash landing is high in a world where predators lie in wait on the ground. In anticipation of B's maiden flight, Rebecca and I took the precaution of covering windows, mirrors, and anything else that posed a navigational hazard. We congratulated ourselves on what a thorough job we'd done in anticipating every dangerous contingency that might confront B when he at last took wing.

"You've spent most of the day with that bird," Rebecca said when I drifted into the kitchen to make a cup of coffee. The insinuation seemed to be that *she* hadn't spent most of her day with the bird and was the saner for it. I could tell from her body language and intonation that my continued skirting of the release issue bothered her. She was chafing to broach it again. "Once he's flying well," she said, "we'll put him in his cage and take him to a park. Every day for a while, maybe for an hour or so each time. There'll be other sparrows around, and he'll get used to them and curious. Then we could start leaving the cage door open to see if he comes out. I'll bet he'll soon want to go and join a flock." I pointed out how worried I'd be for his safety, how we'd never see him again. "You're more concerned with yourself than with him," she told me bluntly. "I'll miss him too, but we just can't keep a wild bird in the house. He wouldn't be happy in the long run. If we don't stop ourselves from getting attached to him now, we'll never let him go, and this whole thing will turn out badly." Expecting a Greek chorus to step out from the wings and chant something, I sliced another strawberry, picked up my coffee, and headed back upstairs. I knew, of course, that Rebecca was right about our duty to release B. All I'd have to do on some rapidly approaching sunny day would be to tote him to a park and be unselfish enough for the couple of seconds it would take me to lift his cage door and prop it open.

I was a little surprised not to hear shrieks by the time I reached the landing—the point at which the sound of my movements usually cued B that food was on its way. Silence greeted me as I opened his door. I walked over to his box prepared to explain that decisions had been made and that he'd better start faking a disability of some kind if he didn't fancy living in the wild. But I never got the chance. B had disappeared.

3

FLIGHT

Only a few small passerines, such as the house Sparrow and the
sand martin, possess enough "spatial intelligence" to find their
way through the windows and doors of a house.
  —Konrad Lorenz, *King Solomon's Ring*

*T*INKER WITH AS LITTLE AS A SINGLE HOUR, AND OUR SCHEDULE IS THROWN
  off enough to irritate B. Daylight saving time commenced overnight to Rebecca's usual complaint that someone has stolen an hour of her weekend, the
fact that she gets it back in autumn notwithstanding. I remember hearing
about farmers in the Bible Belt refusing to adjust their clocks accordingly because doing so tampers with "God's time," a quaint notion for which I now
feel a modicum of sympathy inasmuch as we've violated "B's time." The
immediate problem this morning is that we forgot to set our clocks ahead last
night and are now running an hour late getting out of the house to meet another couple for breakfast. B, outraged that he's getting short shrift as we rush
to make up lost time, is looping the room like a World War II fighter plane
engaged in a dogfight. I'm standing behind the second door into his room (a
screen door I installed for security purposes) apologizing for such a brief first
visit of the day. I hate disappointing him, of course, but the show he's putting
on makes it almost worthwhile. Speed, stamina, incomparable reflexes are all
on display—a far cry from his halting, clumsy attempts at flight on the day he
escaped from his box. When, as I thought, he'd killed himself as a result.

COMPARED WITH BIRDS, MAMMALS ARE SUFFOCATING IN THEIR OWN carbon dioxide. Along with the rest of its physiology (feathers, hollow bones reinforced with internal struts, beaks instead of heavy jawbones and teeth), the avian respiratory system evolved to facilitate flight and does so by keeping a bird's blood oxygenated at levels a marathon runner can only envy and would probably trade water at the finish line to acquire. Unlike human lungs whose simple function of drawing in breath and exhaling never quite manages to supply completely fresh air to capillaries where gas exchange in the blood takes place, birds, in addition to their lungs, which are relatively small, employ a complex system of sacs and connecting tubes to buffer through the system an uninterrupted flow of oxygen-rich air.

Naturally, an efficient respiratory system is only as good as the mechanism that drives it. A bird's heart, a four-chambered counterpart to the mammalian pump, is proportionately three to four times the size of a human heart and beats at a much higher rate. At first blush, this might seem to be nature's way of putting a Corvette engine in a hang glider, but considering how much energy powered flight requires, such equipment isn't excessive. As an animal walks, it has the relatively effortless task of putting one foot in front of the other and by doing so in even the most desultory fashion manages to amble through life. Surfaces upon which it walks are, one might say, faits accomplis, existing in useful rigidity whether pedestrians traverse them or not. Air, however, is problematic and must be manipulated if a creature wishes to fly through it purposefully despite gravity's persistent nagging. We might better appreciate how remarkable a bird's ability is in this regard if, as we walked, it were necessary for our feet and legs to transmute the ground into an element capable of supporting our weight as we moved across it.

Powered flight requires lift and thrust. A bird provides both with its wings, an initial upward boost given by its legs in birds such as house sparrows. Soaring species—hawks, eagles, vultures—often step into space from a cliff side and are carried aloft on thermal currents rising from below. Only a facedown corpse could fail to be impressed by the majesty of these pirouetting creatures held suspended as if by special

dispensation from the Creator. But the proletarian dexterity and ma-
neuverability of the passerines (more than five thousand species) impress me more—the small perching birds, the seed eaters, the songsters,
and the worm gobblers: nuthatches, cardinals, chickadees, grackles, orioles, junkos, cowbirds, cuckoos, bluetits, house sparrows—little poems
in some of these names and certainly in their takeoffs and landings, in
their swoops and breakneck gymnastics through the thickest brush.

A popular misconception based on the unreliability of casual observation has it that birds flap their wings up and down as they fly. While
this technique has worked well for generations of cartoon characters, it
fails utterly in the real world.

Aside from a passion for T-squares and mechanical pencils, my high
school drafting teacher loved old movies and trains. Once or twice a
year, Mr. Weaver would arrange an assembly and show footage of
steam locomotives emerging from tunnels or rounding horseshoe
curves on the sides of mountains, the tedium relieved at intervals by
medium-range shots of train stations where, judging from the obligatory felt hat on all the men standing around, people were waiting to
catch the *Chattanooga Choo-Choo*. But in the second half of the assembly,
Mr. Weaver usually screened a couple of Laurel and Hardy silent-era
shorts along with ancient newsreels of goofy stuff—people trying to fly
under their own power, most notably. I loved watching confused but
determined individuals who'd strapped one-by-eight boards to their
arms before running downhill earnestly flapping. One man, whose
crash looked particularly crippling, wore funny-looking goggles. As
protection, I suppose, from whatever dangers he felt that coursing
through the upper atmosphere might pose to his eyes as he soared his
way into the history books.

Whether or not these early aviators were serious, I can't say; it may
have all been staged for comic effect. I have little doubt, however, that
there will always be someone trying to emulate the flight of birds at its
most basic and seemingly obvious level by beating the air up and down
with ersatz wings. Despite the fact that any motion produced in this
way would be strictly vertical. Such attempts require idealism and an
abiding ignorance of the aviation principles governing heavier-than-air
flight. I salute these dreamers and mourn how sad it is that their attempts will always fail. If nothing else, warfare's brutality would be

mitigated by the sight of air force squadrons flapping their way through bombing missions.

As a bird flies (this is especially pronounced just after takeoff), power strokes beginning with the wings raised above its back are what propel it. The wings descend in a forward sweeping arc not unlike someone rowing a boat with two oars set in oarlocks. In the case of birds, however, the element being pushed against is air rather than water, and since for every active force there is an equal and opposite reactive force, the bird moves forward. A subsequent recovery stroke, providing little, if any, thrust in most species, reverses the power stroke's trajectory and resets the wings to complete the cycle. So this recovery stroke can be made quickly, the wing feathers separate, allowing air to pass through them as the wings rise like pistons to repeat the process.

Lift, to flirt with a mixed metaphor, is a different kettle of fish. How it's produced isn't obvious, nor is it synonymous with flapping, which may explain why it took humans so long to get airborne, taking, as we did, the flight of birds as our model. The secret of producing lift lies in the shape of the wing itself acting as an airfoil and is unrelated to the flapping issue—in principle. In birds, thrust provided by flapping results in air passing over the wing's surface as the bird moves forward. It is this passage of air bisected by the leading edge of the wing and the subsequent pressure differential across its upper and lower surfaces that pushes the wing upward and the attached bird or plane along with it. Airplanes (their engines providing thrust) take off headed into the wind, as do comparatively heavy birds such as ducks and geese, which are otherwise unable to muster enough initial speed to rise off the surface of whatever body of water they happen to be on simply by beating their wings. Waterfowl are sometimes stranded in the doldrums of a becalmed lake where they must wait for a breeze to arrive before they can get themselves into the air.

The physics of why an airfoil behaves as it does is interesting, tied to relatively abstruse concepts such as the first law of thermodynamics (conservation of energy) and the behavior of fluid under pressure (air, in this context, is considered a fluid). I'll avoid these topics and the very real danger of making an ass of myself trying to explain them. Besides, the elegance and rigors of science can obscure aspects of things better apprehended without the specter of calculus hovering in the background. When the great Indian poet Rabindranath Tagore commented that "science may truly be described as mysticism in the realm of material things," I suspect he understood that attempts to quantify reality are useful but inherently limited. Science broadens human understanding but can never complete it. The experience of seeing a bird in flight is not the same as solving the pertinent equations.

Much of what makes avian flight sublimely beautiful are the very things that make it mechanically possible—feathers. Paleobiologists have yet to reach consensus on whether feathers evolved as insulation or to facilitate flight, a question related to, and seemingly as intractable as, the debate over the avian connection, if any, to dinosaurs. While it may be difficult to imagine a family relationship between a chicken and *Tyrannosaurus rex* or between *Brontosaurus* and a house sparrow, there is a demonstrable similarity between bones in an avian wing and those in the human arm. Humerus, radius, ulna, all of them are there. In fact, with the exception of the hand, they are shaped more or less the same and perform the same function. I sometimes remind myself of this when, with a certain amount of envy, I look at B's wings, transfixed as I so often am by the their astonishing ability to lift him on command. It's pleasant to know our kinship is bone deep, and even though this knowledge has not moved me one iota closer to successfully flying around the room, it leaves me content to imagine what that might be like.

David Attenborough begins his book *The Life of Birds* (companion volume to his PBS series of the same name) with a discussion of *Archaeopteryx,* a protobird dating from the Jurassic period whose name is a compound of two Greek words meaning "ancient wing." The fossilized remains of this creature were first discovered in a Bavarian limestone quarry near Solnhofen, Germany, where they'd lain for 150–160 million years until found by a quarryman in 1861. Looking at the accompanying photograph of *Archaeopteryx,* I am stunned by how many eons of silence this relic with a long, bony tail has endured. That such a prodigious amount of time has passed makes me uneasy, as does the thought that so much of it ever existed to begin with. John McPhee was on to something when he commented in *Basin and Range,* "Numbers do not seem to work well with regard to deep time. Any number above a couple of thousand years—fifty thousand, fifty million—will with nearly equal effect awe the imagination to the point of paralysis." I find myself marveling that a creature so long dead could have lived at all, its ending fixed in the relative permanence of stone without a compensating image of its beginning to redress the balance. It could be a symbol of all things fallen—an angel descended from heaven's estate or the hapless Icarus punished by the sun for his father's hubris—and yet it is unmistakably a bird, and unlike Icarus whose wings fell into the sea, its wings are intact, half-opened across the exposed face of its tomb, a clear impression of perfect feathers attached to delicate bones, imparting the sense of an undiminished longing to fly. B's pedigree is an old one, much older I think than mine.

B has stolen my bookmark again, flying it to the screen door, daring me to give chase so he can play keep-away from the clumsy primate. My only hope is to wait him out by feigning indifference to bookmarks and to those who steal them. Usually, though, I'll play the game and lunge around in mock exasperation, pleading for the return of my property as he clatters from one place to the next, me lumbering in pursuit, sometimes getting within an inch of his beak before he flits off to another perch. Since his cargo is longer than he is and nearly as wide, modifications to his flight plan are necessary in these cases. The effect is comic, especially when he takes off with the load unevenly distributed. The tips of his wings slap against the paper in a rat-a-tat-tat until he makes a midair adjustment and corrects the imbalance. He does this by hovering for a split second after takeoff, releasing the bookmark and then grabbing it dead center, looking like a tiny man with a yardstick clamped in his teeth overbalancing with his arms before falling from the top rung of a stepladder. I've tried photographing this performance but always end up with either a very clear picture of the space where he'd been or an unrecognizable blur that reminds me of those images of purported ectoplasm snapped in atmospheric old houses and offered as proof for the existence of ghosts. I now own an assortment of bookmarks embossed with B's beak print along with who knows how many books whose pages bear the same endorsement or, in many cases, a more emphatic sign of his presence— pages with triangular bits torn from their edges.

LOOKING INTO B'S UNEXPECTEDLY VACANT BOX, I DID A DOUBLE TAKE. Our minds preconstruct the salient features of familiar scenes an instant before we return to them, and when the featured attraction is missing, our brains stumble a bit as they rush to catch up with reality. I lifted the towel carefully and checked to make sure B hadn't burrowed beneath it or gotten tangled in its folds. Emphasizing that I'd brought more strawberry, I looked under Rebecca's desk and behind bookcases. I turned over pillows, rifled through papers, and examined the closed windows for a third time in as many minutes. Thinking, "Bird's not here. Bird's got to be here," I repeated the process several more times, panic rising as I widened my pattern by crawling on hands and knees along the baseboards, arriving finally at the heating vent in the wall. The slats were open. Wide open.

When one of my college girlfriends mentioned upon returning to school in the fall that her pet hamster, Schultz, had escaped into eternity by squeezing through a heating grate in her parents' house and sliding as a result irretrievably into the ductwork, I found the idea grimly amusing. Believing B had met a similar fate struck me as evidence that the karmic wheel turned slowly but reliably. I called into the abyss and pressed my ear against the opening, expecting to hear frightened chirps or the sound of claws sliding on metal as they tried to gain purchase.

When I bolted downstairs and announced that I was reasonably certain B had killed himself accidentally by falling into the bowels of the house, I could tell from Rebecca's eyes that this was news she wasn't prepared to hear. I explained the particulars as we hurried back to B's room, wondered to myself how difficult it would be to dismantle a heating system. "Isn't there somewhere else he could be?" Rebecca asked as she checked box, towel, desk, bookcases, windows, papers, and pillows.

"He could be with Michelangelo in Florence if he's got a time machine and an interest in art, but I've checked this entire room, and he isn't here. The only way out is down that damn heating vent."

"I wish you had a time machine and would use it," she snapped. "What are we going to do?"

I'm ashamed to admit that I didn't want to do anything except sit with Rebecca and discuss what morons we'd been for not realizing how close B had been to flying his way out of a box we should have had brains enough to cover with a screen that fit. This, along with all that could be said about our even more boneheaded mistake of failing to close the vent, promised hours of self-loathing and recrimination. Of course, as things stand now, I'd give B a kidney if he needed one and surgeons could somehow make it fit. If he were trapped in the house, I'd tear it down to the foundation, steal a supermarket cart for my stuff, and live in a bus kiosk with my rescued bird. Then, however, when it appeared that he was entombed and possibly dead, the idea of tearing into walls and a serpentine network of ductwork seemed to me pointless and likely to end in expensive destruction or the more depressing circumstance of finding his remains.

"Maybe you should at least take out the grid so we can shine a light in and see if he's down there." This was not a request. Rebecca can be surprisingly persuasive for someone who is only five foot one and weighs scarcely more than one hundred pounds. "I can't stand the thought of him trapped and frightened and waiting to die." She looked as sad as I'd ever seen her look when she said this, fidgeting with her hair the way she does when things aren't right, her voice poised between tears and angry frustration. To be honest, I was close to tears myself, thinking about my stupidity and the resultant loss of a project that seemed to be going so well. As the quality of late-afternoon light shifted, scattering itself differently as evening scudded in with a slight breeze from the west, the pink woodwork (Rebecca cannot explain why she chose such hideous paint, and I cannot explain why I agreed to it) around the windows grew less garish. I remember thinking how cheerless everything looked, how immune to moderation by even that daft color we could formerly joke about.

"We can try," I said, "but I don't think it'll do us much good. That vent drops more or less straight down to the basement, so even if we do spot him, I don't know how the hell we'll get him out." Intending to hunt up flashlights and an assortment of screwdrivers, I shuffled toward the door, thinking how cruel it is that history can never be changed.

When a newspaper erroneously published Mark Twain's obituary in 1897, thirteen years ahead of schedule, Twain responded by saying, "The report of my death was an exaggeration." B is probably unique among house sparrows in having a personal appreciation of Twain's experience in this regard. By neglecting the simple expedient of looking up while searching for a bird (Holmes, you amaze me), we'd reached our lachrymose conclusion in haste, based on the faulty premise that B had dropped when in fact he'd made his way to the highest point in the room. It's tempting to think he amused himself by watching us search, waited until the joke paled before revealing his presence. But since we hadn't known one another long enough to take such liberties, I'd guess the inconvenience of being trapped finally made him gamble that the mammals would rescue him without subsequently eating him.

Built in 1908, our house has a lot of old fixtures. One of these was a rose-colored shade with brass filial hanging from the ceiling in B's room. I still have it, stashed in a closet somewhere along with the mounting hardware. The incandescent bulb whose light it softened we've replaced with one of those circular fluorescent tubes that screw into an existing socket; it's ugly, looking like an artist's conception of a space station in a 1950s edition of *Popular Mechanics.* I miss the old arrangement and the translucent glow it produced, but even a sixty-watt incandescent bulb burns hot enough to blister skin, whereas the fluorescent gives off almost no heat at all. Fortunately, the light wasn't on when B landed in the shade, slid down its concavity, and ended up pinned beneath the bulb. He made bashful chirps and futile bird's-feet-on-glass scurrying noises as he tried to get himself back to the rim.

Rebecca, her attention drawn by sounds from above, noticed B first, or rather a dark spot on the glass that expanded and contracted with the opening and closing of his wings as he tried to scramble free. As I stood on a stool and removed the shade, I half-expected him to explode away from me like a quail flushed from the underbrush—an idea very much at odds with the calm, almost regal indifference he displayed as I lowered him. He might have been a potentate in an oddly designed sedan chair carried by slaves. We placed the shade on a pillow, Rebecca helping me as if it were a ponderous weight far too heavy for one person to carry. B remained inscrutable throughout our jubilation but accepted bits of wilting strawberry with the condescension of an atheist taking communion on a dare.

Over the years I've learned to read B's thoughts and moods—what he wants, how he feels, what he's about to do. And he, in his way, appears to understand me. I'll swear an oath he was embarrassed by what I imagine he viewed as his aeronautical depantsing. And something about the way he remained in that lamp shade for several minutes after we got him down made me think he was dwelling on whatever lesson he'd learned from his navigational error. "It's as if he's trying to atone," I said to Rebecca.

Rehashing the details and reveling in the luxury of a second chance, we sat with our would-be pilot for the better part of an hour following his rescue. After closing the vent, we covered unused electrical outlets with duct tape (we've since traded up to those plastic socket inserts parents buy to protect their toddlers from electrocution) and generally dealt with the room as if it were an enemy we needed to disarm. By the time we returned to the kitchen, I'd admitted to Rebecca that she was right: release the bird as soon as possible. Doing so wouldn't be easy, but it weighed on me that B could have died in a heating shaft or been fricasseed under a lightbulb. We'd skirted these evils, but they undermined my arguments about the relative safety of keeping a bird indoors versus the hazards of life in the wild. And besides, it was hard to pretend that B viewed us as boon companions. He didn't act afraid when we overstayed our welcome after doling out his meals, but eyed us suspiciously as we moved about the room. He'd perch briefly on our fingers, give little more than a token struggle when we picked him up, but I got the feeling he wished that either he or we were someplace else. I reminded myself that birds were unable to exceed their programming, were attractive little automatons but robots nonetheless. After being released somewhere close to home, perhaps he'd take up residence in our area, even visit now and then—one sparrow standing out from the others, lingering longest on the fence rail, last to flee at our approach. I described this to Rebecca, who smiled without comment. I diced another strawberry, had a slug of cold coffee, and went back upstairs where, as it turned out, B had also been thinking things over.

B's tail feathers are bedraggled. He mangles them every year, not because he's a psychotic feather-plucker like caged parrots driven mad by isolation and neglect but because something about tail feathers pisses him off. Following his yearly molt, they are pristine and aerodynamically perfect. Within a week, fraying is noticeable again, and with the passage of another twelve months his tail looks as though it's been run through a pencil sharpener. I suppose Freud would have diagnosed some class of conversion neurosis extroverted through repeated and aggressive tail preening. But Freud never saw B casting a critical eye at those feathers before running his beak along the shafts, tugging vehemently until the ends become ragged and spiky. I've wondered if he reshapes his tail as a countercultural statement of some kind at odds with his overall conservatism in matters of dress—handsome black bib, striking white ruff about his neck; his other feathers spotless and groomed to perfection. It's doubly interesting that regardless of how radically he reshapes or truncates his tail, his skills as a flyer are never affected.

It's a gorgeous day in the middle of May, and B's hopped up on hormones. He's so full of himself and eager to have my attention that he's having what my mother would have called a "conniption fit." I had lots of these as a child, triggered whenever I ceased being the center of everyone's universe for more than five minutes at a stretch. B shares the trait and stands shrieking on my shoulder, annoyed by the way I continue to write on a yellow legal tablet despite his emphatic desist orders. He's presented me with one orange and one blue plastic milk bottle cap, one desiccated leaf, one twig, strips of shredded newspaper, and a bookmark with a phone number jotted on it that I've been missing for weeks. These deliveries (apart from the bookmark) are made rapidly and without wasted motion. I never tire of seeing his determined face moving toward me from across the room with a cap twice the diameter of his head secured in his beak. Mere inches from my nose, he prepares for landing by pulling his body at a right angle to his trajectory, fans what's left of his tail downward to gain wind resistance for braking, reverses thrust with his wings, extends his feet that have been tucked close to his belly during flight, and with an audible flutter, the merest flick of the whole apparatus, veers to his right and steps onto my shoulder with all the force of an unuttered whisper.

B stood flapping on the rim of a brass pot when I returned to his room. He wobbled like an apprentice tightrope walker, alternately shooting out one or the other of his wings in an effort to balance. Rebecca and I removed his box after making our safety improvements, having decided to indulge him for a while in his ambition to fly. We brought in the cage we'd bought at Newberry's and readied it for service by installing the standard accessories—wooden perches set at differing heights; mirror with sliding, abacus-like beads for entertainment;

plastic water and seed dishes clamped in on either side of the entrance. We planned to lock B up overnight, and release him for periodic exercise during the day. Provided the guards were nearby, he'd be a trustee whose privileges included outings in and over the prison yard. I thought about getting myself a truncheon and a pair of mirrored sunglasses.

I walked over and offered B strawberry, but when I got within two paces, he performed a convincing imitation of a bird flying away from a human. Having removed himself to the top shelf of the bookcase, he looked at me as if to say, "Didn't think I could do that, did you, buster?"

I didn't. At least not with such aplomb. Seemed to me either he'd been doing a lot more practicing when I wasn't around than I'd thought or house sparrows in general, if not B in particular, were precocious flyers. And it occurred to me as I watched B watch me that getting him into a cage for the night might now be a challenge. If he'd still take food from my hand, I could possibly nab him while he ate—a ploy that would work only the first time, if then. Depending on his current level of paranoia and how quickly he could get into the air when I made my move, he'd certainly be able to avoid me should he choose that route. "Thank God," I thought, "he has trouble landing." Although slow and noisy by current standards, his flight from the planter was excellent. But his arrival at the bookcase was a graceless skid.

As I've gotten older and my goals have become less lofty, I'm frequently surprised by the importance of what I or others may think of as trifles. When I was a kid, there was an old guy in town named Herbie who my father assured me was "simple," a gentle euphemism for describing someone whose mental capacity falls with a plunk on the debit side of the ledger. My cohorts and I viewed Herbie, to the extent we thought about him at all, chiefly as entertainment of the local-color variety. We referred to him as Herbie the Park Bum. He was always well, if casually, dressed in Salvation Army thrift-store chic and spent long summer days hanging out in Cameron Park, the modest green in the town square that was lined with trees and Civil War mortars, their barrels stuffed with beer cans, condoms, and potato chip bags. Within my lifetime, the park contained an honest-to-God bandstand of the type used by brass players not overly fussy about detail in the march tunes they favored. Where Herbie spent his nights and winters remains a mystery, although, given the number of broken capillaries on his face, Jim Beam may have been with him. I can't remember ever seeing him drunk, but that was the rumor. Another had it that he was a reformed politician. He might have been a seasonal apparition blowing in and out with the robins.

Herbie's most memorable characteristic was his partiality for a toy six-shooter he wore holstered low over his right hip. He was a sight: a lanky, potbellied old man armed by Mattel, wearing, along with a deafening plaid shirt, rayon pants in retina-damaging green—an ensemble in hopeless competition with a nose in need of girders to support it. Encounters with Herbie involved seeing who had the quickest draw. The fact that none of us carried anything resembling a sidearm didn't present a hardship as long as you remembered to form thumb and index finger into an approximation of a pistol, square off with Herbie about twenty paces apart, and twitch slightly as if ready and eager to shoot somebody. In the only actual conversation I had with him, Herbie told me that what made him happiest was having enough spare cash to buy rolls of caps for his gun. Anyway, that was the gist—his speech meandered and was hard to follow. I was sixteen or seventeen at the time and wise enough with inexperience to conclude, based on our little chat, that Herbie was on par with an old lady in town who liked to converse with mailboxes and telephone poles. She wore undersized wigs too small to cover her own matted thatch and had sixty-eight cats running loose in her house.

After staring at me for a minute, B flew from the bookcase to my shoulder and has, in a manner of speaking, never really left it. I can close my eyes or stare into space and relive the surprise and delight of an instant when the order of things reversed and a bird flew to me instead of away. Since that day, I've tried without success to explain the significance of that moment in a way that makes sense to those of my friends who view this whole "bird thing" as proof I'm delusional. It's easy enough finding words and phrases: "Profound experience, life-altering event, magical, charming, sublime, intense, unforgettable, amazing, truly amazing, incredibly amazing, so amazing I couldn't believe it, amazing when I think about it, I know this sounds crazy but . . ."

Descriptions don't work. The essential quality of a remarkable experience doesn't often survive the telling and, like a translated poem, can only be damaged. I wish we acquired a purer language, learned as we mature, inappropriate for expressing anything mundane. Music comes closest but fails on specifics, imparting emotion without context beyond the program notes or the lyrics. But we manage, sometimes deeming one another "simple" on the topics of cap guns and birds. Herbie died more than thirty years ago, and because I suspect whatever marks the grave contains but his name and dates, I propose the following epitaph:

In Life: Possibly Sane. Probably Happy.

"A VERY INTERESTING THING JUST HAPPENED," I SAID TO REBECCA, WHO was busy destroying the living room with her latest attempt to make a belly-dance costume. Her sewing projects involve the production of large debris fields of the sort one normally associates with train derailments. I always walk in expecting to find emergency response teams combing the wreckage. Her goals in these endeavors are apparently twofold. The first and most important is to misplace enough pins and needles to guarantee at least one ending up embedded in my ass or, failing that, in one of my feet. The second is to actually make a costume that doesn't appear as if it were made by someone nodding off in an opium stupor. Rebecca readily admits that she is not a naturally gifted seamstress. She perseveres, however, and with antlike tenacity produces costumes that are really quite lovely. But, I digress.

"The bird flew up to the bookcase when I went in and from there to my shoulder. To my shoulder, can you believe it? It was the most incredible thing."

I wasn't convinced the performance would be repeated since, in my experience, animals relish opportunities to make human beings look foolish. If, for example, you discover your cat wearing a lace apron and serving tea to a delegation of mice, it's a dead certainty she won't do so again when you call in a witness. This is why anecdotal evidence is suspect and good science insists that reputed facts be reproducible. I needn't have worried. B made a sloppy landing on my shoulder as soon as Rebecca and I entered his room. He stood on me calmly, clucking sotto voce, his sharp little toes poking through my T-shirt as he maintained his grip. His vocalizations are varied and, as I've come to learn, subtle in their ability to express a wide range of emotion. This observation is at variance with the common belief that house sparrows are monosyllabic, tone-deaf squawkers whose discordant musical traditions are more rooted in twentieth-century atonality than, for example, the dulcet arias of such celebrated avian singers as the song sparrow or the nightingale.

As B matured and became personally interested in my behavior, his cluckings grew more complex, developing into a muttered stream-of-consciousness commentary he sometimes carries on with himself when I'm inattentive to his agenda or when he's busy with something new, puzzling, or that he finds objectionable. Depending on circumstance, pitch, tempo, and volume change, as do the "syllables" he uses to construct these monologues. House sparrows are inventive, if not melodic—but even here, B often surprises me. I've read differing estimates on the number of vocalizations house sparrows are capable of producing, with the high end ranging between fifteen and twenty. I'd say one hundred or more is closer to the mark, many of them with specific meanings I've been able to decipher—"please," "thank you," "don't move," "come back," to name a few. After all this time I understand a tolerable amount of "Sparrow," but I can't enunciate it. The few calls I've taken a stab at voicing are made with such a broad American accent as to render them meaningless to him. Just as B comprehends a good bit of English but can't speak it worth a damn.

Impressed, Rebecca held out her index finger the way people automatically do when confronting a tame bird. Most trust-based relationships begin cautiously, and B was being careful. I suppose that from his perspective the whole setup—food, box, heating pad, the so-called rescue from the lamp shade, my constant fawning—could have been an elaborate trap we'd built in pursuit of sinister ends. But if he harbored such thoughts, he dismissed them and stepped onto Rebecca's finger, where he stayed for ten or fifteen seconds before leaping back to my shoulder. Thus, B established priorities. For whatever reason, he made a decision to bond with me and has stuck with it for seven years, always picking up where we left off, even after I've been absent for protracted periods. B's fond of Rebecca, and shows unmistakable affection for her, more so as the years have passed, but his relationship with her is distinctly different from the one he has with me; "more circumscribed" is the simplest way to put it.

In the space of less than a minute, B has done the following things: Torn off a strip of newspaper (a valuable commodity in this house, I can tell you) from the sheet spread beneath one of the ficus trees. Winged his way twice around the room, landed on my chest, considered shoving the paper up my nose. It's June, and he's got a hankering to build a nest. Having decided my nostril lacks the necessary square footage, he stashed the paper down the neck of my sweatshirt, flew to the top of his cage (for politically correct reasons, henceforth known as his "house"), surveyed his domain, rose straight up about three inches, turned a half-circle, descended about ten inches, hovered briefly at the entrance, zoomed in to the upper perch, sidled over to his mirror, gave it several vigorous pecks, and returned to me.

That first evening of our alliance with B stands out as the point of departure Rebecca and I made from the relatively normal lives we'd been leading into our current status as "the weirdoes who dote on their birds." We spent most of the remaining daylight watching B practice his takeoffs and landings. Every few minutes, he'd land in our laps, on our shoulders, or, increasingly, on our noses. This fascination with human faces, particularly noses, is a characteristic common to all but one of our sparrows—he's tame but has abandonment issues. For several months after taking wing and coming to terms with us (think of "coming to terms" as Rebecca and I agreeing to furnish them with food, shelter, friendship, entertainment, and full medical benefits for life), they seem to find our mugs irresistible. Perhaps, to a small bird, our faces represent the essence of human individuality, our noses the chairs we've set out inviting them to have a seat and know us better. Their eagerness to accept this perceived invitation can be painful, especially when they lose their anchor like a rock climber with a broken rope and flail down your face to end dangling by a claw from a nerve-laden lower lip.

As we sat with B, my recently acquired resolve to set him free faded with the sunlight. Rebecca remained torn on the release issue—indecision based on concern for B's welfare and on her belief that I became too immersed in him, too subsumed in a routine of cloistering myself with a creature that held her for months in relatively low esteem.

There's no denying that he treated her at times as a menial whose function in my absence was to serve his food and get out. Rebecca claims that by the time dusk fell and she returned to her sewing project, "I was pretty certain B wouldn't be leaving." I reached the same conclusion myself when, half an hour later, I put B to bed in a way that didn't involve penning him in a box—the start of a routine that has become a nightly ritual important to us both.

4

BALANCING ACT

I tie my hat—I crease my shawl—
Life's little duties do—precisely—
As the very least
Were infinite to me—
    —Emily Dickinson, poem no. 443, in
      The Complete Poems of Emily Dickinson

Consistency is the last resort of the unimaginative.
    —Oscar Wilde

THE PARISHIONERS ALL LOOK SO CLEAN-CUT EXITING THE BIG STONE church not far from our house. They flow blinking into the sunlight and collect in little tidal pools that merge into breakers as Rebecca and I pass through on our way to get espresso. This happens every Sunday in what I refer to as "Swimming the Baptist Tide." They've recently installed a big internally lighted sign on a corner of their property, a smaller version of the kind of thing you often see towering on a pole near a freeway exit. I'm a little confused by this week's slogan—"Why church: It's the place where God fans passionate spirituality." To be honest, I'd have hoped for something a little less abstruse from such a venerable Protestant sect. Even after mentally inserting the omitted question mark, I have no idea what they're trying to say. If the sign read, "Why church?: It's the place where God gives you a spiritual wedgy," I'd be tempted to accept their veiled invitation.

I'm not generous when deprived of caffeine and must remind myself how odd, if not positively disturbing, *I* must appear to people (especially older ones) who think Lawrence Welk really knew how to jazz up swing tunes. Rouged and coifed beneath decorative hats, the older women clutch their purses and Bibles as we pass—I with a devil's goatee and a rat's nest of wild dark hair hanging down my back. Rebecca, if it's cold outside, is clad in droopy sweatpants, a full-length coat, and the kind of ear-flapped geek hat Elmer Fudd would endorse. In all probability, there's one or more sparrow turds stuck on her somewhere (and on me, but we won't talk about that), which makes it at least plausible when I tell strangers she's my older sister and has had lots of head trauma.

We could walk to Starbucks earlier or alter our route by cutting through Colonel Summers Park where, for reasons I can't explain, people prefer to sit in their cars while eating their lunches rather than avail themselves of the well-kept lawn and picnic tables set beneath lovely old trees. Had we ever gotten around to releasing B, this is the place we'd probably have done it. The park bears the name of one Owen Summers, commander of the Second U.S. Volunteer Infantry during the Spanish-American War. There's a likeness of the colonel on a bronze plaque affixed to a big commemorative rock that sits near the sidewalk. "Gay" has recently been emblazoned above the plaque. It's marvelous that those who are such deft hands with spray paint have time to research the sexual orientation of obscure nineteenth-century military personnel. Rebecca and I could cut through the park, but I'd miss the Baptists and how wonderfully American it is to see them on the hoof in Sunday morning fellowship. Besides, we've got our routine. It's all Rebecca and I can do to get out of the house before noon without stiffing the birds on one thing or another. They all want attention and aren't bashful about lobbying to get it. I'd like to have them fill out those little customer comment cards like the ones restaurant chains provide—and transfer, I suspect, directly from suggestion box to garbage can. Responses to the question "How Was Our Service?" would probably run the gamut from "Great, couldn't be better" to "Sucked," "Lousy," "There was hair in my seed dish."

We've had birds for more than seven years now, and what they want most, you see, is our time. I can readily believe B would prefer, on principle, that I stay seated in his room at night in an attitude of quiet reverence while he sleeps. To the extent that living with tame birds has a drawback (apart from the considerable amount of debris it generates), it's the extraordinary amount of attention birds crave from people with whom they've bonded. Of course, this is also part of the charm. It seemed to me early on that an instinctual need to belong to a flock, and whatever sense of community such membership provides, would account for their desire to interact with us. I now consider this only a partial explanation.

How much socializing a bird engages in has a lot to do with its species. Raptors are relatively solitary beings, as are several types of seabirds who spend much of their lives over open water, returning to land but once a year to mate, build nests, and raise a family. Many birds that typically gather in flocks appear to band together for mutual protection while feeding. During long northern winters, some exploit the advantage of shared body heat by roosting at night in huge enclaves, but, here again, utility rather than the joys of social intercourse seems to be the motivating factor. These generalizations are just that and don't take into consideration the many exceptions one would expect to find in a class of creatures numbering close to two hundred families and the better part of ten thousand species. This much variety accommodates a behavioral continuum from reclusive to gregarious, embracing an enormous territory of subtle motivations affecting why and how birds relate to one another.

But as far as I can tell, house sparrows enjoy hanging out together as an end in itself. They congregate daily in a big Oregon grape bush hanging over the sidewalk not far from our house and set up a racket that will cease abruptly whenever a pedestrian passes underneath. Some researchers speculate that house sparrows convene these cacophonous chatter sessions as a means of exchanging information about sources of food and water. If this is true, I've undoubtably figured in their discussions from time to time: "That bastard on the corner forgot to scatter seed this morning, and would it kill him to scour out the bird bath more than twice a week?" House sparrows mate for life and are monogamous. Listening to the forlorn chirping of a female whose mate had been killed by a neighborhood cat last summer was keening, mournful, and almost more than I could bear. Even B, who pays scant attention to outside bird voices, seemed affected. He sat on his window perch cocking his head, moved I think by hearing for the first time in his life the extemporaneous poetry of loss. The widow sat on a telephone line until dusk, calling and calling for a life she knew wasn't coming back. It's a wonder to me that ages of accumulated sorrow, both human and animal, have left the world uncrushed by the weight.

Eventually, I gave up trying to figure out why our sparrows love being with us. Finding themselves in a situation far different from anything they'd encounter as wild birds, they adapted accordingly and became an avian aristocracy unburdened by the necessity of toiling for their supper and were freed, as a consequence, to pursue other interests. In their eyes, I'd guess Rebecca and I are members of their flock. But also, their mates, parents, friends, and servants—a strange amalgam that, if thought of in human terms, would also be illegal. It could be argued that we've fostered a dependence in these creatures that demeans them, that a gilded cage is still a cage. As one who has watched a zoo leopard trying in vain to cover her feces on the cement slab she called home, I believe it's possible to demean an animal not just physically, but in ways that reduce its mind to an insane contortion of what it was or might have been. I hope I'm correct in inferring from our sparrows' joie de vivre that fate has spared them these ghastly alternatives.

On the other hand, we have friends who insist that we're the ones demeaned by our self-imposed dedication to a bunch of birds, of all things. One popular theory has us lavishing on our sparrows a virtual Niagara of misplaced parenting impulses that could be directed more profitably toward rearing offspring. Both Rebecca and I admit to an occasional twinge of regret at not having a child, someone to park us in a low-budget nursing home when we finally become incontinent. The ship has not sailed on this possibility but has nearly cleared the harbor headed for open water. Most likely, a jaded bureaucrat will sign the commitment papers. If, indeed, I end my days propped in a chair marinating in my own urine, all I ask is to be able to cast my mind back to the happy past I'm presently living.

Our sparrows need individual attention—games, for example, and the chance to sit on our shoulders and preen. They need breakfast and fresh water. They need their rooms tidied. A descent into chaos would be the rapid, inevitable result of skipping daily bird-room maintenance. Those who haven't lived with umpteen birds flying freely around the upstairs of their house can amuse themselves by speculating about how much entropy or tendency to disorder such a circumstance entails. By noon, we've usually fretted over and ignored the more general household chores such as vacuuming, laundry, dishes, and gardening. I like watching Rebecca do her morning sit-ups with a bird on her chest, another clinging to her head. Think of her as a human carnival ride for sparrows.

Emerson might find us guilty of "a foolish consistency," but routines evolved over seven years constitute a system we all can live with. Because B and the others don't like tardiness, sleeping in past seven is difficult, especially in spring and summer. Birds, naturally, are early risers and see absolutely no reason Rebecca and I shouldn't be, too. B has not been sympathetic to my informing him that I'm basically nocturnal. You should see the look I get if I disturb him when *he's* sleeping—a sidelong, squinting, "Do you *know* what time it is? This better be good" sort of face. He likes War Bird by eight, breakfast by nine, cookie and games no later than eleven.

Life is on track by the time Rebecca and I find ourselves wading through Baptists. We sometimes joke that this flock of reliable churchgoers is a sort of indicator species that tells us all is well in our little niche. We're having a pleasant walk, anticipating an imminent nip of caffeine, a late breakfast to follow. As we walk by their medieval-looking church with its crenelated battlements from which one could pour boiling oil should the need arise, I wonder about the social aspects of ministering to the soul and about the tangible structures that grow from the human need to gather in groups. I suppose we find the same comfort in numbers as do birds of a feather gathered in a field.

Content to let me lead our late-afternoon room-cleaning waltz, B flits about on my upper body, shifting position for a better view as I complete my appointed rounds. I couldn't tell you why he's so interested in this daily fifteen-minute series of tasks. It's as if he thinks I'll screw it up if he doesn't keep tabs.

Today's musical accompaniment is Franz von Suppé's Light Cavalry Overture. *I'm looking forward to the part that so successfully evokes an* image of cantering horses that it's become a cliché. B likes this selection and stays in my palm as I bounce him rhythmically to match the music's goofy cadence. If he were wearing riding boots, the effect would be perfect, inasmuch as a squatting bird's posture is not unlike a human jockey tucked up in that uncomfortable-looking way their profession demands.

Removing the sliding plastic tray from inside B's house, I brush from underneath his perch the little pile of dried turds that accumulated overnight. These particular specimens are pink, the result of B having gobbled nearly half a Bing cherry last evening before bedtime. The ordinarily white paste commonly found in avian feces is uric acid (the bird's urine) and is typically ejected along with solid waste that forms the dark part of each shipment. Birds don't have bladders—another weight-saving adaptation.

Squatting near the garbage bag, I blow twenty-four hours' worth of chaff from one of the room's two seed dishes and then pick out a dozen seed-encrusted finch turds deposited there by B's hillbilly roommates. It's like digging for prizes in a cereal box, and I feel childishly elated each time I come up with one—nobody can say I don't enjoy life's simple pleasures. B loops the room, lands on my knee to evaluate the harvest, preens his wing feathers, and gives me a delicate peck on the nose when I lean over to kiss his head.

If finch dung were gold, I'd have just found El Dorado. Some days the zebras concentrate on greens and a slice of hazelnut bread, but today they've been tromping around inside the second (and larger) seed dish eating and defecating with abandon. The efficiency with which they service two biological imperatives simultaneously is perversely admirable, an example of such perfect symmetry I long to stencil the yin-yang symbol on their fuselages. B stands on the rim of the dish when he eats and finds it inexplicable, I think, that the finches refuse to follow his example. B accompanies me to the closet but reverses course when I emerge carrying the yellow broom, an item that has two attributes he dislikes: it's yellow and it's a broom. He's learned to tolerate most things for which he has an immediate and visceral antipathy, but not the yellow broom. Yellow appears to bother him on purely aesthetic grounds (he grumbles if Rebecca comes into his room wearing a yellow shirt but will, on occasion, play with a yellow bottle cap), and he absolutely draws the line when it's the color of an infernal human contrivance capable of swatting him from the air. Since an evening three or four years ago when a friend of mine (with whom my relationship became for a time a wee bit strained) described using a broom to beat two juvenile house sparrows to death when they entered her living room by the fireplace chimney, I've stopped viewing B as irrational when it comes to brooms.

While I sweep up seed hulls and shit, B sits nearby, watching me shepherd whatever I find into a central pile that he'll disperse by flying over it at low altitude when my back is turned. I've switched off the music because I need to hear where he is when I'm moving around occupied. Despite mistrusting the broom, he's been known to fly onto my back or thigh or butt while I'm sweeping, and because he's light enough to land surreptitiously, my failure to detect his approach has led to several close calls—accidentally brushing him off me by lowering my arm, for example. No injuries resulted, but these incidents startle him and frighten the hell out of me.

Satisfied that I'm following protocol, B resumes playing with the new Popsicle stick I gave him yesterday after I retrieved an old one from behind the couch where it had lain long enough to acquire a shroud of dust, finch feathers, and hair. He watched me unearth this antiquity and staked an immediate claim to it by trying to snatch it from my hand. Such disagreements are inevitable whenever one of my salvage operations uncovers some long-missing item he once found diverting. Passé objects are supposed to wind up in B's wicker toy basket but are often mislaid and forgotten. Our tussle ended with a victory for me and an indignant bird shrieking the equivalent of "Stop, thief, stop" embroidered with expletives.

Still testy about the theft of his property when I returned to his room half an hour later, B immediately searched my hands, pockets, and down the neck of my T-shirt. A bird ransacking your person is a unique sensation that feels as if you've been waylaid by a self-directed feather duster that's equipped with several things that can poke you. He found what he was looking for in the waistband of my jeans but hesitated before tugging it out, suspicious of the switch I'd pulled by substituting a new and therefore less weathered stick for the original that was far too revolting to clean off and give back. Considering how sharp B's vision and memory are, I don't doubt he was able to detect discrepancies in the wood grain between the two.

Stick mania is in its second day and shows no sign of abating. Floor sweeping has caused a delay of game by disrupting the playing field, but now that I'm headed to the closet to put broom and dustpan away, B risks shoving his stick in my face. When I toss it across the room, he pounces on it like a hawk nabbing a mouse. Although B's playful enthusiasm temporarily trumps the broom issue, he remembers that the closet is a dark place, an area to be avoided in the commonsense way any portal to the underworld should be given a wide berth. He therefore flies his toy to the top of the television—which is covered with a pink place mat and serves as a feeding station stocked with bread, apple slices, and greens—and waits for me to return from my foolhardy excursion into hell's vestibule. All I've got to do now is empty his water dish into the five-gallon bilge bucket, use a paper towel to wipe out the dish, and then refill it from one of the water jugs we keep on hand. Without the broom to ward him off, this simple operation is complicated to the brink of impossibility by B's insistence that I get my priorities straight and play the damn game. The stick when I toss it slides beneath the futon frame. While B cautiously retrieves it, I gain enough time to complete the water project before he makes it back to my shoulder for round number two. When I leave to get his dinner, he clings to the screen door and shrieks.

REBECCA AND I NEVER FORMALLY AGREED WE'D KEEP B, JUST MADE incremental adjustments furthering that end while tacitly maintaining we'd release him as soon as he was ready to fend for himself. It could be said we're still waiting, that any day now he'll be an outside bird surviving by his wits on the street. Rebecca said to me recently that we've been living with birds for such a long time now that she sometimes has a hard time remembering what it was like when we didn't. She once told me that it seemed scary to her to think that on the day we found B "we knew less about more bird-related things" than she would have thought possible. I laughed at this, not because I disagreed, but because her phrasing reminded me of something one of my relatives said when I was a child.

Uncle Ralph, oldest of my father's five siblings, lived out near the northwestern tip of Pennsylvania, in Warren, and had been, like Ernest

Hemingway, an ambulance driver in World War I. Ralph was an accomplished pianist, a dedicated Mason (as was my father), and, by the end of his long life, the kind of cranky old coot who yelled at neighborhood kids to get and stay off his lawn. His widow, now nearly one hundred years old, only recently gave up bowling. Once a year, Ralph drove down to see his baby brother, and he and my father would paint the town red by going out for beer and steamed shrimp at the Moose or the Elks or at one of the local "Hose Houses," which is how people referred to the social clubs maintained by volunteer fire companies in the area. You haven't experienced the best of small-town life until you've seen a contingent of heavy drinkers clinging to a raffle-financed hook-and-ladder truck as they weave their way to a four-alarm blaze.

At any rate, the thing about Ralph is that I recall him asking me if I knew how to play "Turkey in the Straw." I was seven and had taken approximately two violin lessons and was less of a prodigy on that instrument than a mannequin might have been expected to be. I said I didn't know any such tune, and he asked why not and looked at me as if I were the first person he'd run across who possessed this particular deficiency. Our musical discussion, however, left less of an impression on me than overhearing Ralph comment to my father later in the day that "Al knows less about more things than anyone I've ever met."

Al married my aunt Stella in the late thirties, their union the result of a correspondence carried on for several months after one or the other of them answered a "So-and-so wishes to meet a like-minded so-and-so. Object: Matrimony" newspaper posting. Stella eventually boarded a train, traveled to Sacramento, California, and took Al as her husband. A year or two later, they moved back to my hometown, Sunbury, Pennsylvania, and spent the rest of their lives there. By the time I heard this story, Al had been years dead and Parkinson's disease had wrecked Stella who, stooped and shuffling when she walked, sat listening to Chopin and Strauss until the clock ran out. She left me $1,282.63.

Early photographs of Stella show an attractively plain young woman wearing rimless spectacles and a look suggesting that for her, trigonometry had not been much of a challenge. Indeed, she had been her high school class's valedictorian and Ralph's equal as a pianist. It was to her, kneeling across from me, that I took my first unassisted steps, her arms wide open in the classic toddler-welcoming gesture at which childless people sometimes excel. This, my oldest intact memory, is a mental heirloom I'd be the poorer without.

To think of Stella journeying three thousand miles to marry a guy she'd never met startles me even now. I'd as easily believe my timid little aunt hustled pool in her spare time or was a renowned kickboxer, but there you are. Al, as it turned out, was somewhat less scintillating than suggested by the elegant prose of his letters. Speculation quickly morphed into certainty that the words Stella found so enticing had been the work of a latter-day Cyrano. Al looked a bit like Jimmy Durante but with a more conventional nose and did well enough as a handyman to end up leaving at his death five or six thousand dollars in large bills that Stella found stashed in his basement workshop. I understand that he had several children in California from whom he was estranged. Perhaps it was of a reconciliation with them that he dreamed when I'd see him once a month snoring in an overstuffed armchair until Stella's announcement that Sunday dinner was served. According to my father, Al was an ill-informed blowhard who believed the government was suppressing water-powered cars, that sort of thing. I gather it was this side of his personality that prompted Ralph's bon mot and explains, possibly, the modest turnout at Al's funeral. I can't remember that he and I ever exchanged words beyond "hello" and "good-bye," and had he been a fictional character, he could scarcely have been more peripheral to my life. What was said about him is more real to me than whoever it was he may actually have been. It's a sad commentary on a man's life to be remembered as the butt of a cruel observation, but after more than forty years, I still think Ralph's comment is funny. Maybe it was his delivery.

When B moved in, Rebecca and I probably *did* know less about more aspects of living with birds than just about anyone around. We managed to save his life because we had someone to call for instructions and sense enough to do so. If Craig hadn't been home when we phoned, I'd be writing on some non-bird-related topic and our cats would still have free rein of the upstairs. People now call *us* with bird questions. They assume that we can identify a species based on nothing more than a hazy description, "Well, it has feathers and what appear to be feet." They fancy we'll know what to do if a bird they've found is injured or sick. To some extent, their faith is justified. I can say, "Why, yes, sounds like a young Steller's jay with a broken wing. Drive it to

Audubon—that's a species they'll care for and release." I can tell callers that birds won't abandon a nest because humans have touched it, and while they may reject one of their young for reasons of their own, they won't do so because it's been tainted by our scent. And I make a point of mentioning that fledged juveniles on the ground are usually fine and should be left alone. I can promise them that a downed bird, motionless after flying into a window, is not necessarily dead, that it might revive and fly away. But the questions I'm not asked are, you understand, the ones I can answer with absolute authority.

I can say that house sparrows make little chewing noises when they're tired and rub their eyes like children fighting sleep and that it's possible to feel breath exiting their nostrils as they drowse in your hand, and I can tell you they sometimes wake from a nap, stretching and preening themselves out of a lingering mist but that the transition from sleep to perfect alertness is usually immediate and with no intervening state, rather like ice sublimed into steam. I can tell you that their feet gripping your finger is the most delicate strength you will ever feel and that their upper mandible is made up of two conjoined halves, a line of demarcation running lengthwise down the middle, and that in males, pigment lost in autumn turns these appendages from shiny black into lustrous tan, when, in a nod toward androgyny, their beaks for a short time match those of the females.

I can report to you that B sometimes decides against one particular seed or another, rejecting it repeatedly even though to my eyes it's identical to those I've collected in a pile and fed him one by one. I can describe B curving back on himself as he accesses his uropygial gland, a flesh-colored nubbin hidden by feathers on the up-side base of his tail and from which he obtains a necessary oil, valuable in preening, without which feathers quickly lose their sheen. I can let you in on the following tidbit: on average, a house sparrow's brain is more than 4 percent of its body weight, a human's but 1.5. As a cultural oddment, I'd be happy to mention Robert Burton's seventeenth-century *Anatomy of Melancholy*, one of the most sententious yet quirky and readable books ever written. Composed by Burton to relieve his own depression, it repeats Aristotle's assertion that sparrows are short-lived due to excessive lust or, as Burton phrases it, "salacity." Of course, Aristotle also claimed women had fewer teeth than men.

Armed as Rebecca and I are with the twin secrets of puppy food and heating pad, house sparrow infancy is easily managed, requiring only a relatively short period of manic attentiveness on our part and enough dexterity to wield a toothpick accurately. A number of people, including some who are knowledgeable about birds, consider our record remarkable—four baby birds found, four baby birds saved. But our parenting success probably rests primarily on luck and on the innate toughness of house sparrows.

The advantages Rebecca and I have in maintaining this madhouse are a reasonable amount of patience and what the conventional wisdom of our peers views as a masochistic desire to be inconvenienced. Understanding why some of our friends think this way is simple enough if you consider that many animal lovers don't necessarily want live samples cluttering up their homes. It's a sentiment I appreciate whenever I step in one of our cats' strategically placed puddles of puke. Failure to factor in how radically our inconvenience threshold has shifted upward in seven years is the flaw in the way people look at our situation. They underestimate the extent to which, for a number of reasons, Rebecca and I have ideal dispositions to do what we've done.

Frankly, we're odd. When it comes to fending for ourselves at home, we may as well be a couple of unsupervised ten-year-old kids who have been unaccountably set up in housekeeping. After we sweep our floors, they're still littered with debris; when we dust furniture, nothing really changes; after we fold our clothes and put them away, they're still strewn everywhere; when we clean out litter boxes, they instantly refill, as if from the stocks of a perverse cornucopia. We swab out our toilets, but they retain their fur. With the completion of the human genome project, I look forward to an explanation as to why we're unable to descumify our tub. Sometimes I despair. Especially after visiting other couples we know, all of whom live in houses that appear to be equipped with invisible yet perpetually hardworking domestic staffs.

Even before some ethereal functionary said, "Trust me on this, let's send them birds," we'd had intimations from the earliest days of our cohabitation that living like adults, at least in the sense of holding chaos at bay, was largely beyond us. Ironically, the effort required in providing for sparrows, although siphoning off time from our combat with the house, has imposed a different kind of order, a discipline that makes hours spent with our birds an unfolding meditation. I tell myself we live in tarnished but comfortable elegance with functional plumbing and a few good pieces of furniture. There's a particularly nice oak bed in which my father was conceived, a mahogany vanity at which my mother powdered her nose, a cherrywood bureau with heavy glass knobs that has held my underwear every year of my life, the mirror in which I've watched myself age.

Since B's arrival, we've done alot of shuffling around. In the first place, Rebecca wanted her room back. When she decided to move up from San Francisco to live with me, one of the inducements (possibly the only inducement) was my promise that she could have four walls to herself for use as a dance room and study. Aside from painting the window trim pink, she did a good job with the space by hanging colorful saris on the walls and spreading out small oriental rugs that looked as if, were the right spell cast, they could double as flying carpets. Given that she'd recently left communal living in an apartment with a fluctuating number of itinerant roommates, she liked having sole proprietorship of an area unrelated to sleeping. She hadn't anticipated sharing it less than two years later with creatures whose toilet habits were expressive.

By the third week of July after B's arrival, we moved him into our guest room, which also doubled as my study at the time. Owing to a sharply sloping ceiling on its south side, it feels like a garret. It contains a kitchen sink and countertop with shelving framed in above—remnants of the house's incarnation as a duplex during World War II when many single-family dwellings in Portland were converted into apartments in order to accommodate an influx of shipyard workers. Most of the changes (separate outside entrances, for example) were undone after the war, but the place is still listed on property-tax rolls as a duplex. We have two electric meters, one for upstairs, another for down— a fact that haunts me with the specter of Axis aggression as I write individual checks to Portland General Electric each month.

We locked an outraged B in his house for the short trip down the hall. He shrieked and threw himself against the bars until we passed through his door, a move that struck him, I suppose, as a departure from the known universe into whatever lay beyond. He continued to sit quietly on his upper perch even after we set him down in his new room and worked at coaxing him out. After three or four minutes, Rebecca tried reverse psychology. "The bird better stay in its *cage*. We don't want the bird getting out of its *cage*." He fell for it. With several loud, interrogative chirps, B stretched himself into a willowy bird, emerged craning his neck and flicking his tail. Because of their habit of frequently puffing out their feathers, house sparrows give the impression of being stout little birds. In *Peter Pan in Kensington Gardens*, J. M. Barrie noted this tendency sparrows have to "puff and blow."

B didn't trust his new room's wall-to-wall carpet. He'd gotten used to bare floor in Rebecca's study, skittered around on it as if ice skating for the first time. He kept glancing at the dark-blue nap spread below, thinking perhaps that we'd adopted a pond as well as a bird and had decided to maroon him on its shores because we were insane. He stepped onto my finger after I began making the soft clicking noise with my tongue against the roof of my mouth that I've used as a palliative since the day we found him. Rebecca says it sounds as if I'm telling a tiny horse to giddyap. B recognizes it as a signal that everything's all right, appearances to the contrary. Countless times he's been poised for flight in response to an alarming sight or sound—Rebecca in a yellow tie-dyed shirt, a car backfiring—when, after one or two clicks, I've felt every muscle in his body stand down from alert. It works like an audible Xanex.

Although to my knowledge he avoided landing on the carpet for a day or so, he was soon flying over it without hesitation. He liked sitting on top of my computer monitor, the flashing cursor evidently telegraphing a message he was keen to decipher. He'd bend over the screen's edge as far as he could without losing balance, stand peering at that blinking phantom like a fat man straining for visual confirmation his genitals hadn't vanished. As if charting an island, he enjoyed hopping on the bed, inspecting its perimeter. Until Rebecca and I figured out that uric acid wasn't water soluble and tended to clump in the drain when wet, we appreciated that B took to perching on the water spigot and crapping in the sink. We still clung to the idea that caging was what sensible people did with a bird living in their house but fortunately never followed through on our intention of locking B up when we weren't around.

Most days during the workweek, I took my lunch in restaurants, usually somewhere on Southeast Hawthorne between Thirtieth and Thirty-ninth. Sometimes I'd kick around the shops, buy a used CD or a book before returning to work. This area of Portland is often compared to San Francisco's Haight district because of the way it blends over-priced boutiques with panhandlers outside them in one convenient package. Actually, the stores are interesting. The kinds of shops where you can find Tibetan prayer mats, futons, hemp clothing, handmade jewelry. With B in the picture, I started going home for lunch, leaving work early and returning as late as I could plausibly defend.

Part of this change was driven by my paranoia, only word for it, that B would drop dead unless I checked in. The heating vent and lamp shade incidents loomed fresh in my mind, and I continued to labor under the wrongheaded beliefs that birds are not only alien to the point of being incomprehensible but fragile to the virtual exclusion of all other traits. Whereas even feral dogs or cats can be said to be domesti-cated beasts and therefore bred in a sense to live with humans, it oc-curred to me that a tame bird is always wild—at least in its family con-nections, chances being slim that any of its forebears had taken seeds from a person's tongue (a pastime B and I were experimenting with at the time) or had tried using blue carpeting as a substitute medium for taking a dust bath. It felt as if B and I were negotiating. He appeared willing to renounce what lay beyond his window and to resist job of-fers pouring in every morning from the choir of house sparrows gath-ered in the photinia bushes whose branches brushed the house. The least I could do was give him my time.

I'd rush back home, hurry to his room but walk in slowly, careful not to smash him with the inward-opening door that he'd taken to loitering around once his distrust of the carpet wore off. I'd usually arrive about 11:45 and was expected. Some days I'd be delayed an hour or more and in that event was certain to find B brooding, perched high up, flaunting the symbolism of "I am above you." Nothing I could do but wait until he par-doned my tardiness and descended to my shoulder. I came to know many of his foibles during these early days and to accept that a mind must surely lie behind them, a conviction, the implications of which I'm still working through. Humans are jealous of their sentience and, excepting a foreknowledge of death, begrudge self-awareness to all other creatures.

I'm a slow eater, still gnawing on my entree long after Rebecca finishes a second helping of dessert. This annoyed her, especially when we'd eat in restaurants and were pressed for time. She'd fidget, go all sullen, and plot my death. Things have improved, and B gets the credit. He'd call me back from the kitchen with a medley of ever changing shrieks, chirps, and other sounds he'd audition at the top of his lungs. The most affecting was a slowly uttered "cheooh-cheooh" number that descended into a lugubrious grace note I can't figure out how to spell. The day he premiered it, I ran back upstairs with my mouth full of shredded wheat. I thought he'd either finished watching *Old Yeller* or impaled himself on a spike. I took to eating faster after this, and with the time I gained was able to give B an additional ten or fifteen minutes before I returned to work.

Because my earliest coherent memory of someone making an emotional connection with an animal directly involves my mother, I inevitably think of her when remembering my first year with B. It was my fourth birthday, also Mother's Day. As a combined gift, my father drove the three of us to a kennel in the country run by a woman who raised cocker spaniels, a breed of dog for which my mother had a particular affinity. The woman lifted a small door on the side of a whitewashed outbuilding, and a jumble of twelve-week-old puppies came bounding down a metal chute into an area secured by a cyclone fence. To a four-year-old child, one cocker spaniel looks pretty much the same as any other, but I recall how taken my mother was with one of the puppies and how she held both of us in her lap on our way home in the car. At her suggestion, we made a kind of game out of which of us could be gentle enough to pet the dog without waking it.

There's a framed picture of my mother in our dining room taken on her wedding day to my father in 1951. It shows a very pretty middle-aged woman who is not visibly pregnant with her third and last child as she stands in a stylish red suit on a patch of close-cropped grass with spruce trees behind her—the composition jaundiced overall by whatever happens chemically to color photographs from that era. Strange to see the unborn ghost of myself in her eyes and in the clenched set of her jaw a presentiment of the edginess I carry within me. She looks out as if regarding this very instant when she endures only in memory, herself long dissolved in earth, her spirit part of whatever meaning her survivors attach to the world. I don't know what to make of the rigidity in her shoulders or of her barely perceptible smile that I've seen in photos of myself I'd no idea were being taken. Was she defending herself from the cold? Did she wish it had been spring, that it was forsythia behind her, blazingly yellow and cheerful? Was she frightened at the prospect of raising me? Can't say as I'd blame her. The passage of almost fifty years blears all this to pointless speculation, reminds me that I've no more idea what she was thinking on that day in late November than I do for saying with certainty what small items the purse she held in her left hand contained.

Hard to believe she'd be ninety-one were she still alive, a concept impossible to square with any image I have of her. Even at her sickest, her face retained an uncanny youthfulness that snipped ten or fifteen years off her actual age. The last time I saw her, she lay in a fetal position in a hospital bed, her dark eyes open but fixed elsewhere. I sometimes return to that room in my mind and, with more than the perfunctory tenderness of a duty performed but not understood, hold her hand as she dies. I undo the isolation of her death, transform the visits I made every day into something other than a sense of relief when it was time to go home. "Stay where you are in the future," she'd say. "My death wasn't as bad as you think." Clearly it was, but she loved me unreservedly.

Part of the reason I think of my mother as often as I do stems from not having known her well. I was twenty-three when she died and what with having been away at school and then traveling, I segued from being a kid with a mom into a self-centered young adult who grudgingly returned home to Pennsylvania and found a cancer-ridden woman rummy from pain killers. The pregnant woman in the photograph is not so much the one who carried me, birthed me, loved me, or who vowed to put me on a Canada-bound bus should I ever be drafted, as she is a person whose experiences seem to stand entirely apart from my own even though I know her history in outline form. As if it were a sketch of the Civil War or Edison inventing the light bulb. When, in 1941, her first husband dropped dead from a heart attack, she was left with financial worries and two small boys. I can't imagine how shattering the news from Baltimore must have been, the telephone call or telegram that said in effect, "Your husband, a rising officer in the merchant marine, is dead at the age of thirty-one. His heart gave out as he shaved himself in a hotel washroom." There's a bit of sadness you never quite drain from your bones. My oldest brother, J. D., has but three distinct memories of his father. The last, as I've set the scene in my mind, is Dickensian in tone and of a time when Americans allowed their dead to come home: a boy not yet five leaves his bed in the wee hours to sit in a dimly lit stairwell, peering between the banister's dowels at an open coffin lying below. Frightening how tragedy renews itself with each reenactment of spouse losing spouse, child losing parent, each repetition singular, a sucker punch from the hand of all you believed in and from which we arise remade whether or not we know it at the time.

There are many reasons I wish I could have had an adult relationship with my mother, not the least of which is that I might have had a chance to understand the essential sadness that seemed to lie at the center of her psyche, to find out why, for reasons never explained, some days she spontaneously wept. When I was a small child, her behavior frightened me; later I often responded in frustration, sensing perhaps that we shared not only blood but a sometimes tragic view of the world. A view bred, I suspect, from the same chemical imbalance I live with and for which better treatment options now exist than the small amount of Valium my mother took to geld whatever grim ideas were in attendance when she'd wake in the morning anxious and depressed.

My mother forged ahead unbeaten by whatever it was that left her no choice but to pull herself by an act of will through those days when an indefinable grief seemed perched on her chest. I admire that she retained an ability to laugh, as did my father even after losing an infant son—my half brother Lon, whom I know only as a grave marker in West Side Cemetery. I admire that my mother could often be droll, sometimes by acting out of character, which, I must say, was fairly prim regarding anything below the waist. Hemorrhoid jokes at her own expense are a pretty good example of what I mean.

At the time we found B, I was as depressed as I've ever been and although happy enough that Rebecca and I were engaged, I feared marriage was one of those milestones better anticipated than passed. What was I depressed about? Don't know. Was I suicidal? No, too much the coward by far. Some days better than others? Yes, but unpredictably so. Good at hiding how I felt? Not bad, but it was hard getting things done.

Any anxiety? Decidedly, that's the way this free-floating crap some-times works when a sense of dread is thrown in as a bonus. Any midlife-crisis stuff going on here? I think so.

When Rebecca and I decided to marry, the bargain completed over a stack of receipts for plumbing supplies I'd bought in anticipation of redoing our bathrooms, she mentioned how nice it would be to have a wedding big enough and catered enough on which to hang one hell of a party. I liked this idea because aside from the advantage of not hav-ing to testify against one another in court, compelling reasons to tie the knot didn't seem all that prevalent to me. Rebecca loves reminding me that my immediate response to her wedding plans was, "Other than help pay for it and show up on time for the ceremony, will I actually have to do anything?" I felt that additional responsibilities would in-terfere with the frequent naps I relied on to get me through more days than I care to recall.

Rebecca is also quick to relate the specifics of a phone conversation she had with her mother three or four months after B moved in. To Bev-erly's question, "Aren't you angry about all the time he spends with that sparrow?" Rebecca replied that while she still had reservations about the situation, she could truthfully say I was in a better humor than I had been for months. She was thankful, she said, and willing to make allowances. "Chris still gets home from work bitching about his day, but the minute he gets in with the bird he relaxes and is happy" was, I believe, how she put it. Since 1995, when I spent two months in England and Rebecca found herself promoted to B's chief of staff, she tells this story with a modifying coda—"I didn't really appreciate the bird back then, but now I understand what my husband found so com-pelling." You can almost hear her listeners thinking, "Bought into his madness, poor dear."

Rebecca is not the only one whose thinking has changed. I've seen a parade of skeptics walk into B's room with a condescending smile and leave an hour later not necessarily ready to acquire a bird but willing to agree that my lobotomy can be indefinitely postponed. Even my sister, Lola, who'd once been attacked by parrots in a Manhattan pet shop—no one knows why—and who, as a result, was chary around birds, con-ceded after meeting B that I hadn't significantly exaggerated his abili-ties or overstated his capacity to dominate a room.

So, is B really who I say he is aside from the demonstrable reality that he lives in our house and flies to me when I enter his room? I've often wondered this myself. Are any or even all of the more intangible qualities I claim he possesses mere projections of my own self-absorption? Have I constructed my own little world and placed B at its center in the mistaken belief that his actions and reactions are other than robotic? Have I made B the homunculus and myself the ghost inside the machine?

If I could answer these questions with objective precision, I suppose I'd be well on my way to effectively unraveling most of the unyielding mysteries that touch on the nature and limitations of consciousness. Unfortunately, I'm not up to the task, nor do I ever wish to delude myself that I am. It's too easy to obsess over puzzles in which pieces are missing, some of us ending up like John Berryman when he wrote, "All the black same I dance my blue head off!" The last line in the last poem in his last book of poetry, *Delusions, Etc.* He killed himself in 1972. I'm content to stand by the validity of one central thing I, at least, know to be true: B is a thinking being with an inner life. The rest, as Ezra Pound said, "is dross."

B finishes his daily portion of sugar cookie and washes it down with three sips of water. Rebecca started baking these treats after deciding that the hydrogenated oils in store-bought cookies weren't substances that should be inside our birds. I'll tell you this for free: her ability to refrain from consuming every sugar cookie she bakes is an amazing gesture of ferocious self-denial. I once asked her to tell me, all joking aside, how many sugar cookies she thought she could eat at one sitting—assuming that considerations such as becoming wretchedly ill would not apply. Her conservative estimate: fifty. To my relief, I discovered that her sugar cookie passion is based on nostalgia rather than a Seven Deadly Sins type of gluttony. It reaches its zenith between Thanksgiving and New Year's when memories of her mother's holiday baking are acute. I'd worried she might have other cravings. Disturbing ones. I asked her if she ever had Donner-party survival dreams.

It's late August and B is molting again. So far only his bib looks ratty, but he's so dear to me that seeing again the start of his yearly unraveling fills me with an autumnal sadness. Another year passed, another cycle ineluctably grinding away. And yet, B's doing extremely well. He's just vacuumed up cookie crumbs and brought me his blue milk-bottle cap before settling into my hand. My mood brightens when he scratches the right side of his head and neck followed by the left. It seems impossible that he's able to move his leg that quickly, must do it somehow with smoke and mirrors. I never see him at this without remembering the zany musical phrases that accompanied the cute forest creatures that scratched themselves in every Walt Disney nature program I saw as a kid. Mostly rodents, I think. Chipmunks, squirrels, rabbits; sometimes the cavorting offspring of large mammals such as bears or cougars as they paused in alpine meadows to address an itch. Birds too, providing they were cute. The music convinced me that nature was indeed a very funny place.

It's early afternoon on a humid Sunday; B is alert but ready to drowse on top of my hand. Although I'm sweating, he seems oblivious to the additional heat my hand puts out. I envy his temperature control. He opens his wings in response when I purse my lips and send a current of simulated wind through his feathers. He's now like a mandala on which I fix my gaze. My fingers themselves become feathers where they touch him, weft me into a middling doze, into an airy fabric of finch chatter, traffic, and voices in the street.

B decides after ten minutes that I've been disembodied long enough. He stands on my shoulder, nipping my right ear lobe. This is tolerable as pain goes but sufficiently annoying to convey his imperative: "Wake up immediately and be entertaining." If I don't respond or if I pull my head away and tell him to stop, he'll relocate, focusing attention on the tender skin of my forearm. In a testy cut to the chase, I toss out his red cap because I know it's in disfavor and has been for weeks. He flicks his tail and dons his "Christ, do I have to do everything" look. He jumps to my knee, picks up the blue cap, carts it up, and drops it in my hand.

Even after I leave the room, "Fetch the Cap" can go on indefinitely in a solo version that B invented. This involves flying the cap to a ledge, pushing it off and then nabbing it again as it rolls on the floor or spins in place like a fumbled coin. I go about my business guilt-free when I hear him clicking away with his toys. I keep an ear open for the frustrated chirp he'll make when (inevitably) his prey escapes by skidding under the couch or something else scary. When I go in to assist, he'll usually lead me to the place where the cap went missing. I can rest assured that he's searched his toy basket for an identical spare.

I throw the blue cap over to the futon, watch it descend in a lazy arc, B in pursuit like a heat-seeking missile. He subdues it with a series of pecks, then pauses a moment as if dictating terms. Because the cap has landed top side down, he tugs deftly on the futon cover until the cap turns over, a technique that saves him the more difficult maneuver of sliding his beak underneath in order to flip it open side up. Faced with a similar problem on the floor, he'll snowplow the thing into an impediment weighty enough to act as a brace against which to push while he rights it. He then snatches up his toy and returns to me.

We've spent hours playing this game—it, or one of its variants. Today, B's enthusiasm wanes after the fourth play, and he settles back in my hand. In deference to his progressing molt, he husbands energy for growing new feathers. He'll soon lose interest in sport until the last week of October. Apart from languidly tugging a troublesome chest feather, he's about as indolent as it's possible to be without a mint julep in your hand and Gulf Coast humidity. I often talk to him when he's sleepy, and from the way his head is drooping it would seem that my update on the Baptist sign is boring him into a nap.

Two recent postings: "Why Church: It's where God uses our uniqueness." "Why Church: It's where God is doing a new thing." God, of course, can do as he pleases, although I don't see what help a human being's pathetic individuality could possibly be to the architect of the universe. But if he wants to fiddle with someone's distinctive qualities in front of a congregation, there's not much that can be done about it except, I suppose, avoid church. Rebecca wonders if God's "new thing" might be a dance.

Naturally, it's always the other person's beliefs that lend themselves to unflattering analysis. Ridiculing my growing insistence that B is fully self-aware has no doubt provided hours of harmless entertainment for many of my friends and acquaintances who think I'm otherwise a reasonable fellow. In fairness to the person who cooks up this stuff for the sign, I'm willing to admit the possibility that he or she employs a certain amount of poetic license. On the other hand, it's difficult to dismiss the fact that these people base their creed on a so-called literal interpretation of Scripture. I'm concerned, therefore, about the implications of a Supreme Being so jaded by his customary pursuits that he's been reduced to searching for novelty at a church in southeast Portland. I would respectfully remind the sloganeer that the Bible states pointedly, "There is no new thing under the sun."

In a larger sense, I wonder what happens to cultures in which words are valued in public discourse as the building blocks of the come-on and the blandishment rather than as instruments of plain speaking without a disclaimer, of subtlety without intent to mislead, a culture in which marketing departments trade on language as the means of invoking the demons of transient desire. Our ability to respond to the uplifting properties of metaphor is eroded and with it our ability to find and describe connections where none were thought to exist—things that don't add much to a spreadsheet tally. Signs become commands; directions become assurances—the antithesis of omen, suggestion, and the merely possible. Thus, we are pointed away from any number of instructive wrong turns that eventually bring us home. To the tranquillity of having a tame house sparrow nap in your hand, you might say. It would appear that institutions charged with maintaining the intangibles of spirit and morality feel they can no longer rely on either the depth or the beauty of their core beliefs in order to remain competitive, resort instead to the expedient of vacuous catch phrases tarting up their parking lots. Frankly, I don't know which is more troubling, that they've got the *cajones* to post this drivel or that people's souls are impoverished enough to be moved by it.

I find it appallingly easy to be peevish about this sort of thing until I recall with aching fondness the mainstream greeting cards I'd get from my father at Christmas and again on my birthday. Predictable rhymes that expressed what the sender himself was unable to say. I think of my father in the drugstore picking out a card for a "Wonderful Son." He signs his name, pads to his desk for a stamp, phones me a few days later to ask, "Did you get my card?" Being a snob is harder than it seems.

AS A GESTURE OF THANKS, WE HAD CRAIG (OUR BIRD CONSULTANT) OVER for dinner on the Saturday following B's move into the back bedroom. A rather shy man, he'd been too reticent to call for an update on B. We knew, however, that he'd been making inquiries through one of

Rebecca's coworkers, a guy named Mike Duncan with whom Craig had gone to high school. He was eager to meet the bird he'd been instrumental in saving. While the pasta overcooked, the three of us headed upstairs. I liked Craig right off.

People accustomed to living with tame birds move differently from those who are not, at least when they're in the presence of birds. Put me in an empty, well-lighted room, and there's a reasonable chance I'll trip and fall; come visit when I'm with one of our sparrows and you'll find me walking or sitting or moving my arms and head as if precision in these things were a matter of life and death—which, of course, it is. There's no specialized vocabulary of motion to describe this, no first and second positions, no arabesques, no jetés, only an ongoing awareness ("B consciousness") of my body's position relative to a creature I could crush without knowing it. Sorry to belabor this, but it's a topic of fundamental importance to a person in my position. Although moving cautiously in B's presence is now second nature with me, I remind myself often that my subconscious has screwed up before and could do so again. Assuming otherwise is to court disaster.

"He looks great, really healthy," Craig said with what I thought was a touch of justifiable pride as I made the introduction. B flew up when we entered and perched on a picture frame that hung above the bed. He acted wary and as if he'd like to have a word with me in private on the subject of guests. Craig, extending his hand palm side down, moved slowly toward B, who surprised me by not shifting to higher ground or making a break for my shoulder. "Sometimes birds don't feel comfortable with an open palm," Craig explained, as if anticipating my question. "I guess they think it could be a trap." It hadn't occurred to me that B might be hip to the mechanical possibilities of the human hand, intuit somehow that fingers could contract into an incarcerating fist. When Rebecca called Craig with the dinner invitation, he told her he'd bring with him a large cage he no longer needed. He laughed when I suggested that this was why B refused to get on him.

The cage in question is a large rectangle, two feet by four feet square. It's constructed from six sections of stout wire that form grids with one-inch-by-two-inch openings. It looks like a place you'd harbor chinchillas until you felt their pelts were ready for market. Craig built the thing himself and used it for years in connection with his pigeon rehabilitation activities, a pursuit that living in cramped quarters forced him to abandon. When Rebecca mentioned our dilemma over what to do with B, Craig said he'd donate the cage if we thought it would help.

Imagining a time when I believed cages were a sane solution to living with birds is difficult, almost like trying to convince myself I used to be Stalin or some other lunatic. "Why, yes, I deceived, abused, and killed millions of my countrymen, that was me." I hate to be peremptory, but people shouldn't have birds if they can't do so without caging them. I don't care how merry their budgie, canary, finch, dove, pigeon—or sparrow—or whatever they happen to have seems to be. I don't care if it hops, burbles, dweets, sings, and chirps. If it's caged, it's miserable. If it could tie bedsheets together and hang itself from a water pipe in its cell, it would. The smaller the cage, the more heinous the crime. Birds, especially small ones, must fly, and most cages, as opposed to properly set up aviaries or large rooms, allow for little more than wing-propelled jumps from one perch to the next. Even clipping the wings of larger birds such as parrots seems to me less an issue of protecting the bird from injuring itself (certainly a valid concern in the majority of captive situations) than a question of human convenience and control.

Caging a bird punishes it, in effect, for possessing the ability to fly, the sine qua non of, well, birdness—might as logically box up your cat or dog because it insists on walking every chance it gets. A small bird without space in which to fly is an ornament that just happens to be alive. A wind chime hanging in a cage next to a fan would serve the same purpose—pretty, tuneful, moving. Unless you embrace a "Might makes right" philosophy or, in this case, "I cage because I can," the immorality of restricting birds to a few cubic feet should be obvious. By remaining obtuse to the ethical questions raised by preventing creatures from exercising an ability honed to perfection by roughly two hundred million years of evolution, I certainly missed it. Prior to meeting B, I would have considered these opinions naive.

Here's the position I was in that Sunday morning when Rebecca and I hauled Craig's cage up to B's room and set it in position by a window: Liked B very much, touched by how friendly he'd become. Except jokingly, didn't credit him with anything approaching vigorous intelligence and assumed he probably didn't possess enough inner life to be meaningfully aware of whether he spent most of his life in a cage or not. Wasn't wild about having everything in the room festooned with bird shit. Still guilty over not releasing him even while suspecting he might not integrate well with outside birds due to private-school upbringing. In spasm of tortured logic, figured cage would legitimize B's status as a domesticated bird housed in quarters society would approve. Wanted to be normal. Keeping bird unpopular decision with fiancée.

Until I banged into an open cabinet door, B watched calmly as we carried in his penitentiary. His comments, delivered while standing on my head, were brisk and choice. A chattering diatribe voiced in what I'd call "alarmed juvenile house sparrow," which to my ear lacks much of the volume and nuance present in the adult equivalent. I wondered if the crashing of metal into wood and my attendant burst of profanity had activated one of his presets, some ancient house sparrow algorithm that ran a subroutine dealing with untoward noise in otherwise nonthreatening situations. Be this as it may, I was more amazed that he flew to my head than by his vocal response to an event he might have easily found frightening. Consider: The two boobs he employs as servants come barging in with a big object he's never seen before. The larger of the two boobs (the one he'd been grooming as a valet/companion) stumbles and rams said object into a cabinet door that shouldn't have been left open to begin with. Discordant crashing noise is followed by bellowed invective. Boob might try looking where he's going next time, needs improved anger management. Smaller boob looks startled, annoyed.

I'd have thought that flying to a higher perch or ducking beneath something or freezing in place would have been a bird's predictable response to a comedy duo wrestling with an enormous cage. It wasn't until some days later that I toyed with the possibility that B had paid me a compliment. Not, certainly, for being clumsy. He probably considers that part of the human condition. I think he was scolding the cage, willing to commit all twenty-five of his grams to my defense. On the other hand, maybe he simply trusted me enough to know *I'd* protect him while he vented spleen. Either way, this incident prompted me into thinking about what happens when animals make choices. In B's case, for instance, was there an "I" choosing between alternatives? Assuming yes, how were these choices framed? As images cast on a tiny backdrop (undoubtedly, I thought, such a minuscule brain wouldn't have much of a screening room), as constructs in a language of simple emotion, as competing neurons hollering "Follow me" to the rest of the network? And what of the "I" itself? Is it an entity as elusive in birds as in humans, as apt to hide in plain view? Is it lashed together with an equally elusive "me," one personal pronoun defining the other?

"Look, here's your new house," I said to B, using that chipper tone one adopts with idiots and tantrum-prone children. He'd simmered down considerably and hopped onto the extended finger I moved slowly toward the cage while delivering my sales pitch. He cocked an ear to my voice and an eye to the cage, inside of which Rebecca had already secured two or three wooden perches. "This might actually work," she said. "He doesn't seem afraid of it." I was already visualizing awed visitors commenting on what an unusual pet a house sparrow made. I could see B hopping from perch to perch, accepting food treats through the bars and, as the pièce de résistance, flying to my shoulder when I opened the cage.

I knelt, undid the latch, and swung open the door that now squeaked slightly as a result of the collision. B remained on my finger as I moved my arm inside and nudged him onto the closest perch with a goose from my thumb. He preened a neck feather with the casual air of a gangster filing his nails while an immigrant shopkeeper coughed up protection money. Not what I expected. I thought he'd throw himself against the bars as soon as he realized he was trapped. I'd budgeted emotionally for his shrieks of betrayal, knew I'd need to ignore them until he accepted the reality of life behind bars. Indignation prickled through me as I thought myself ill-used—all I'd done for B, and he couldn't even register a token protest regarding the physical barrier now existing between us. Petty, of course, considering he'd been in the cage only about thirty seconds. I closed the door, stood up, and said to Rebecca, "That was too easy."

I'd barely gotten out the words before B was on me. Having zipped through one of the cage's one-by-two-inch portals as if it weren't there, he liberated himself with so much precision that I doubt a single feather touched metal as he passed through the grid. It must have been displays like this that prompted Lorenz's glowing assessment of the house sparrow's "spatial intelligence." Someone with better visual acuity than mine or Rebecca's might have looked at the cage and been able to predict B's escape, might have said, "He'll eventually squeeze through those openings—better get a different cage." Had I paused to consider how much of B's apparent bulk is actually feathers, I'd have conceded the point. But I'd also have tested the theory. After all, a free cage is a free cage.

The impressive thing is that B apparently *knew* he could free himself at will. No wonder he didn't feel trapped. I'd say it was a good fifteen or sixteen inches from where he'd been perched to the exit point closest to me, plenty of distance in which to build up an embarrassing, if not dangerous, amount of momentum by the time he reached an opening he hadn't examined closely.

Let's say you find yourself climbing around on craggy rocks near the sea. After a long ascent, you reach a point above deep, clear water sparkling below in tropical sun. You're a strong swimmer, a good diver, and you're hot and grimy from the climb, maybe even bleeding a little from the scrape on your knee that you expect will sting when it hits saltwater, but what the hell? The problem with diving will be to thread a narrow passage between two sheer columns of rock that rise from the water and extend far above your precipice, columns made of the same lichen-encrusted stone that so efficiently abraded the flesh on your knee. Of course, having your skin flayed off will be the least of your troubles if you miss; you wonder how long it will take the authorities to recover your body. You'd feel better were you able to rappel down and inspect the gap you're hoping to glide through, but that would require equipment and training and you're itching to get on with it. What to do?

That's more or less the situation I once chickened out of in Mexico. I mention it because the memory came back to me as I marveled at B's precision escape from Craig's finely wrought cage. As a teenager, I dove with my friends off thirty-foot cliffs into an abandoned coal-mining pit that had long since filled up with water and that was plenty deep enough to warehouse the scads of New York City gangland murder victims stuffed in cars and reputedly lying in its murky depths. I can't say whether the facilities were actually used in this way, but the idea added an extra thrill to swimming in that pit. None of us ever drowned or laid open our skulls by hitting the ledge of underwater rock that protruded about ten feet out from the cliff side. Our repetition of the life-saving mantra "Push off far enough to clear the ledge" probably saved our lives. As for me, I might have been a gangly bird standing up there on spindly legs. I envied the barn swallows skimming over the surface of the water and often wished I had wings to swoop me from danger if a dive went wrong.

Without, however, the incomparable sense of my body that birds possess of their own, wings would not have served me well. Orientation in space is, I think, more finely tuned in them, a sense of the world measured as the distance to, from, around, and through everything else, creatures for whom inactivity itself is probably an aspect of motion. Just as the human facility with symbolic language dominates our merest thoughts.

B stood on my shoulder waiting for the next move in whatever game he thought we were playing. Simple rules: place bird in cage, bird flies out of cage. Whereas I found this immensely entertaining, B moved on with his life after several repetitions, flying off to resume his decoding work with the cursor. "I can't cage him," I said to Rebecca.

≈

REBECCA'S MIND IS EXTRAORDINARILY ACTIVE WHILE SHE SLEEPS. IT cranks out dream after vivid dream accompanied by a soundtrack of screams, sighs, gurgles, yips, and other sounds that range, depending on what's showing, between the mewing of kittens and the fall of Troy. Wake her up, discuss the commotion, and she'll acknowledge your complaint, apologize for disturbing the peace. She then resumes sleeping and picks up seamlessly at the point she left off. I'm astounded by the tenacity with which her subconscious mind holds its ground. I love getting reports next morning of frogs riding bikes near the ceiling when she "woke up" around three o'clock. You can't buy this kind of entertainment.

Although it's not a complete wasteland, there being intermittent scraps of vegetation to relieve the barren plain, my sleeping mind is a dustbowl where crops tend to fail. I generally wake no wiser than when I went to sleep, the night only occasionally enlivened by the dream about my grandmother's canary or by images of indistinct faces or of other prosaic objects such as the day's newspaper sitting on the porch in its plastic baggy. A really extravagant night features disorganized clips of recent events. More than this must surely go on, but I've no way of knowing.

I think my impoverishment as a dreamer is self-imposed, rooted in a fear I've had of what lies below ever since I woke in terror from what I call the "janitor nightmare," the composition of which relates to three events: my paternal grandfather's death in July 1957, seeing the ocean for the first time the following August, entering kindergarten one month later. The dream—short on action but long on affect—went like this: our school janitor floated in a sealed milk bottle that bobbed in the surf at Atlantic City, New Jersey. That's all, just floated and bobbed. I couldn't tell if he was living or dead, those concepts being somewhat confusing to me then. He wore the outfit I saw him dressed in every day at school as he pushed an oiled mop over floors that were already spotless: gray work pants and shirt with a black bow tie—it was a different time. Days passed before I shook off the suffocating pall of entrapment cast by that nightmare. I think the whole thing derived its power from someone's kindly meant comment at my grandfather's viewing, "See, it's just like he's sleeping."

All things considered, I'm glad I've been exempted from wrestling with sleep the way Rebecca does. She dreams of our birds, often frighteningly so—the house is on fire, one of them is lost and unreachable in a hellish landscape, they've been attacked by cats, pestilence strikes, or they're beset by some other unbearable thing. She deals with this regular assault by suspending suspension of disbelief whenever the show becomes gruesome. She's aware that she's dreaming long before she wakes. I, on the other hand, have had only one dream about our birds, a recent one involving B.

We're in a hardwood forest, mostly birches and maples. The birches look spooky even in daylight with strips of white bark hanging from their trunks like tattered cerements. The underbrush is sparse, so I don't have trouble walking through it, but I wish I could find the old trail I'm certain should already be underfoot. B rides on my shoulder but flies ahead every few minutes in a gesture of independence I find surprising given how frightened he was when we entered the woods.

Having walked a long time, we're both thirsty, and I apologize again and again by saying, in reference to the swiftly running stream I promised I could find, "It should be here; I know it should be here." B vanishes from my shoulder, but I don't remember seeing him leave.

Before I panic, the scene changes. I find B dipping his head in the elusive stream, silently drinking. He's so much a part of the setting that I hesitate to call his name. After several seconds he turns, and the sound of the stream is activated by the sight of water drops hanging like gems from his beak.

Final scene: I put B to bed in the bifurcated trunk of a birch tree at the place where the massive halves split to form the arms of a Y.

Freudians, assuming such people still exist, will have less fun with this airy bagatelle than Jungians hungry for archetypes. There's nothing sexual here, not even the crotch of the tree was appreciably vulvate. More a gentle commentary on ineptness or confusion. I couldn't find the trail, couldn't find the stream. Probably a fair assessment of my abilities. Beyond that, who knows? An old friend of mine insisted that B and I left our bodies and meandered in the woods I knew as a boy. I might have given credence to this theory had it not been advanced by a person who claimed that extraterrestrials lived beneath Mount Shasta. That the dream ends with my putting B to bed is interesting, though.

Bird bedtime is a big deal around here, especially B's. Any doubts concerning our credentials as fanatics should be laid to rest once it's understood that Rebecca and I *never* miss getting our sparrows settled for the night. In the event one of us is out for the evening, the other is home taking up the slack. This is why Rebecca and I haven't vacationed together in years, why we're not available as a couple in the evenings until after our birds have gone to bed. This plays hell with our social lives, especially in summer when the days are long (we refer to this period as B-light slaving time), and it's often well after ten o'clock until we've gotten all of them down for the night. "Can't they put themselves to bed?" incredulous friends ask when we decline invitations or duck out early from things. Well, of course they can put themselves to bed—it's not like they'd sit up wide-eyed staring into darkness until we got home. Not the point, really. What an immense relief when we gave up dissembling. Manufacturing headaches and visits by out-of-town relatives became both tiresome and morally untenable. Better to be thought crazy than dishonest.

Long before I had birds, I found in reading *An Exaltation of Larks*, James Lipton's enduring book on venery (the art of assigning names to different groups of like animals; a *pride* of lions, for example), that not only are larks an exaltation but that taken en masse, turtledoves are a true love, ravens an unkindness, owls a parliament, and sparrows a host—a designation that dates to the 1400s. Please note, as does Lipton, the military connotation of "host," the implicit suggestion that sparrows resemble an invading army.

On the evening of the day B first flew to me, it became clear he didn't want me leaving the room at dusk, his insistence on this point directly proportional to the fading of the light. By the time it was nearly dark, Rebecca had long since decamped, my bladder was filling up rapidly, and I was also very hungry. With B perched on my finger, I tried several times to put him in his "house," but by backpedaling up my arm, he outmaneuvered me at every turn. Frustration and urine compelled me at last to dump him on Rebecca's desk and dash out the door. While standing at the toilet, I decided to forget about locking him up. I assumed he'd find a suitable roosting place on his own, probably on the bookshelves. I could always go in later with a flashlight to check.

An excellent plan except for the chirp after depressed chip I heard after I walked out of the bathroom. Had I not been drunk with the novelty of B having flown to me, maybe I could have resisted his pleas. By tabling the question of what to do at night with a clingy bird, I could have gone downstairs and eaten my dinner.

I saw B sitting near the door when I peered inside. Dim light from the windows revealed him hunched on the floor, small and alone. I found myself uncomfortably aware of my relative enormity, of the power I held over him. Nothing about him resembled a "host" or any part of an army. He flew to me when I stepped inside the door, without, I should think, a very clear picture of where he was headed. In terms of color vision and resolution, a house sparrow's eyesight is superior to a human's. But in low-light conditions, given that sparrow eyes and human eyes are believed to contain a similar number of rods—the ocular cells useful in night vision—B and I probably see about equally well. After flapping into my chest, he ricocheted into the cupped hand

I brought up quickly enough to save him from crashing and burning like a befogged plane hitting an alp. Other than a nearly inaudible cheeping as he oriented himself into a forward-facing position, he settled immediately and without comment into my hand, his beak protruding from the aperture formed by my index finger and thumb.

With my father's favorite starvation image running through my mind ("I'm so hungry, the big guts are eating the little guts"), I stood in place for several minutes, unsure about what I should do, fearing that movement on my part would be a diplomatic blunder. B did, in fact, respond with a series of defensive snaps and pecks when I moved my thumb. Otherwise, he seemed perfectly comfortable and surprisingly wide awake as he shuffled around and preened in my hand. I'd rather assumed that birds, excluding owls, of course, more or less conked out when it got dark—another theory shot to hell. He seemed unconcerned when I eased my way over to the couch and sat for twenty minutes holding him under my chin. "What took you so long?" Rebecca asked when I made it down to the kitchen. "What," indeed?

I didn't know how to answer her. Events, I could describe: "At dusk, B didn't want me to leave. He chirped sadly when I left, flew blindly into my chest when I returned, ended up in my hand. He preened, tucked his head, and went to sleep. We'd still be sitting there if I hadn't roused him by stroking his head with the tip of my nose. He perched on my finger as I lifted him through the door to his house. As far as I know, he's now asleep on his upper perch." The emotional content of this experience was as difficult to explain to Rebecca (and to myself) as had been the "Wow" sense of awe I felt when B first landed on me earlier in the day—that broad, unforgettable stroke on his part, his public declaration of where he wanted to go with his life. Calling for me, flying to me in the darkness, sleeping in my hand were private gestures that sealed the bond.

Rebecca is away on the third day of a business trip; I'll be gone early next month and will have my revenge. Running this place solo, especially in the evenings, is an endless series of avian-related tasks. It's taken years, of course, but there are now twelve birds in this house. Sparrows, finches, canaries—the upstairs is filled with them. It sometimes seems they arrived overnight.

I'm in with B after an hour spent attending to the needs of the others, all of which are finally in bed. Nominally, at any rate. Chirps, rattles, and clangs coming from the adjacent room tell me that the second of our four sparrows is restive. I know what his problem is: he and Rebecca have a relationship similar to the one I have with B, and he's upset by her absence. I've given him loads of time today even though I'm stretched thin trying to accommodate everyone else, not to mention a petulant B. I should put in a few hours of paying work, attend to the grievances of three geriatric cats, go buy groceries, and feed myself.

B dislikes changes in routine, believes himself victimized when I don't live up to his expectations. I've been in here five minutes, but he has yet to join me on the couch. He prefers to stand on his window perch feigning interest in wind-driven rain pelting the glass the way it does every day during November in Portland. His new feathers are spectacular, fairly glowing with an electrified sheen in the reflected light of the window. I'm sure he feels that my effusive plumage compliments are a transparent attempt to compensate for showing up half an hour late with his dinner— ass-kissing pure and simple. Because he can't stand being ignored, I've found that a more effective way to get his attention is if I assume a posture of nonchalance.

But not tonight. Another couple of minutes have elapsed since I stopped speaking and broke off eye contact. I'm forced to admit that, of the two of us, B is better at remaining blasé. In a smarmy French waiter's voice, I recite the menu, point out hidden virtues of the plate I've prepared for his dining pleasure: "Kernels of organically grown corn hand selected by me, hazelnut whittled by thumbnail into beak-tempting slivers, one crescent-shaped apple slice, one crisp spinach leaf complementing a main course consisting of `goop' moistened to perfection using fresh Portland tap water and mixed with one of our fine stainless steel spoons into a nutritious paste of flawless consistency. Plum compote served on the side, compliments of the chef."

Were Rebecca here, she'd now be delivering her nightly report on how things went with the other birds. Details of who did what to whom, who ate heartily and who did not, who went to his or her perch without screwing around, who appeared to go to his or her perch without screwing around but then thought better of it and flew back out. As often as not, I'd be removing some sort of bird debris from her hair and making chimp-like grooming sounds as I picked through the strands. We'd have a game of "Hit the Cap."

Hit the Cap evolved from Hit the Ping-Pong Ball and is played with me sitting to Rebecca's left, my left arm draped over my stomach and the upper part of my right thigh. By forming my hand into the male masturbator's classic position, I make a silo in which B hides and out from which he pops each time Rebecca drops the cap onto the opening. He's capable of knocking a cap two feet or more, often inserting the virtuosic touch of hitting it twice in one play—once straight up, again as it descends. He celebrates really superb hits by twirling 360 degrees in place and rapidly snapping his beak. On average, he'll give Rebecca about six seconds to retrieve the cap before emerging from my hand to investigate the delay. He glances at me frequently to make certain I'm watching his performance, halts play if my attention wanders. Some nights his interest in games is tepid; others, his desire to play is obsessive. At Rebecca's nightly announcement from the hall that "I'll be there in a minute, B," he loops the room in exuberance. Once she's in and seated, he grabs a cap, worms his way into my hand, and, if necessary, nips my fingers until I form them into his bunker. I'd like to have a pastoral ren-dering of our gaming tableaux painted on a Greek amphora—Rebecca and me in white robes and sandals, B topped with a laurel leaf crown.

A quick calculation tells me that I've spent almost 50 percent less time with B today than I normally do. Rebecca will be calling in a couple of hours, and will barely get past "Hello" before asking about the birds. Three days is about her limit before she begins suffering bird withdrawal. She rarely travels without a supply of bread and seed in her purse and will probably tell me she teared up while feeding a troop of house sparrows as she waited for a cab. Details of B's dissatisfaction will dominate tonight's conversation, lead into an obligatory discussion of how tough it is when one of us is away.

I figure the only way to motivate B into ending his boycott is to pretend that I'm leaving. Before I'm halfway to the door, he's in the air banking past my head to a landing on the bookcase gremlin. Now is when we deal with face-saving issues. My reading of the situation tells me B believes he's made a significant concession by symbolically blocking my exit. By offering him my finger (which he accepts) I admit guilt for every-thing that's gone wrong with his day. Detached observers might suggest, logically enough, that granting an inner life to a bird is one thing, pre-suming insight into its motives quite another. B would likely agree. But re-gardless, I've proved to Rebecca's satisfaction how skilled I've become at reading nuance in his body language. If I were able to conceal a reason-ably gullible person in this room, I could make it appear that B and I are telepathically linked. With astounding accuracy, I can say to Rebecca, "He's about to scratch the right side of his head," or "Within a few min-utes he'll be taking a bath," or "He doesn't want apple, try the spinach." You must take my word for it that this sort of thing happens often enough to make it statistically convincing that I'm not just guessing. Perhaps I'm a bit like Clever Hans, a horse that "counted" by stamping his hoof however many times his examiners requested. As it turned out, Hans knew when to stop by watching the unconsciously made facial cues of his trainer. Quite a remarkable feat in itself.

B's on my knee tucking into a piece of corn; next he'll want millet and a ride to the water dish. It's late, but the finches have gotten their second wind and are zooming and chattering and arguing over some bit of finch arcana that appears to be the focus of an ongoing dispute. They often pick inconvenient times to revisit such issues. Although they've been known to carry on their fractious posturing in almost total darkness, switching off lights tends to dampen their combative little souls. B is yawning and rubbing his eyes on my sleeve; I offer him his cap, but he grabs it from my hand and tosses it away.

After turning off the overhead light, I return with B to the couch; we'll sit for five or ten minutes while the finches deflate in the subdued glow of the table lamp. Although B has been hinting that he's tired by rubbing his eyes on my thumb, he'll use this period to stand on my shoulder and preen. He'll voice a few haunting nighttime chirps, an unadorned recitative, his paean to nightfall. Very different behavior compared with how things go when it's me forcing the bed issue. He'll twirl in my hand as if battling demons, snap them dead as they rise from the shadows.

The finches have stopped jockeying for position in the ficus tree. Two of them are already tucked and sleeping, the whole contingent looking like a collection of ingenious ornaments I've placed among the leaves.

Because I understand the cheeky bastards, I think it's probably now safe to kill the remaining light. This is when Rebecca would say goodnight to B. She'd promise him a visit and Cheerios first thing in the morning. At the words "morning" and "Cheerio" he'd incline his head as if imagining the scene. He'd watch closely as she collected her belongings and prepared to leave. I mean to say, he really scrutinizes her as she gathers pens, notebook, pocket calendar, hair clips, cups, magazines, address book, and everything else that's forever caught in her gravitational field. As she squeezes through two doors and out into the hallway, it's fascinating to watch her move that much freight without actually exploding.

I turn off the table lamp and return with B to the couch. My thoughts at this time of day are diffuse. Hundreds of barely formed ideas shift their way from birth to extinction as my eyes adjust to the darkness and the heat from B's body flows into my hand. One night out of a hundred I can nearly banish the hissing of images and allow myself a dip in the void, but I'm always too frightened to do so—fearful, I think, of misplacing the world and myself along with it. I'd be a lousy Buddhist, preferring that my ego savor the calmness that comes from sitting in darkness with a sleeping bird. Have it and know that I have it, dig in my heels, and nod with affection at the way this room looks right now, durable even in shadow. I'm unwilling to risk the blister on my hand where I burned it today or this horrible woodwork enduring in its pinkness.

B has tucked and untucked a couple of times during the past ten minutes and is, at the moment, preening his bib. A person licking his or her own Adam's apple would be the human equivalent. I'll soon put him in his house, wait to make certain he's content before I leave for the night. There isn't generally a problem unless he decides to fly after me as I head for the door—a touching but risky gesture I try to discourage. A month or so ago, midway through his molt, was the last time he pulled such a stunt.

It may be that Rebecca and I are the only people who know that house sparrows purr. Not the localized gurgling that cats make in their throats, but more a full body vibration, a silent shivering unrelated to thermal issues or fear. B is so relaxed he's doing it now, making it that much harder for me to bring myself to rouse him. Before lifting him over to his house, I'll wait until a car passes or some other distraction wakes him. I'll nudge him onto my finger and from there to his perch.

The transfer goes smoothly, and there's no practical reason for me to linger, there being almost no chance he'll try following me tonight. But I wait anyway, studying what little I can see of him protruding from beneath his canopy—an old, faded dish towel decorated with pictures of teapots and cheerful-looking houses that have bouquets of flowers growing from their chimneys. There have been many nights when B has comforted me at least as much as I've comforted him.

5 ≋

MIND OVER MATTER

Intelligence is a vernacular word that we apply to the large set of relatively independent mental attributes that build, in their entirety, something we call "mind."
—Stephen Jay Gould, *Questioning the Millennium*

Man thinks and God laughs.
—Yiddish Proverb

MARLOWE (NAMED AFTER RAYMOND CHANDLER'S PRIVATE detective) was my favorite cat. Black and white with half a white mustache, he was big—large-boned, heavy, and weighing more than twenty-five pounds before I imposed a diet and got him down to fighting trim at twenty. He intimidated Rebecca after she took up residence. He'd block her path, swipe at her heels, and move those small items of hers he could get his mouth around, placing them downstairs by the front door—cassette tapes, books, candle holders, lip gloss, shoes. He never touched anything of mine. Their animosity flourished until, in retaliation for one of his ambushes, Rebecca poured a cup of water on his head. Marlowe respected her after that, and by the time he died four years later, Rebecca mourned him as deeply as I did.

The problem began with Thea, the cat Rebecca brought with her from San Francisco. Upon her arrival, Thea astonished Marlowe (I can

102

still see the look on his face) by swiping him across the nose when she emerged from her carrier. Our fault, really. We didn't follow correct procedure for introducing a new cat into a household, just sort of flung the two of them together. We thought Thea was still tolerably drugged on the kitty tranquilizer Rebecca had gotten from her vet and to which Thea responded forty-five minutes after receiving it by going from manic to unconscious in one fell swoop, as it were. Her eyes rolled back in her head, tongue hung out, back legs collapsed—the whole ataxic performance that a strong downer facilitates. And it was a good thing this happened when it did because less than a minute before the drug kicked in Rebecca said to me, "The pill didn't work; let's give her another one."

Marlowe, typically gentle around other cats, refused to let bygones be bygones and persecuted Thea for the next several months. He reduced her to a closet-haunting ghost who no doubt wished she could exorcise herself back to San Francisco and that nice big flat that she and Rebecca shared on Page Street. She'd venture partway down the stairwell at night, but Marlowe invariably chased her back up. The war lasted until almost Thanksgiving—Rebecca and Thea had arrived in July.

Because he was strictly an indoor cat, birds were mostly hearsay to Marlowe. But having a noisy sparrow in the house aroused long-dormant hunting instincts. As leader of the opposition party, he molded himself and our other two cats into a small guerrilla army whose principal activity centered on watching B's door in eight-hour shifts. I told Rebecca they looked as if they'd willingly swap a week's worth of kibble for a battering ram and munitions. I once went upstairs and found Rebecca looking out at Marlowe through the door of her study (the upper half of the door is windowed) and saying to B who was attentively perched on her finger, "Cats are savages, B. That's a cat, evil pussycat." It became a real pain in the ass shifting an obsessed feline every time I wanted to visit B, but the hunter-prey memento mori aspect of the situation helped solidify my antirelease bias and led to the era of screen door construction I inaugurated a few months later. The Appalachian theme of our upstairs will be complete after I install an outdoor privy in each of the bedrooms.

In thinking about Marlowe, I realize that I tended to credit *my* cats with inner lives, as if their association with me somehow endowed them with the requisite mental powers they needed to be at least marginally self-aware. This way of approaching the question of consciousness in other creatures didn't reflect beliefs that I'd reasoned out. I never thought much about it one way or the other until B came along and undermined my entrenched chauvinism. The idea of stepping inside a cat's brain for fifteen minutes to see what exists there besides images of food and instructions on how to obtain it seems far more interesting to me now than it would have been in the era before I had birds. He'd never permit it, but I'd love to get inside B's mind, too—maybe rig up a comic-book transference device involving metal skullcaps and pulsing electrodes.

Even assuming that such a mad-scientist approach were viable, structural differences between the avian and mammalian brains would likely scuttle the project in a cloud of blown and smoking synapses. Our respective brains are, to be sure, variations on a theme built around the older reptilian model. They both contain mid- and hindbrain sections that regulate the body's autonomic processes while controlling such basic drives as hunger and aggression. When, however, the line of descent from reptiles diverged—birds going one direction, mammals another—so did the physical evolution of their respective brains when it came to accommodating those higher mental activities that, taken in the aggregate, form what we think of as intelligence.

In mammals, these functions—learning, memory, emotion, insight—are fixed in the upper part of the forebrain or cerebrum (another legacy from the reptiles) in an area known as the cerebral cortex, a feature virtually nonexistent in birds but massive and heavily encephalized in humans. Leaving aside philosophical debate over mind-body duality, questions about how and from whence consciousness derives and speculation concerning the existence of a soul as the unique, enduring essence of being, the cerebral cortex is unquestionably the seat of our formidable intellectual power. In nonhuman mammals, as well, a positive correlation exists between the size of the cerebral cortex and correspondingly higher levels of intelligence. Or at least intelligence as we're capable of measuring it. This is why primates and dolphins with their relatively large cortical areas are better problem solvers than, for example, mice, cats, horses, or dogs. But it's critical to understand that absolute brain size is far less important than brain volume relative to body mass (as noted in Chapter 4, house sparrows compare extremely well in this regard). Large animals may indeed be very bright, but they also need large brains simply to regulate the demands of large bodies. By the same token, tiny brains in tiny animals are often capable of re-markable things: with a brain that may be charitably thought of as a speck, honeybees manage to fly, coordinate six legs, navigate, gather nectar, build hives, defend themselves, communicate with one another about sources of nectar . . .

Based on the assumption that any creature lacking a respectable cerebral cortex exists without the neural anatomy necessary for intelli-gent, flexible behavior, the dominant scientific view of birds as rigid stimulus-reflex machines has until recently remained pervasive. Has done so despite a wealth of anecdotal and a growing body of experi-mental evidence to the contrary. But as so often happens when obser-vation runs counter to theory, someone questioned the underlying hy-pothesis. In this case, it was Stanley Cobb, a Harvard Medical School neurologist, who did pioneering research that resulted in a favorable reassessment of the avian brain. In their 1968 *Scientific American* article, "The Brain of Birds," Laurence Jay Stettner and Kenneth A. Matyniak report that "Cobb concluded that the avian `organ of intelligence' was not the cortex but the hyperstriatum." They also note that Cobb per-ceived a "negative correlation between cortical development and intel-ligence," deducing that "the principal function of the cortex in birds was in relation to the sense of smell, and that as the more advanced avian species came to depend less on this sense, the cortex shrank in size and importance."

The hyperstriatum, absent in mammals, is an enlargement of the striatum, which, along with the cortex, is one of the two major struc-tures forming the mammalian and avian cerebrums. The link between the hyperstriatum and avian intelligence is now well established. As with the mammalian cortex, bigger is better. This is indicated by the su-perior performance on intelligence tests of ravens and parrots, both of which have large hyperstriatums—as compared with chickens, quail, and pigeons, which do not. There is an expanding body of scientific ev-idence to demonstrate that some birds are easily equal to chimps and gorillas in cognitive ability. I nominate the house sparrow for inclusion in this group.

In his recent book *Bird's Eye View,* David M. Bird (yes, he's aware of the irony of his name), professor of wildlife biology and director of the Avian Science and Conservation Center at McGill University, relates a story about house sparrows learning to activate automatic bus door openers, a tale passed on to him by friends of his after their return from a trip to Hamilton, New Zealand, in 1990. Evidently keen to board buses in order to search for food dropped by human passengers, "The clever birds set off the sensor in one of three ways. They either flew slowly by it, hovered in front of it at a distance of a few centimeters, or landed on the top of it and then leaned over to stick their fat little faces in front of it." A bus company employee noted that the sparrows had "picked up the technique fairly quickly." In fact, shortly after the new doors went into service, two months previously.

I'm standing outside B's screen door scanning the room. Today is the first day this week I've been able to spend a generous amount of uninterrupted time with him. By turns, he's been playful and relaxed. After an intense game of Cap, he spent half an hour napping on my knee as I read. I've just returned from running errands. I expect he'll be either desperate to see me (looks unlikely) or frosty because I'm late with his afternoon grape (seems probable). I heard a veritable Babel of bird chatter when I entered the house, but wasn't able to distinguish greeting calls from B amidst the chorus of jabbering that streamed down the stairwell.

It's now a game of hide-and-seek. My job is to find B with my eyes before entering. He's not on the bookcase gremlin, not on the sword, not on one of the shelves, not on the television or the Cheerio container. He's not crouched behind the table lamp or in his house; he's not on or around his toy basket, and he isn't trying to pull a fast one by standing on the other side of the door, flush against the frame. I don't see him peeking out from around one of the speakers on the floor or from behind the mirror that's propped up on a wine crate. As a rule, I spot him more quickly than this.

Now that I'm worried and think about forfeiting the game by walking inside to begin a proper search, I notice the tip of a black beak pointing out ever so slightly from behind a water jug that sits on the floor. I'm constantly amazed by B's ability to find new hiding places in such a static setting. "I wonder what happened to the sparrow that lived here," I say. "I wonder where he's gone. Clever finches have commandeered his room and driven him away." Although this begins endgame, it doesn't get a response, nor was it meant to; it's only one more step in how this thing is played. Until I exclaim, "There's the bird," he won't break cover and invite me in.

B loops overhead as I enter, lands on my finger chirping and bowing. The idea of having lived most of my life without him seems to me a monstrous fiction I invented to frighten myself. He stands on my shoulder and chatters in my ear—like a sports fan reliving an exciting play. And as this image pops into my head, I wonder if anthropomorphizing will ever catch up with me. Will secret police come at night and drag me off to a reeducation camp?

THE VAUX'S SWIFT IS ONE OF THE FASTEST CREATURES ON EARTH. Weighing but two-thirds of an ounce, its modest four-and-a-half-inch frame is equipped with a twelve-inch wingspan capable of propelling it better than one hundred miles per hour in level flight. Virtually its entire waking life is spent in the air feeding on insects. Swifts belong to the relatively exclusive order Apodiformes that also includes one other family of remarkably fast, dexterous flyers—hummingbirds. It's neither here nor there, but bird's nest soup actually exists and is made not, as one might infer from the name, of unpalatable, not to say indigestible, grasses and sticks but of congealed saliva painstakingly deposited on sheer rock and formed into a cup by a species of southeast Asian swift. Considering that the broth of this delicacy is said to be tasteless and that obtaining the main ingredient involves scaling walls in bat-infested caves, I'm unable to explain why such an item made it into the human diet. How someone hit on the notion of boiling up bird spit for dinner will remain, I suppose, one of life's little mysteries.

For the past nine or ten years, a growing colony of Vaux's swifts (currently estimated to number some forty thousand birds) has visited Portland during the month of September, roosting at night in the smokestacklike chimney belonging to Chapman Elementary School in the northwest part of the city. The flock makes its sojourn here while migrating south to wintering areas in southern Mexico and Central America, returning again in spring when the birds head for their summer range, which extends as far north as Alaska. In a culture where wildlife is often deemed expendable when it becomes inconvenient, it should be noted with admiration that while the swifts are in residence, students, faculty, and staff at Chapman go about their business in an unheated building. That they've elected to do so year after year has obviated the alternative of killing the birds by firing up the school's furnaces or of taking steps to prevent the swifts from gaining access to the chimney. Money raised by the Chapman School Swift Project has defrayed the considerable cost of installing a new metal chimney as far away as possible from the existing masonry structure coveted by the swifts. With the work of converting the boilers completed, the installation of the new chimney is ready to proceed pending the resolution of last-minute engineering details.

Chapman School, Ionic columns dominating its neoclassic facade, sits in a quiet residential area adjacent to a small park. Unlike many elementary schools in large cities, it feels exactly like the place people wish could have been the setting for their own introduction to academia. It offers a comely building set on an enormous lawn where, in my day, the more bellicose kids would have waled on their schoolmates. A delightful place to congregate every fall with hundreds of other people who have come to watch a colony of birds retire for the evening.

The chimney, forty feet high and several feet in diameter, is a freestanding brick structure situated at the rear of the school. From my usual vantage point leaning against a sapling around front, it appears to rise from the building's center with enough industrial authority to suggest a factory where they rend, smelt, or construct something. Each evening during the month or so the swifts are in town, many of the spectators bring picnics and install themselves on the grassy area sloping down from the sidewalk toward the school's south-facing wall. This is where Audubon volunteers set up display tables and answer questions. Kids run around, and there's often a volleyball game in progress next door in Wallace Park. Under most circumstances, a gathering of this many Americans outside on a warm evening will reliably produce an ambient sound level considerably above a murmur, but something about this yearly spectacle compels an almost reverential silence. Conversations are held as if privacy were a concern; music doesn't blast from portable stereos.

The first swifts arrive well before sundown, black dots coasting in from all directions to begin a lazy orbit of the chimney. A man nearby says to his friends, "I can't believe I'm spending my Sunday evening watching birds go to bed." While the tone of his voice suggests regret, I notice his gaze seldom strays from the sky. It would be easy, at first, to think you were watching bats, there being a similarity in size and in the occasional jerky dips the swifts make as they change course to capture an insect. Bats are admirable, if idiosyncratic, flyers in their own right, but compared with swifts and viewed aesthetically, their flight is a series of spastic blunders. As the flock thickens, your options dwindle, the difficulty of not looking at the sky increasing with each additional bird applying itself to the vortex.

Strange the way this happens: glance back at the chimney after your attention's been drawn off a moment by a skateboarder whizzing past on the macadam path, and you find there now seem to be far more circling birds than the last time you checked. I track individual swifts as they appear over the tops of surrounding houses, fixing them in my binoculars until they merge with the others—adding, as it were, their shoulders to the wheel. One instant I'm viewing an individual life, the next moment it vanishes like an idea subsumed in a busy mind. Light dwindles; the formation tightens.

From the time the initial smattering of early arrivals begins to assume the proportion of a flock, one's sense of being in the presence of a coordinated organism grows along with the ever increasing number of birds joining what is fast becoming a funnel cloud simulacrum turning clockwise, draining itself into the chimney. Responding now and then to an external stimulus (rumor of a hawk, perhaps) or to a request or command from the body politic, rotation reverses and the mass of descending birds billows upward and outward, scribing a languorous counterclockwise curve that in the end loops the birds back again to their rightward-turning spiral.

Vaux's swifts roost vertically on chimney walls or, in a more natural setting, tree snags—increasingly scarce thanks to old-growth logging. Their tail feathers end in what amount to specialized spikes acting as kickstandlike stabilizers that help prop them in place while they sleep. By the time they've all settled into the chimney, they're roosting three deep, one swift clinging to the wall with another on its back and yet another on the back of the second bird. Older swifts, in deference to their enhanced social status, are allowed roosting positions near the center of the flock. This perk, according to an article in the *Audubon Warbler*, affords not only a more desirable thermal position but also greater protection from predators striking the perimeter of the colony. If this is true, and I have no reason to doubt that it is, think of the logistical problem this presents as forty thousand birds shoehorn themselves into a poorly lighted smokestack in accordance with the dictates of an age-based seating chart. The spectators cheer and applaud when, a little after eight o'clock, the last bird packs it in for the night.

While I'm watching swifts, Rebecca is at home reassuring B he can rely on my promise that I'll be back in time to put him to bed. It's an outrageous claim, I know, but Rebecca insists that he's less agitated when, in a sense, I tell him beforehand that I'll be stepping out. I'm used to feeling like a mooncalf, so I don't mind outlining my itinerary to a house sparrow. And because I don't think Rebecca is deluded or that she's lying about the particulars of B's behavior when I'm absent in the evenings, her theory about why he acts as he does seems plausible to me. She doesn't believe that B responds to the specifics of where I'm going and when I'll be back but to whether I say "soon" or "later" as I exit his room. She notes that during the normal course of a day I always say, "See you soon, B," whenever I leave him unless, that is, I don't plan on being back for his bedtime. In that event, according to her, I linger by the door and say, "See you later, B," when I finally manage to go. His expectations are thus set accordingly, problems avoided. But if I screw up by using the former valediction in an instance when I should have used the latter (easy enough to do through force of habit, the ratio of "soon" to "later" being at least a hundred to one), he expects me back shortly and gets upset when I don't return.

Rebecca's experience from about six years ago illustrates why I make it a point to keep B informed. I was quite late getting home from work when she rang me at my office worried because I hadn't called with an explanation. B, in her words, was "having a cow," shrieking and flying back and forth to the window, hanging on the screen door, listening by the heating vent. His distressed chirping ceased after Rebecca got me on the phone and was able to verify for B that predators hadn't killed me. I suppose it's possible that he reacted empathically to

Rebecca's mood, first to her uneasiness and then to her relief. Or maybe the sound of my voice soothed him when he heard it leaking out from the telephone. Who knows? I remember him gluing himself to my shoulder that evening with an extraordinary amount of determination.

Because I'm convinced that B has consciousness, it seems only sporting to assume that each Vaux's swift must own a measure of the same commodity. Within six months of B's arrival, I could no longer walk outside without the eerie sensation that hundreds of bird minds were ticking away in the vicinity—not necessarily taking notice of me but capable of it. That Vaux's swifts amass, swirl in perfectly synchronized flight, and then ultimately disappear inside a smokestack is, if nothing else, a triumph of communication. You just can't have thousands of birds flying in tight formation, changing speed and heading as a single entity, without commands and feedback passing to and from each individual bird. I mean to say, creatures flying wing tip to wing tip do not have much margin for error. The rather lovely thing right now is that no one knows exactly how they do it.

Solving a mystery ends speculation and the fun of not having the facts. Still, I'd be the first to look up the explanation of how the swifts do what they do, fully aware of how disappointing and prosaic the answer might be. Despite how wondrous it is that Earth is not supported on the back of a giant tortoise or on the shoulders of Atlas and despite how marvelous it is that we derive light and warmth from the fusion of hydrogen into helium within a flaming ball of gas and not from Phoebus Apollo driving a fiery chariot across heaven's vault, surely some part of us is diminished by this knowledge. Wordsworth said, "We have given our hearts away, a sordid boon!"

My mother liked telling a story that involved her great-uncle Parker and a supposed encounter he had with a ghost one evening after church, the action taking place in the closing years of the nineteenth century at a crossroads in the village of Stonington. I know this place and the country church and boneyard hard by the road; relatives from both sides of my family are buried there. It seems that the figure of a white-clad woman began appearing regularly, but not consistently, following Sunday evening services. Since no one questioned initially whether or not she was metabolically viable, she must have seemed corporeal enough not to send screaming parishioners diving into their buggies. She confined herself to hanging about the edge of the grave-yard opposite the church, refused to speak when hailed, but sometimes ventured into the center of the road, right arm extended to her inter-locutor as if she wished to introduce herself with a handshake. Some-thing off-putting about the setup, however, discouraged anyone from accepting her offer. Until, that is, Uncle Parker hit upon the idea of draping a handkerchief over his palm before grasping hers. Hard to say what he hoped to gain from the encounter, let alone what lesson, if any, the experience taught him. Either my mother didn't know or Parker never said. He may have wanted to be neighborly, but evidence sug-gests otherwise. Until well into senility (a state of mind hastened, pos-sibly, by the way things turned out), Uncle Parker remained quite a lad for the ladies. The old goat probably found the strange woman attrac-tive, an infatuation that evaporated along with his handkerchief when it burst into flames at her touch.

I'd love to believe this story is true, take it at face value and live out my life convinced that ghosts exist and, by implication, so does life after death—even though in my experience people concerned with living forever have more trouble planning vacations than those who aren't. But even if one puts stock in the irrational, how then to reconcile intu-ition and inkling with the more palpable reality exposed by observation and logic? How to separate fear, bias, faith, and hope from the cause-and-effect world we find ourselves mired in? I've looked at B on occa-sion and wondered, "Is all this because he's cute?" What I call the in utero conundrum: if human fetuses bristled with spines and scales, I daresay the abortion controversy would be considerably moderated. People respond favorably to adorable things. One theory has it that evolution selected this tendency as a means of inducing us to care for our squalling, but otherwise valuable, offspring. I'll own up to a weak-ness for cute. Probably explains why, as a child, I was always dragging home kittens.

≈

ASIDE FROM ENABLING ME TO ADD, SUBTRACT, MULTIPLY, AND DIVIDE, arithmetic never did much for me. It wasn't until I was in my teens and came to grips with Euclid and the seemingly immutable correctness of plane geometry that I began to appreciate precision for its own sake and as a telling indicator of governing principles open to inspection and verification by anyone willing to take the trouble of looking. Everything appeared reducible to measurable points in absolute time and absolute space, a conclusion not lost on Sir Isaac Newton. His physics convinced me that while the universe may be a cold, indifferent place, it's at least comfortably predictable, consisting as it does of well-behaved atoms and simple forces acting upon them independently of whether anyone observes their movements or not. Newton's equations fueled the scientific revolution in the West—apart from capitalism, our dominant cultural paradigm. A practical application of classical physics got astronauts to the moon and returned them to earth because it's a damned good approximation of how matter and energy interact on the macroscopic level. If you're curious to know with how much force a freight train bearing down on your stalled car will hit you, Newton's your man.

But thanks to two major developments at the beginning of the last century, few scientists any longer believe that classical physics represents anything approaching a complete description of what we think of loosely as reality. Relativity theory and quantum physics are twin pillars of what is sometimes called the New Physics and suggest, among other things, that no single frame of reference is qualitatively better than any other. Events that seem simultaneous to two observers may appear as sequential to a third. There is no objectively "right" answer to what happens when. Of equal importance is the discovery that on the atomic level, at least, observation affects not only the outcome of experiments but even when and if a particular event will occur at all. We live, it seems, in a participatory universe.

I hate mentioning any of this. In the first place, references to "relativity" and "quantum" seem pretentious, the kind of crap some paunchy guy would throw around at a party as part of his mating display. And in the second place, few people (myself included) possess the mathematical sophistication necessary to a genuine understanding of physics at this level. And make no mistake about it, these theories, tested and confirmed in particle accelerators, are mathematical constructs. Even Albert Einstein, who at times wrote for a lay audience, is said to have remarked (with, I suspect, a self-deprecating kernel of truth, given that he was less a mathematician than a theoretical physicist) that once mathematicians got hold of relativity theory, *he* no longer understood it. The great danger for a layman dabbling in quantum physics is that it's devilishly easy to draw inaccurate or fanciful conclusions. Among other things, quantum theory does not somehow overthrow physical reality, nor does it offer any credence to notions of the supernatural. Believe me, anything that happens plays by the rules, even newly observed phenomena that challenge existing orthodoxy. But it's probably not much of a stretch to assert that the line between physics and metaphysics begins to blur way out on the hairy edges of this stuff.

Quantum theory does unquestionably point to aspects of reality that are counterintuitive, a place where particles are also waves, where uncertainty prevails, where potential is as important as actuality—the so-called quantum vacuum containing an unmeasurable yet infinite ocean of possibility that forms the source of all things actual. In truth, quantum theory recognizes aspects of reality wherein the whole exceeds the sum of its parts. It is this property of emergence inherent in complex systems—minds, for example—that interests me here. Some physicists now believe that the ambitiously named and elusive Theory of Everything must, in order to be complete, unite not only matter and the four fundamental forces of nature—the weak and strong nuclear forces, electromagnetism, and gravity—but consciousness as well. I can't be the only one taking immense satisfaction in contemplating what amounts, broadly speaking, to a scientific basis for believing that although consciousness may have a physical basis in the brain, it is unlikely to be explained as a mere electrochemical process deriving from millions of neurons secreting and discharging in concert. Yet, for the most part, neuroscience remains faithful to the reductionist model, and while it has seen great success in explaining, for example, visual processing in the brain, it has had precious little in putting forth a convincing theory to describe what it is that *experiences* a perception or how it is that consciousness, presumably derived from and embedded in all those firing neurons, is bonded into a single contemplative entity. A robot could be said to "see" an object, but it's doubtful it has any sense of what it's like to do so. Reductionists would say, "Build a better robot."

Francis Crick, who, along with James Watson and Maurice Wilkins, is best known for his work on the discovery of DNA, has in recent years interested himself in neuroscience, becoming an ardent proponent of a reductionist model of consciousness. In his 1994 book, *The Astonishing Hypothesis: The Scientific Search for the Soul,* he asserts: "'You,' your joys and your sorrows, your memories and your ambitions, your sense of personal identity and free will, are in fact no more than the behavior of a vast assembly of nerve cells and their associated molecules." As succinct a formulation of the reductionist position as you're likely to find. And Crick may very well be correct, despite a somewhat apostolic faith in the ability of a number of exotic chemical compounds to produce a "Francis" capable of persuading a "me" or a "you" to go out and purchase his book. William James had it nailed when he said, "The greatest empiricists among us are only empiricists on reflection: when left to their instincts, they dogmatize like infallible popes." Crick will forgive me if I hope we continue searching for an answer without ever finding it. Nice joke if human consciousness is programmatically incapable of explaining itself.

How touching, though, that it fears for itself, grows melancholy when pondering what an elegant nothing it might actually be. Looking last night at a video of B's first weeks, I wondered how much of my dearest friend was captured there beyond images of a young and still awkward bird, beyond intimations of his inquisitiveness and affection caught in the bright summer light we had that day. In attempting to preserve the who and what of our lives, we demand a great deal from our contrivances, hoping that photographs or film will validate our history more reliably than memory, endure when the reality has washed as irretrievably into the past as waves that have broken on shore. And what *of* memory? I have my delirious mother wheeled from the house on an ambulance stretcher, and I have B riding on my head, chirping with curiosity, as I crawl on the floor pursuing a screw that recently held my glasses together. Interesting how we all carry wreckage and the means to repair it. Or, depending on what kind of face you feel like putting on the human condition, maybe it's that our joys are moderated in the interest of humility. Either way, I can hold B in my hand and think how pleased I am that he is with me now, that it is neither before his time, nor after his time, that our minds build from the same instants the evolving specifics of who we are.

I'm home after seeing the swifts, and B greets me with a merry chirp, flying to my shoulder when I enter his room. There are a number of downy feathers on Rebecca's knee where she says B sat alternately preening and napping for the past half hour; she says he's been an "angel love." By the time I'm seated, he's settled in my hand, drowsy and yawning. I'm pleased to reflect that whereas the swifts are specialists, B is a generalist with an accommodating palate and no seasonal yearning to be south of here or in the process of getting there. Rebecca listens to my observations, points out that B migrates from the top of his mirror to the hilt of the sword. She flatters me by pretending I manage to convey something of the found poetry forty thousand swifts leave in eddies behind them.

"WHY DOESN'T THE BIRD LIKE ME?"

"Thinks you're a jerk."

Although I answer more tactfully, this is the gist of a conversation I've had with visitors that B finds beyond the pale. Such exchanges are embarrassing because these perfectly nice people usually have a fol-low-up question, "Why would the bird think I'm a jerk?" Generally, some external—an article of clothing, say, or unacceptable hair or painted fingernails or teeth crying out for orthodontia—explains why B takes issue with one person and not with another. Even Rebecca, as I've said, falls from grace over fashion faux pas. I appear to be immune from censure. I could walk in wearing a suit of armor without upsetting him. But I'll be damned if I can figure out what B's got against certain peo-ple that causes him to shriek and chatter every time they visit: they dress unremarkably, are not abnormally large or small, don't ooze or drool, and they comport themselves in a civil manner. It's as if he peers beneath their surface and is appalled.

Others are more fortunate. As demonstrated by a willingness to land on them after a modest evaluation period, B seems to hold them in relatively high esteem and remains as consistent in whom he prefers as he does in whom he dislikes. Most newcomers, however, fall into an undistinguished middle ground, tend to be people he'll warm to given time, especially if I leave the room for fifteen or twenty minutes. These guests usually describe their encounters with B in a similar way—"I kept trying to coax him to me, but he wouldn't budge from that perch by the window, just stared at me and flicked his tail like you said. I was about ready to get up and leave when he flew over and landed on my knee. He wouldn't get on my finger, though." B will present caps to an elite few when they visit. I call them "The Elect."

"How did you guys train him to do that?" initiates ask me.

"We didn't."

B's playfulness didn't manifest itself until after we moved him into the back room and began efforts to wean him away from the toothpick. He showed virtually no interest in any of the bird-entertainment crap we picked up at the pet store—sliding colored beads, a hanging bell, a surreal pivot-mounted plastic bird designed to bounce back dementedly every time it's pecked. The only item that drew a big reaction was an eight-inch-high rubber bath toy facsimile of Woodstock from the comic strip "Peanuts." It was, of course, yellow. Rebecca presented the thing as a surprise by coming up behind me and placing it on my shoulder. B, who'd been playing coy, zoomed off the computer monitor in full attack mode and gutted Woodstock in spirit, if not in fact. After separating real bird from fake bird we stashed Woodstock in a drawer that B eyed with suspicion for almost a week. Nothing else we introduced as diversions sparked any interest. I suspected that house sparrows were incapable of play—my polite way of thinking they lacked either the brains or inclination to recreate, were hardwired for little else than beak-to-the-grindstone survival. But our big concern at this time was B's disinclination to eat seed, his taste for which had been retarded, I think, by our continuing to slavishly feed him baby food whenever he begged. He'd flutter his wings and gape, and I'd serve up another heaping portion.

We laid in a supply of seed from the pet store called "Finch Mixture," choosing it because it appeared to contain seeds appropriate for small birds and because the manufacturer had labeled the package "Vitamin Enriched," an irresistible phrase to American consumers. I'm surprised someone hasn't marketed vitamin-enriched paint as a healthy alternative to the nutritionally barren stuff currently covering our nation's walls. I remember thinking what a lovely mosaic the seeds made after we poured them into a Pyrex pie dish along with a bluish sand-based mineral supplement that Rebecca dubbed "blue rocks." Because birds lack teeth, many ingest tiny stones or gravel that's used in their gizzards as the medium against which food is ground before it passes into the stomach proper where it's digested chemically. Grinding action by the gizzard is especially important in birds that consume seeds whole, less so in birds such as house sparrows that husk their seeds before swallowing. This is a good thing because B has never, as far as I know, eaten a single blue rock. I suppose, however, he'd do so if he had to. He likes the white mineral blocks we supply, gnaws on one periodically throughout the day, but they're chalky and provide little grit. Our other three sparrows love blue rocks; the finches, also seed huskers, eat them readily; our canaries are ambivalent.

Rebecca took B's refusal to eat seed as an affront to her parenting skills. She'd follow him around the room pushing sprigs of millet in his face, a strategy that failed, naturally, to make her case for the edible properties of seed, resulted instead in our first exposure to "The Look." Expressive of bewilderment, irritation, contempt, The Look encourages you to stop whatever you're doing and go off somewhere to rethink every decision you've made since birth. Whereas the road to hell is paved with good intentions, the road to anthropomorphism is paved with the faces of the animals we love. Fellow mammals are easiest to read, their expressions congruent with our own, written as they are on a familiar palimpsest of nonverbal emotion and response. The higher up the primate ladder, the closer the match. I know any number of people for whom staring an ape in the eye would be to confront the better angel of their own humanity. That birds have beaks where there should be lips and nothing visible where there should be ears makes it harder for us to distinguish distinctive traits within a species (no trouble, of course, telling a duck's face from an eagle's), each countenance carved apparently from the same mute stone. Short of remembering where I put my glasses, I've had few epiphanies in life, but getting The Look has rather made up for it. One minute I had a bird, the next minute a bird with a face I'd have no trouble picking out of a lineup. "Yes, officer, second from left, that's the sparrow that brutalized Woodstock."

A few days after our trip to buy seed, Rebecca and I were hanging out on the bed in the back room trying to figure out how we could exclude the lunatic fringe from our wedding. B periodically circumnavigated the room, stopping for a quick preen or scratch on the mirror frame or the spigot before returning to burrow in my hair or gaze in my ear. This was the day I discovered B's fascination with minute irregularities on human skin and how painful it is when he uses his beak to excise some tiny excrescence I didn't know I had. Since learning that I react badly to these ministrations, he's grown circumspect and generally contents himself with merely looking at my manifold blemishes. Still, he'll occasionally touch one of these imperfections so delicately with his beak or tongue that I often can't tell whether I've felt him do so or not. If such gentle explorations didn't mean that his willpower is flagging and surgery imminent, I wouldn't coil so tightly when he indulges himself in this way. I try to view his efforts as affectionate interest in my welfare, remind myself that he's ever so tolerant when I nuzzle his head despite how innately troubling it must be for a bird to have mammalian breath whiffling its feathers.

After B bit down on a small mole I have on my neck, I fished him from my hair and placed him on the bed between Rebecca and me. While he investigated the folds in my pants, Rebecca, who is nothing if not persistent, reached around to the pie dish and grabbed a pinch of seed that B, of course, ignored. Instead of eating, he began work on extracting the sapphire from Rebecca's engagement ring, a project he pursued with enough initiative to make Rockefeller look like a drifter. Realizing after a minute or so that his prize wasn't budging, he switched his attention to one of the small accent diamonds on either side of the central stone—yanking with the kind of maniacal enthusiasm you'd expect from a man whose tie is caught in large turning cogs. I guess he figured that something was better than nothing.

The knack women have of extricating themselves from bras must be related in some way to the sleight-of-hand smoothness they employ when removing their earrings. Rebecca reached up as if shooing a mosquito and returned with the silver hoop from her right ear. The same task would have taken me five minutes, resulting in an inflamed lobe the way it did back when I sported an earring as part of whatever statement I thought I was making. My twenties, fortunately, did not coincide with the current mania for pierced mucous membranes that I expect will evolve before long into the cosmetic amputation of digits and limbs.

Seizing her earring by the garnet-colored bead dangling from its center, B didn't hesitate when Rebecca offered it to him. He grabbed it, flipped it, banged it, tossed it, rolled it, threw it from the bed, rocked from foot to foot while I hurried to retrieve it. This resulted in our first tug of war, and Rebecca still laughs when remembering B's triumphant flight around the room after he snatched the earring from my fingers. We've never discussed it, but I'd be surprised if this initial play session didn't begin undermining Rebecca's resolve to return B to the wild.

Most of the video we have from B's infant days shows a relatively undistinguished house sparrow eating, sleeping, and defecating, a bird too concerned with life's basics to worry about the camera. But it frightened B to have one pointed in his direction on the day Rebecca attempted to record the events just described. We spent more time trying to coax an encore than we did enjoying the original performance. It's curious that we diluted our appreciation of B's first play session by working to preserve a facsimile. We put the camera away after ten fruitless minutes of pleading with him to quit the upper perch of his house where he sat scolding us with the same outraged chatter I've heard neighborhood house sparrows direct toward an approaching cat. "No one will believe he played with an earring," I whined. "It's something he'll probably never do again."

"Could be," Rebecca replied, "but he still doesn't eat seed. This baby food routine is a pain in the ass."

I walked in a few days later and found B on the rim of the pie dish expertly pecking. He staged intermittent begging routines for another couple of weeks, but having once learned to feed himself the dietary staple his kind evolved to survive on, he was for all practical purposes a self-sufficient bird. You'll think me starved for entertainment, but I must tell you how entranced I became watching B dispatch seed. After all this time, I still enjoy watching him do so. Until you observe the process closely, it's hard to appreciate what a precise operation a sparrow's consumption of a single seed represents, let alone how much dexterity it takes to down a slew of them in rapid succession. Try the following: Mark a piece of paper with a series of dots only fractionally larger than the point of your pen. Now, see if you can hit each dot on mark with your fingernail, and do it as quickly as you can intelligibly count out loud. Of course, what B does is somewhat more challenging.

He not only picks up seeds with astonishing speed but, as noted earlier, removes their husks before swallowing the meat. This means you must cut your dots in half after stabbing them.

Although I find the taste disappointing, all our birds love millet. B buzzes through these tiny seeds like a combine through a wheat field. The husks pile up and adhere to the outside of his beak until he shakes his head and clears them away. He sometimes overlooks this detail and returns to me looking as if he's afflicted with an exotic beak disease that's broken out in unsightly lesions. Reminds me of a cat neglecting to retract its tongue and of how I forget now and then to zip up my fly. Luckily, I've got Rebecca around to say, "Hey, sailor, trying to tell me something?"

B, like most birds, tends to gobble his food, instinct telling him to get it while he can. Thus, it surprised me one day to see him eating slowly. And although I thought at first he was either ill or had been replaced with a flawed doppelgänger, relaxed dining gradually became a part of his regular routine. That he could eat as contemplatively as a toothless man gumming a Tootsie Roll suggested to me that he valued food beyond its usefulness as fuel. This led to the first of many puns on his name: "How did B like his grape? Thought it was B-licious." He probably realized how pointless it was to rush meals in the absence of meaningful competition over resources. He shares his room with finches, but he's nearly twice their size and doesn't take them seriously, seems to view them more as an irritation than a credible threat. As far as I can tell, he considers them jabbering subnormals that, strictly speaking, aren't really birds.

As with most activities that don't specifically involve him, B acts as if my talking on the telephone is wasted time that profits him little. He's burrowing in my hair at the moment but is perfectly capable of shrieking into whichever ear doesn't have the receiver pressed against it. He'll comment loudly into the mouthpiece, attempting, I assume, to inform the person on the other end that I'm not really free to talk right now. A caller once asked me, "Is this a bad time? You sound like you're in a jungle." A reasonable assumption when B's in full voice and the finches are rehearsing a composition that could be aptly titled "The Sounds of Castration." I enjoy informing telemarketers I have to hang up because a team of nurses has arrived with my lithium.

The older of my two brothers and I are having one of our twice-monthly conversations. I look forward to these calls not only because I love J. D. and enjoy talking with him but also because, aside from Julia, my one surviving aunt, he's the last real link I have to my hometown and to the life I lived and to a life I chose not to live—a place I can't abandon entirely in any sense beyond the strictly geographical and even in this, when I think "landscape," I flash automatically on the river and mountains of home, the place where I awoke into myself from the long sleep before birth. "Home" for me is an ever receding point of return, a destination impossible to find without the assistance, you might say, of outdated maps.

As usual, J. D. and I establish pretty quickly that nothing significant is new since last we spoke. We discuss cats and the mounting vet bills associated with keeping our respective geriatrics cobbled together. He has the best of hearts when it comes to animals. Some years ago he acquired a neglected rabbit from a neighbor who'd kept the creature penned outside year-round on the off chance one of his demon spawn would haul it out of its cage and play with it. J. D. gave the rabbit a room in his upstairs and a good life for two or three years until it keeled over from an apparent heart attack. I remember J. D. telling me, "It's a good bunny," with an emphasis on "good" that made it sound as if bunnies, as a rule, were morally dubious. Then there's the time he held up traffic in both directions on a two-lane bridge over the Susquehanna River while trying to rescue a cat that had leaped from a car in the middle of the span. A truck driver complained (can't blame the guy, I suppose) but elected to remain in his cab after J. D. invited him to dismount—a wise decision. It's only within the past couple of years that J. D., now in his sixties, has scaled back an exercise regimen that included bench-pressing more than three hundred pounds. He was a skilled boxer in his youth, had considered turning pro.

B's settled in what amounts to a hammock of hair behind my left ear. He's too far back for me to see him with a sideways glance, but by leaning forward and looking in the six-paned mirror that's propped a few feet away atop an old wine crate, I can discern the end of his tail protruding from about where my ear lobe should be. I cover the phone's mouthpiece and say, "B, how about some corn?" He ate a large helping of goop before I got on the phone, but I'm not surprised to see his beak emerge when I pose the question. He's passionate about corn. J. D. is explaining to me the logistics of "fish night." It happens every Saturday and involves doling out portions of fresh haddock to his five cats. Alerted by the smell, they twine themselves into an orgiastic frenzy.

While J. D. describes the machinations involved in keeping one cat from stealing another cat's fish, I locate the plastic baggy containing corn, extra spinach, and apple slices that I packed this morning as part of B's breakfast. I don't know how he emerges so quickly from my hair without getting tangled. When I open the baggy he exits, as my father might have described it, like shit through a tin horn. I've got the phone cradled between my right shoulder and ear, B waiting on my left index finger for me to squeeze out the insides of the kernel I've selected. An unusually juicy one, it emits a jet of water that grazes B's head. He rises backward off my finger, lands near the water dish, and turns a couple of full circles while snapping his beak at invisible pursuers.

I can tell you from experience that a house sparrow's beak can be a formidable weapon and that the twirl-and-snap procedure B uses when alarmed is not something I take lightly. He'd been with us nearly nine months when I flew Beverly, my future mother-in-law, up from southern California as the surprise guest at Rebecca's thirtieth birthday party. Since then, whenever I ask Rebecca what she'd like as a gift she tells me that she wants what I gave her the year she turned thirty.

Beverly was curious to meet the creature we'd been referring to as her "grandbird," and so, the morning after her arrival, we all shuffled into B's room. He wasn't, I must point out, all that accustomed to visitors at that stage in his career but had already shown a tendency to make the kinds of eccentric judgments about people he's now notorious for making. Fortunately, he's also grown more philosophical about guests popping in, better able to accept that he's got a public whether he likes it or not. The thing to keep in mind here is that all four of our sparrows understand that Rebecca and I have eyes, that our eyes are important to us and are not to be poked—even when they're littered with sleep goo first thing in the morning and therefore untidy. Because B spends lots of time close to my face, I'm often asked if I'm afraid of losing an eye. I'm not. Accidents can happen, of course, but I know that B would never intentionally harm me.

Beverly brought up the rear as I entered first, followed by Rebecca. B flew to my left shoulder right away, and stood flicking there in his "What the hell is all this?" pose. Rebecca and I sat on the bed as Beverly worked *her way over, moving the way someone might if they suspected the floor-boards were rotten. Muttering at her approach, B tensed, ready for take-off, but maintained his composure until Beverly stepped on an empty cas-sette tape container and sent it bouncing and clattering across the floor. Things would have been fine had I not chosen that instant to kiss B on the head. He turned and snapped.*

Although this took place on a Sunday morning, my optometrist friend, Bill Berman, was in his office catching up on paperwork. He told me to come right down. My left eye hurt, watered copiously, and showed a marked sensitivity to light. The day was brilliantly sunny. Bill, who I always thought bore a slight resemblance to Franz Schubert, took me into the examination room and sat me in front of an interesting contraption that looked like binoculars on steroids; he peered in one side, I peered in the other. "You're missing a triangular piece of epithelium from your left eye that looks like it was removed with a scalpel, no ragged edges that I can see. Tell your bird he does nice work."

"Permanently damaged?"

"I don't think so," Bill said. "The wound's not deep. You'll have blurring on that side for a week or ten days and probably some low-level pain, but it should heal nicely. I'm going to give you antibiotic drops I'd like you to use a couple of times a day to ward off infection. You'll be fine; you lucked out."

Bill was correct in all particulars regarding my prognosis, failing only to predict that for several days every character of every line of text I read appeared to have an umlaut over it. When I asked how much I owed him for the exam and the drops, Bill said, "What, you kidding?" his tone suggesting it was more likely a planet would leave orbit than that he'd charge for helping a friend. He was a good and generous man, and it pains me to report that he died a year ago from a heart attack. He left a wife and three young children. Hundreds of shocked and grieving people attended his funeral; it was literally standing room only. I'd be lucky to get Rebecca belly dancing and four paid sparrows at mine.

B has finished his corn and is now on my shoulder performing a spot of bib maintenance. His intermittent clucking leads me to believe he's just about had it with my being on the phone. His interest in games has been tepid lately, but I might be able to defuse his impending snit by asking him to find me a particular cap—the red or the blue one, say. He's demon-

strated an ability to perform this task correctly, but it's not a sure thing. He may not feel like cooperating, which, inferring from his mood, will be the case today. Or he may bring me a cap other than the one specified, doing so either out of perversity or from "Ignorance, Madam, pure ignorance," to quote Samuel Johnson's famous reply to a woman in Plymouth who asked him to explain how it came to pass that in his monumental dictionary he'd incorrectly defined the word "pastern"—which, in case you're dying to know, is the part of a horse's foot between the hoof and the fetlock. Not, as Johnson defined it, a horse's knee.

"Hang on a minute while I ask Lucielle [my sister-in-law] if she remembers the guy's name." J. D. is responding to a question I've posed regarding an unsolved murder that was committed years ago in Sunbury. The victim had been strangled—a circumstance that a small American town could just about cope with in the early 1950s. The fly in the ointment was that the corpse, found in bed, was guilty of being that of a young man partially clad in women's clothing. I'm talking about a town that found Barry Goldwater a trifle liberal in 1964, so you can imagine what attitudes were like a decade earlier. Cross-dressing young men were not a feature of daily life, and if they had been, there would have been a bounty on them. Rumors surfaced implicating prominent townspeople in the killing and with the sensational "perversions" associated with the case. That men known as pillars of the community were donning women's undergarments and trussing one another up in interesting sexual positions might have a certain Old World charm had it not resulted in someone's death. As it stands, a man was murdered, and no one ever paid for the crime.

J. D. tells me he's standing on his deck as we speak, looking across Korten's field to a row of well-kept houses on Susquehanna Avenue not far from where the murder took place. I can visualize what he's seeing because I used to play in that field—or very large yard, depending on how you wish to define it—that's associated with the mansion-cum–funeral home on the corner. I remember watching different species of birds that congregated there and in the maple trees bordering the street. Blackbirds, grackles, orioles, flickers, jays, robins, cardinals, starlings, house sparrows. This was before J. D. and Lucielle bought the house from my parents and we moved to a larger place outside of town. Back when birds were just birds to me and the property where men in drag got strangled was just *another house I'd pass as I walked to school. Sitting here now, I'm able to project a sense of invigorating dread into my second- or third-grade self as it meanders past the crime scene. And I watch as I scatter stale bread crumbs in Korten's field after my mother suggested that "I go outside and feed the birds." No point in it, but I try sending that early edition of myself a retroactive prevision of things here in the present.*

Although I've been an hour on the phone, B remains tolerant. Lying on my leg in the posture of a hen warming an egg, he squints up at me as if in contemplation of a massive and badly executed piece of public art entitled Victory Lets the People Down. *Since I haven't had my shower yet, this is not a big imaginative leap. J. D. and I wrap up our conversation by establishing who will call whom two weeks hence, a formality that includes mutual promises to phone sooner should "something come up." I needle him for the thousandth time to come visit me in Portland—a journey we both know he will never make. He'd enjoy seeing me, and I know he'd be charmed by the birds, but for someone who hasn't been outside Pennsylvania in nearly forty years, flying to Oregon may as well be a dogsled trip to the Arctic.*

B rides on my shoulder as I walk over to the futon and place the phone back in its cradle. There's great pleasure in feeling B's muscles alternately tense and relax as he maintains balance in response to my movements. The way he's bobbing along resembles a friar riding a burro. Too bad he won't wear a burnoose that's cinched in the middle with a knotted rope. Clucking and chirping, he responds to my announcement that I'm leaving for a while. Often when he's like this, I have to peel him off me when I reach the door. But today he flies to his toy basket, searches for a moment, and returns to me with a cap—the blue one I asked him to bring me half an hour ago.

I expected Rebecca to revisit the release issue in earnest once B passed his final developmental hurdle by learning to feed himself seed. I thought she'd do so before winter set in and brought with it impossible images of B outside, frightened and wet. I knew she was capable of standing on her convictions but also of biding her time while she sorted through conflicting emotions. This meant eviction proceedings were possible as long as the days remained warm. "I noticed B looking out the window today" was, however, as close as she came to broaching the topic. No carefully chosen words suggesting that once B flew off into the trees (fat chance) our achievement would be complete—champagne all around. The day after Halloween she came to me with a proposition.

From the day she moved in with me, Rebecca coveted my bedroom closet, a large walk-in with plenty of shelving. I'd have given it to her right away, but it was filled with my stuff, and I'm lazy. I preferred to maintain the status quo rather than spend hours sifting through and moving a lot of crap that seemed happy where it was. I was also hesitant to cede additional territory. By my reckoning, Rebecca held sway over more than 50 percent of the available space—a hotly disputed calculation that I continue to defend. But excluding her wistful sighs when she'd see me emerge from my closet pulling on a shirt or a pair of pants, Rebecca never made a land grab, and the issue lay dormant. She made do with the smaller closet in my study, also a walk-in. She slept in the middle bedroom with me but dressed herself in what had now become B's room. The idea of sharing a closet we dismissed as unworkable since our individual approaches to order are markedly different—make that incompatible.

"I'd like to cut a deal," Rebecca said, coming straight to the point. "I want your closet, and I'm willing to give up my study to get it."

Rebecca made this startling declaration while I was showing B the ceramic gremlin and the assortment of inexpensive silver rings I'd bought for him at Saturday Market, the large outdoor artisans' fair that runs nearly year-round beneath the Burnside Bridge—one of nine spans crossing the Willamette River in Portland.

"What's that you say, my delicate petal?" Actually, I said, "You're kidding." Had I been quicker, though, I might have said the petal thing, there being something imperious in Rebecca's tone and hands-on-hips posture that seemed to warrant a W. C. Fields kind of response.

"I really want your closet. I have more clothes than you do; I need the space. I'll set up an area in the basement where I can practice dance. With the way the ceiling slants in here, B doesn't have much room to fly; he'll be better off back where he was." An honorable man would have told Rebecca that she had deplorable bargaining skills, that if you want closets, you don't open negotiations by offering rooms in exchange. We moved B into his permanent quarters the following Saturday.

I don't doubt that Rebecca wanted my closet. But with the benefit of hindsight, I think that coming out of the deal with a better place to store shoes, dresses, and pants was less important to her than establishing domestic harmony prior to our marriage. Giving up a room was her wedding gift to me, a dowry containing one house sparrow and a place to keep it. Other than her ring, I'm not certain what she got from me—perhaps the belief that I might have relinquished B had she insisted upon it. In any event, it's unlikely B would have left me had I tried to release him, our bond being too well established by the time he returned to his original room. Picture the scene in the park: B not understanding, me weeping as I tried to shoo him away, Rebecca sobbing, "He can stay, he can stay, he can stay," some kid yelling, "Look at those people, Mommy."

I'M SITTING WITH B IN MY USUAL SPOT, LOOKING OUT AT THE EAVE FROM WHICH he fell. The most unlikely things assume great significance once we've remade them into symbols—private points of reference that are meaningless to everyone but ourselves. I have an entire B-related inventory: eave, toothpick, cap, box, cage, seed, beak, feather, wing . . .

He heads for my shoulder, alights on my elbow instead, a nonce choice signaled before landing by what seems to me a shrug of his shoulders. I'm not certain what prompted the change—air currents not to his liking, avian prerogative, maybe a decision to stand back and examine me from a farther perspective, consider my construction as if he's thinking of painting my portrait. His gaze is probing but not one that would, as a da Vinci's might, flay me open in search of how my flesh is layered, my muscles tensed; it's more an impressionist's evaluation of light and mood. And I study him, his form unblemished by any defect that I can see, by the least imperfection that would have caused reasonable parents to consign him to death. In our mythology, he simply hurried into our lives, wasn't by any means cast from the nest.

Rebecca never complained that, relatively speaking, she got the swamp, B the ocean-front property. She retained doubts about the wisdom of keeping a wild bird in captivity, doubts similar to my own, doubts that can never be allayed unless B's English improves and he one day says to us: "Chris and Rebecca, I just wanted you to know how happy I am to be here with you. Life on the outside might be all right for the average bird, but it's not for me. Thanks for the years of friend-ship and service, however flawed your efforts might be."

B had been away from his original room for more than two months, so I assumed he'd have no memory of ever living there and would spend the day adjusting. I expected he'd now view uncarpeted floors with suspicion. But he showed no distress when we carried him in. When we opened his house door, he exited promptly, looped the room twice, landed on the sword, and adjusted a wing feather. He flew to the bookcase, my shoulder, and the floor in that order. If, as I did, you find it unlikely that a bird's brain would have much in the way of memory capacity, consider this paraphrased item I cribbed from *Bird Brains,* a beautifully illustrated book by Candace Savage: The Clark's nutcracker, a small member of the Corvidae family (crows, ravens, jays), stores seeds for retrieval during winter. Research indicates that despite alter-ations in the landscape occasioned by snow, this bird can, with 70 per-cent accuracy, remember the *precise* location of seventy-five hundred caches for nearly a year.

The only drawback that attended our moving B out of the back bed-room was in losing the convenience of having a sink and faucet on hand when dealing each day with B's water requirements. When he first lived in Rebecca's study, the water chore involved carrying his dish over to the bathroom to be emptied and refilled—an onerous procedure that made for spillage. This is why after the closet deal went through I adopted a bilge bucket as a place to dump old water and began keep-ing the fresh on hand in one-gallon jugs. These unremarkable contain-ers are of the opaque plastic variety; one originally contained apple cider, the other one milk. Aside from winging over and giving the jugs a cursory examination a few minutes after the move, B paid no further attention to them until I was ready to fill up his dish.

He rode on my arm as I padded around putting the finishing touches on the new arrangement. But when I moved toward the jugs, he flew to his wall mirror—standard procedure whenever he feels the need to put a little distance between himself and anything out of the or-dinary. The glass was (and still is) draped with a pillowcase, a holdover from the days when B was learning to fly and we covered windows and mirrors as a precaution lest he crash into them. We later removed the window coverings but not the one on the mirror, retaining it because B enjoys lying in what amounts to a hammock formed by the way in which the material hangs. I've since lowered it a bit so that he can lounge there and admire his reflection. When I picked up one of the water containers, he assumed a kind of forward-facing launch position with tail feathers pressed straight up against the mirror, his wings slightly open and pulsing, beak half-parted. He reminded me of a fighter plane about to be catapulted from the deck of an aircraft carrier.

I unscrewed the cap from the jug, held it in my left hand, and poured water out with my right, said, "What's wrong, B? Water jugs won't hurt you." As I concentrated on not spilling, I heard the whoosh of his wings as he dove in a swooping pounce and snatched the cap from my fingers. It's unclear to me why a house sparrow should know how to execute such a hawklike maneuver; I doubt there's much call for it in the wild. B zigzagged through the air with his prize, visiting each corner of the room as if in obeisance to the four cardinal directions. This done, he landed on my shoulder and dropped the cap in my hand.

As a pastime approaching organized sport, "Cap" has been a household boon. It's also a minor financial drain considering that B routinely gets bored with one color and requires a replacement. We ran through the primary colors quickly, compelling Rebecca and me to search for chromatic exotica in caps on every conceivable type of potable liquid. We've spent two or three dollars to obtain the mauve-colored cap from a bottle of "Rutabaga Spritzer" or some other equally revolting product. Until you pay attention to this stuff, it's impossible to imagine how desperate juice manufacturers are to market something novel. Sadly, after seven years, we've about exhausted the possibilities, although by traveling to other parts of the country, I can still find caps subtly different in color or size from anything in B's collection. To his credit and my relief, he's willing to recycle, and so the orange cap that's passé today may again be in vogue three months hence.

Our screen door deficiency, a deficit I should have corrected the day B became airborne, was the only bird-related detail needing swift attention. Considering the feline menace (they no longer camped outside the bird-room door, but I thought of them as restive warlords patrolling the downstairs province) and B's penchant for trying to tag along when I'd leave his room, we were definitely pushing our luck. A disturbing incident occurred when B got out ahead of me one day and hovered in the hallway at the top of the stairs. If, instead of screeching, I'd have offered him my finger, he'd have landed on me without a problem, and that would have been that. But because I flailed my arms and accidentally banged my head on the door, B panicked and sailed down the stairwell, turned left at the bottom, and disappeared. Screaming, "B, B, B," I followed (bounding, as they say) and met Rebecca along with three very alert cats sitting in the living room. B whizzed past, banked in through the dining room and on into the kitchen where I caught up with him as he idled near the ceiling fan. He alighted calmly on my shoulder, and I carried him cupped in my hands to his room—cats still in the living room, still gazing upward. They must have wondered if they'd actually seen what they thought they saw. The episode lasted little more than a minute.

Within an hour, I'd completed measurements and was at Mr. Plywood buying pine one-by-fours, angle braces, hinges, and screening. To the right of the entrance into B's room the wall runs at a forty-five-degree angle for about six feet (in the middle of which is the doorway into a small closet) before coming to a point where it meets the east wall of the room. Thanks to this design oddity, I was able to install my screen door in such a way that in the closed position, a small vestibule is formed between it and the outside door. The only mistake I made that required a return trip to the store was in choosing nylon screen instead of metal because I didn't want B poking himself if a strand unraveled. But until I removed the roll from its shrink-wrap, I didn't realize how badly plastic screen stinks when it's new. Actually, it reeks. Knowing I didn't want B inhaling whatever petrochemical vapors were off-gassing from it, I went back to the store and exchanged it for the metal.

B showed no concern when I entered his room carrying a big door. Nor did he climb the walls when I fired up the electric drill—climbing walls being the escape method our cats attempt when the vacuum cleaner emerges from its slumber and, like a rampaging dragon, lays waste to their kingdom. B, by comparison, will ride on my shoulder and sing as I vacuum. He clung to my chest as I hung the door, perched on my fingers when I changed drill bits, vetted the screws with his beak as I got them started in the pilot holes I'd made. "The Time of Shattered Assumptions" might be a good name for my first year with him.

After installing the door, I was bewildered to find that it functioned perfectly. You can pretty much bank on most of my carpentry efforts looking as if I set out to build objects I'd never seen or heard of before. Because I'd worried that B's claws might catch in the mesh, I was relieved that he viewed it from the start as a recreational device to be climbed on, hung from, and flown into with enough kamikaze panache to suggest to an observer unfamiliar with his tricks that he should, by rights, be bursting into flames. Rebecca listened as I described B's fearless interest in a project that involved power tools, and although she gushed over the "great job" I'd done as I pointed out all the traditional door characteristics I'd incorporated into my effort, she was vastly more impressed watching B on the screen hanging upside down. I made the following journal entry that evening, "B seems interested in everything. If he were a college student, he'd take every available elective." I still believe this is true.

B, civil but not chummy, is nursing a minor grudge because I put him to bed early last night so Rebecca and I could keep a commitment with a friend who's visiting from out of town. I've been sycophantic this morning: served breakfast early, sacrificed both my hands in "Double War Bird," haven't talked on the phone, haven't dashed in and out distracted by other concerns, didn't get testy when he hopped across my papers pecking at the print. I even thanked him for reshaping my cuticles. I've been mostly forgiven.

We're like an old married couple who have learned to weather one another's moods, which, in B's case, can be subtle. He's a few feet away cleaning his feet with exaggerated attention to detail. This strikes me as contrived even though he may have legitimate reasons for dragging out the process other than prolonging what I fancy is a lingering chill in our morning's interaction. A full acceptance of B as a thinking being has required that I recognize the essential mystery of who he is. I suppose we are all little gods in this way—supreme in our own agendas, ineffable behind the faces we turn outward to observers.

B has finished his pedicure and is examining fringe on the dish towel that drapes part of his house, pulling one of the strands as if evaluating material he'd like made into a suit. I realize that I know him and I don't, that in any event, I should try harder to remove my ego from calculations of what he thinks and what he feels. I can truthfully say I've gotten better at doing so over the years, having worked through my guilt about his life in captivity and the attendant belief that I owe him perfection.

Three days after my father died I awoke choking from a dream in which he embraced me so tightly I could not breathe, the agony of loss—and by extension, the danger inherent in every attachment—manifested in gasps, palpable in my sweat. The instructive irony in this resurrection of my father's form lay in recognizing his utter separation from me, not as a function of death, but as a condition of existence that dictates terms: we must always love in isolation.

I ponder B's separateness as he loops the room low over my head, his mind in its efficient package moving above our share of the world. He now stands high up on my chest, tugging my whiskers in the way he pulled on the tea towel's fringe. Psychologists and neuroscientists, those who make it their business to know these things, say that consciousness plays itself out in a sequence of more or less seamlessly bound intervals roughly three seconds long that moment by moment make up the "specious present" in which we live. It is thus a feature of mental life that who we are is an ongoing question of who we were. As if to insist on his presence, B pulls me into his unfolding history by yanking hard on my beard and standing back when I wince, his head cocked in an attitude of pure mischief that seems to say, "Let's have some laughs. Look at me, look at yourself, look at the finches in their madness. Isn't it miraculous we're all here together?"

6 ≣

FINCHES

And smale fowles maken melodye.
   —Chaucer

Zebra finches are relatively quiet and only make consistent
little peeps.
   —Pet store ad copy

QUIET RELATIVE TO WHAT, SOMEONE MANGLING A CONSIGNMENT
of bagpipes? As for "little peeps," well, here again, the problem's
in the modifiers. "Only" and "consistent" they most certainly are not. A
truer assessment would read: "Zebra finches are horny little birds that,
excepting occasional eerie lulls, produce a racket that will drive you to
distraction until you either lose your hearing or resign yourself to it.
They're the species that never shuts up!"

Zebra finches are native to Australia, where they are as ubiquitous
as house sparrows are everywhere else. Capable of breeding even after
death, they're the most inveterate fornicators outside of Dante's *Inferno*.
Put a breeding pair together in a room, and they'll get down to business
immediately, will, in fact, continue getting down to business in single-
minded devotion to the principle of geometric progression. The
Malthusian implications of their efforts are staggering.

Popular as pets for well over a century, zebra finches are a fixture in most pet stores and because they're colorful, active, and inexpensive (usually fifteen dollars or less for a pair) are often purchased for the hell of it or because a kid lobbies his or her parents into ponying up the dough. Inasmuch as even hand-raised zebras never become tame, they're not considered "companion birds" and must be accepted strictly on their own terms. All but ignored by their owners, many of these creatures live out their days in cramped quarters, hopping restlessly between perches set but a few inches apart. Some subside into a catatonic stupor. Aside from the dismal, pointless existence these birds endure, it's a lost opportunity for the people involved to watch the evolution of a madcap little society—something that will develop only outside the confines of a small cage. It took a long time for Rebecca and me to grasp this fact and begin allowing our finches the freedom they needed to pursue their version of Manifest Destiny.

We bought our first zebra finch from the store where we buy seed, doing so within two weeks of B taking up permanent residence in Rebecca's old study. Employing the kind of long-handled net you'd use to remove fish from an aquarium, the clerk captured the bird we'd chosen, putting him in a small, flimsy box with "Small Animal Carrier" emblazoned across it. The box manufacturer evidently wished to emphasize its product's versatility by illustrating the sides with a canary, parakeet, mouse, and what might have issued from the improbably fertile coupling of a teddy bear with a hamster. I was uncomfortable watching our finch being nabbed and crated. If he had friends among the twenty or thirty other finches with whom he shared a cage, he didn't get time to say good-bye.

We operated on the assumption that B would like having a companion during the day while Rebecca and I worked. There was emotional blackmail going on in the mornings when I'd leave the house— some of it self-inflicted, I'll admit—but B doing his part to make certain I felt as guilty as possible for leaving him alone. Indignant face plastered against the screen, he'd shriek minor-key laments Monday through Friday mornings when, after delivering his breakfast, I'd oil out of his room dressed in my work clothes. I appreciated Rebecca's attempts to take up the slack. Without explicit prodding from me, she gravitated to B's room on the days she telecommuted, said it was a pleasant place to set up her computer and go to work.

In addition to one boxed finch, we left the pet store early Sunday afternoon with a new cage twice the size of B's house, another pound of "finch mixture," a cuttlebone, more blue rocks, an assortment of perches, new water and seed dishes. The bird was silent all the way home, and I began to think it had died from a coronary. Rebecca and I discussed the prophetic aspects of Monty Python's "Dead Parrot Sketch," and I wondered out loud if the store would accept the corpse for refund or exchange. Our acquisition, however, blew out of its container like a champagne cork after we held it against the opened cage door and lifted the flap. Disoriented and frightened, he then caromed off the bars like a feathered pinball, coming to rest on the bottom of the cage where he hyperventilated and waited to be eaten. B watched the proceedings from his vantage point on the sword, flew over as soon as Rebecca and I stepped back from the cage. He landed about a foot away and bipedaled over to its base, slipping on the polished tabletop as he went. He appeared to will each foot forward in conscious defiance of an impulse to hop—the method of locomotion house sparrows prefer when they're on the ground.

Arriving at the cage, B peered beneath it in this way he has of bending into the horizontal, not unlike a low ceremonial bow acknowledging an opponent. Anatomically impossible, of course, but if I could mimic this posture, I'd be able to look under a sofa while remaining flat on my feet. After scanning the area beneath the cage, he withdrew into the vertical, the finch voicing a single "Oh, shit" peep and skittering backward when B craned his head over the cage's plastic base. I thought of Mowgli seeing another human being for the first time in Kipling's *Jungle Book*. But the novelty of meeting another bird appeared to hold no significance for B. There certainly wasn't any outward indication that he sensed useful clues to his own identity in the guise of a cowering zebra finch.

Rebecca and I had only a general and, as it turned out, overly optimistic idea in the back of our minds that two small birds living together would, despite the possibility of racial strife at the outset, find enough in common to support a friendship. B's utter indifference to finches has been unwavering. He viewed the first as beneath notice and the ensuing tribe as a collection of ciphers. We may as well have brought in birds fashioned of clay: "Look, B, made you entertaining friends; you'll have lots to talk about when I'm away from your room." B stared into the finch cage for perhaps a minute, inclined his head at the occupant, and returned to me without comment. I felt like a broker of arranged marriages who'd badly miscalculated the needs of his clients.

So, there we were with a ten-dollar bird in a forty-five-dollar cage and no immediate payoff beyond the fact that we had a pretty little finch. A classic of his type: gray head, red beak, orange cheek patches, black-and-white-striped tail (which did have a certain zebra quality about it), and a vertical line descending from beneath each eye as if mascara had run. I very much regret that we didn't grant him room privileges immediately, that when it came to the issue of birds in cages, Rebecca and I remained barbaric for more than a year. Hemingway's line from *For Whom the Bell Tolls*, "There are many who do not know they are fascists but will find it out when the time comes," has taken on new meaning for me.

We purchased a second finch two weeks later—another zebra male built along the same color scheme as finch number one except that his tail stripes were less sharply defined. We named the pair Akbar and Jeff. They appeared to have catching up to do, so maybe they knew one another from their pet store days. Zebra finch males advertise their virility with a cackling vocalization that reminds me of the sound electromechanical calculators used to make. Even during cold weather when our storm windows are closed, I can hear the four males we currently have boasting about themselves while I'm in the yard or walking up our porch steps; it's often the first sound I hear upon waking. Although these calls are stylized, there's enough individual variation that I can usually identify a given bird by the distinctiveness of his voice. One finch in particular, Kess, always appends a "hee-haw" coda to his song that is as much like the braying of a jackass as you're likely to hear outside of a barnyard—or Congress.

Getting finch number two (Jeff) seemed like the right thing to do after it became apparent that B and finch number one (Akbar) were not a marriage made in heaven. There wasn't any animosity between them, just a mutual disregard that was obvious the day I put B in the cage with Akbar—a stupid thing to do given that I had only my gut feeling to go on that there wouldn't be a fight. Sparrow and finch took up positions at opposite ends of the long perch spanning the width of the cage. B looked as if he was waiting for me to outline his part in what must obviously be a practical joke. Akbar stared out the window with a "Nobody in here but us chickens" detachment that he self-consciously maintained until I lifted the cage door and B flew out.

I picked up a book, *Zebra Finches: A Complete Owners Manual,* by Hans-Jurgen Martin, that emphasized how social these birds are. I quote, "A Zebra Finch that is kept by itself misses very acutely the company of others of its kind. . . . The results are disturbed behavior, susceptibility to illness and, all too frequently, death." With the exception of intermittent periods of intense activity that centered on banging about on the sides of the cage or repetitive jumping from perch to perch, Akbar had certainly looked unhappy to me. I don't know what a depressed finch feels—images of broken wings and inedible seeds, perhaps. For that matter, it's difficult to say what runs through the mind of an elated finch. One thing was indisputable: Akbar and Jeff liked each other—*really* liked each other.

Although their libidinous activities were shockingly uninhibited, theirs was a love, as it were, that dared not chirp its name—not literally, of course, considering the bursts of exuberant crowing that accompanied their frequent mountings and remountings. The question of who should be on top was something they never managed to settle.

But when they whispered their postcoital nothings, Akbar and Jeff made a very sweet pair. They'd groom one another's head and neck ("allopreening" is the technical term for these tender ministrations between bonded individuals), dig nuts together out of a piece of bread, nap side by side on the upper perch—one facing north, the other facing south. I invented the term "homofinchiality" to describe their relationship. Rebecca found this extremely funny and rerouted a mouthful of tea through her nose when I coined it. An acquaintance to whom I mentioned our finch arrangement asked, thinking, I gather, that we ran some sort of avian Sodom, "And this doesn't bother you?"

The only problem with Jeff and Akbar's setup, likely related more to cramped quarters than to anything else, was that after about a week of connubial bliss, their lovers' spats escalated into feather-pulling tussles that we feared would result in denuded birds. Although I'm convinced that cabin fever lay at the root of their discord, I'd like to know what, specifically, they argued about. Much of the posturing and vocalizing zebra males indulge in seems to say, "I have perfect genes to impart and can thus sire many strong sons." Maybe each accused the other of withholding eggs.

B naps on his gremlin, the contours of his body adding to the humorously macabre aspect of the ceramic face on which he's perched. He is deeply asleep, doesn't stir when I part the curtain covering the window on his outside door. Doing so is usually enough to roust him from even a middling doze, wakefulness brought on by a change of light and shadow attending the movement of the cloth as detected behind those interesting eyelids of his that unlike ours rise up instead of down. In the early days of our association, it struck me as unnatural that a bird would sleep during the day; indeed, excessive sleeping is a sign of illness and would result in a trip to the vet, but our birds all treat themselves to an afternoon nap. I believe B's gremlin is a favored roosting place for him because it affords a measure of privacy away from carousing finches, the orbits of which tend to revolve in other parts of the room.

I offer B my right shoulder after I walk inside. He puffs and stretches, glances at the papers in my hand before hopping down. We've gone through this routine innumerable times, yet I ponder each repetition as the steps unfold, knowing that I'll one day be desperate to recall all B-related things. Every day I vow and every day fail to take nothing for granted regarding those tricks time plays on complacency. It's not for nothing that Kronos, Greek god of time, was often depicted devouring his own children. One moment I'm eight years old standing in our yard, dry snow falling in swirls that might be sheered-off bits of sun that are struggling to survive on a late afternoon so close to the solstice; the next minute, B's on my shoulder, and I must take my own word for it that several decades have intervened.

Another December, another Christmas approaching, five finches left from a high of nine, life and death playing out in a room that, could I work my will, would confer immunity from loss of any kind. B sits preening in Hugh's house. Ancient Hugh, the oddball finch, surviving member of a pair of red avadavats (a tiny Southeast Asian finch) Rebecca acquired four years ago from a friend of hers who inherited the birds from her father. Hugh of the beautiful trilling song, Hugh of the deep red feathers and matching beak. Hugh, who arrived here as "Hugs" from life in a minute cage hung in a kitchen; Hugh, widower of "Kisses." Hugh, who worked out a time-share agreement with B that allowed each to vacation in the other's house; Hugh, the shyest member of the household. Hugh, whose body I found two mornings ago when I came in for the day's first visit saying, "Morning, B. Ready for Cheerios?" And that evening, the pituitary tumor causing Thea's Cushing's disease pushed its way out into other parts of her brain. Rebecca's San Francisco cat, Marlowe's old nemesis. She convulsed, slipped into quiescence, convulsed again, and died in our arms. I hate that we viewed her illness as an imposition—the expense, the tending, the futile hope we nursed that she'd have a few years left if we did everything right.

Christmas Eve in less than two weeks. I'll sit with B in the early evening, Handel's Messiah playing on KBPS. In keeping with a tradition said to have originated with King George II, I'll rise to my feet for the Hallelujah Chorus. I never hear this music without imagining the composer's ghost walking the streets of London searching out an orchestra to conduct. There could be fates worse than pursuing in death what we loved in life. A more appealing alternative than an eternity spent in conscious disconnection from the world, from even the underrated details of living that we dismiss as chores. Longing to pee, not because we must but because the ability to do so no longer exists.

Having vacated Hugh's house, paused at the entrance, and glanced back inside, B arrives on my stomach, stands flicking in expectation that I'll agree with him that today has potential. He sets to work removing an untidy flap of dead skin that hangs near the nail on my right index finger. The piece being too thick to shear off by scissoring it with his beak, he bends it back and forth as if working to fatigue a paper clip into breaking. He gives up after half a minute but rewards his hard work with a bath interrupted now by all five finches who've suddenly remembered that a tub in the room is one of its amenities. Typical for birds that view bathing as a social occasion. B issues three or four "Do you mind?" warning snaps at Lisa who brazenly joins him in the dish. He directs The Look at the four voyeurs standing on the rim who, ignoring the hint, plop into the water and are now splashing like river nymphs that decided on whim to be birds for a day. B sputters away to flap himself dry.

B UNQUESTIONABLY SUCKS YOU IN, BUT THERE WERE OTHER REASONS
Rebecca began increasing the amount of time she spent in his room. She
discovered, despite finches screwing in the background, that it can still be
rewarding to visit a bird that will sit in your hand even when otherwise
ignoring you. Rebecca appreciated more quickly than I did that B's tame-
ness is far more interesting because of his insistence on boundaries—or at
least a set of pliable limitations he applies at will to his dealings with us.
"Do not pet the bird's feet" is one of his rules that I have difficulty re-
specting. He perches on my finger and it's almost more than flesh can
bear to refrain from stroking his long front toes with my thumb. In most
cases, he pulls away as if he's stepped in a cow pie. But sometimes he
watches my thumb and endures. On rare occasions, he'll make little satisfied chewing noises that suggest I'm doing him a kindness.

By late spring of 1994, Rebecca was immersed in the details of planning our wedding. I'd look at her and wonder what defect in her
makeup accounted for her steadfast commitment to marrying me.
Brought to mind Groucho Marx's line about not wanting to belong to a
club that would have him as a member. I'd get home for lunch on Rebecca's days off and find her in B's room talking on the phone with
caterers or some other class of merchant whose secure retirement
seemed to depend on us. For a person who traded a room for a closet,
I must say that she drove hard bargains. B benefited during this process
from Rebecca's list-making proclivities—the most outwardly visible
manifestation of her status as someone whose devotion to chaos is
checked by an equally weighted allegiance to order. Lists of things to
do, when to do them, how to do them, where to do them are the balance
points in this epic struggle. Set her to work with a list she's composed
in tranquillity and there are few people more efficient; hide one of her
lists (purely as an experiment, you understand) and the molecular
bonds holding her together start to decay. It's like watching a bridge
collapse during rush-hour traffic.

B lit up every time Rebecca installed herself on his bed with a handful of lists. Many were written on pieces of paper that were strips she'd
removed from formerly larger lists that may themselves have been
sloughed-off fragments from what I fancy is an enormous master list
she keeps hidden in a vault. "Come on, B, I really need that piece of
paper, please give it back," is a phrase she used a lot in those days.

"God, the finches are noisy. It makes me crazy sometimes" is another comment that Rebecca often had on her lips when emerging from B's room. A couple of months after getting Akbar and Jeff, we brought home Pat and Lily. The arranged marriages that ensued were a mixed blessing for the two males who, it seemed to me, assumed the mantle of heterosexuality with grim determination. They stared at one another from out their now separate cages, conversing in what sounded to me like slang they'd invented to deceive their wives—avian pig latin, perhaps. Whatever else it may have been, it was heartfelt and emphatic. At least we'd remedied the feather pulling.

Pat, who had a distinctive white patch on her forehead, we paired off with Akbar, placing them in the large cage Craig had given us for jailing B. We made it escape-proof by covering the outside with sheer netting fastened in place with a series of safety pins. Lily, as exceptionally diminutive as Pat was large, we placed with Jeff in the much smaller cage he'd shared with Akbar. My regrets over the unequal real estate distribution are mitigated slightly by memories of Lily's consummate timidity, her refusal to leave the cage even after we began our open-door policy. The guy at the pet store asked two or three times while flailing with his net, "Are you absolutely certain that's the one you want?"

Lily was, in truth, a pathetic little thing that wouldn't have topped most shopping lists. "I got sloppy with the glue when I built her from a kit" is how I explained her to visitors. Many pet store finches are products of a level of inbreeding that makes our southern states look incest-free. Lily may very well have issued from parents who were brother and sister out of parents that were themselves mother and son. She didn't look deformed (no third wing protruding from her forehead or anything like that), but you just got the sense that her genes were probably factory seconds. I like to think she had a happy life for the two years she lived with us. She wouldn't have survived in nature, and it's unlikely she'd have risen in the pet store pecking order above her station at the bottom of the cage where, judging by her feather deficit, she'd been relentlessly attacked by her fellow inmates. Jeff was a dutiful husband to Lily, although a bit distracted by his fantasy life. He spent days calling for her after she died.

They probably don't, but I wonder if animals identify themselves and each other symbolically. I'm addressing Christmas cards and find myself pronouncing the names of this year's lucky recipients—Ju-li-a, Bri-an, Er-ic, Lin-da—as I scrawl on the envelopes. The history of each person bulges from the syllables I associate with them. Faces and settings condense a moment in context before evaporating back into the ether with a residue carried forward into the next name. Images of people don't flourish any better in isolation than particles known by the company they keep and by the trails they leave in a cyclotron. Unfamiliar with words so laboriously phrased, B inclines his head as I speak. He looks alarmed, as if I'm having a neurological event that concerns him.

Unlike the signature cackling of the zebra males, I can't discern anything unique in their "consistent little peeps," a sound both sexes make and repeat ad nauseam when the fit is upon them, "Here I am, here I am, here I am." They bear human names for our convenience, our need to make clear distinctions in the world. Bart and Lisa (siblings and erstwhile lovers), Bert (patriarch—father of the latter and Lisa's current beau), Monday (hatched on the corresponding day of the week; extremely good looking. If zebra finches had matinee idols, he'd be one. Bart and Lisa's half brother, eldest son of Bert out of Pat, who is now deceased), and Kess (along with Bert, the only remaining pet store bird; almost pure white, first of the finches in bed at night) are the current members of this busy, cheerful, noisy, often fractious assemblage. A trigger I don't register jolts through the finches' collective nervous system and sends them winging as one into the ficus tree—the one their depredations have rendered bare. B's feet tighten on my finger as ten small wings wallop the air in a rush to flee the latest phantom in an endless string of ravenous finch eaters. On those increasingly rare occasions when B's habituation to "finch folly" deserts him and he finds himself fleeing to higher ground, carried in the wake of yet another false alarm, I swear to God he looks embarrassed first and then defensive. "Look, we all agree the finches are needlessly jumpy, but I'm a bird too, so give me a break. It's not easy willing myself to stay put every time those idiots panic and send out danger signals."

Jane Austen points out in *Pride and Prejudice* that "it is better to know as little as possible of the defects of the person with whom you are to pass your life." Excellent advice if, following the ceremony, newlyweds were assured of never again seeing one another. I find it immeasurably touching that despite living with my moodiness for three years, Rebecca still wanted to marry me, still insists that she got a bargain—an assertion based, I'd wager, on the fact that I'm good with money and know absolutely nothing about professional sports. Rebecca claims that it was my loyalty to B that impressed her more.

We set August 5 as the date and made arrangements to hold the ceremony in the Shakespearean garden section of Washington Park in the city's southwest hills. Climate and soil conditions here are so conducive to growing roses that Portland refers to itself as the "Rose City." And aside from the view it affords of downtown, Washington Park is the setting for an international rose test garden that contains row upon row of hybrid rose bushes with such thought-provoking designations as "Virgin's Yelp" or "Fragrant Stool." Brass plates in one corner of the park are set into brickwork paving, each one inscribed with the first name of a Rose Festival queen (typically a high school senior selected from a field of less attractive "princesses") and the year she reigned—a regal line stretching back to Queen Flora in, I believe, 1907. If I get exactly the right tone of sincerity in my voice, I can just about convince tourists that Rose Festival queens are ritually sacrificed when their tenures end. I explain that the cremated remains are then interred with corporate-sponsored pomp beneath the shiny plates they see before them.

Interesting how 365 days compress into a few outstanding incidents that represent most of what we have to show for another year's junket around the sun. After decades of forgotten living, we arrive at death's door (I plan to be disguised as a process server when I do) with a modest collection of trophy memories. Ask me to free-associate on the year 1994, and I'll give you a kind of contrapuntal riff on the themes of "War Bird, Finches, Trapped Sparrow Incident, Wedding." I'd mention how I came that year to understand Rebecca much better.

She's simply more reticent about most things than I am. If, for example, there's some problem with a meal she's been served in a restaurant, I'm the one delegated to send it back. This means it will always be my soup into which the waiter hawks phlegm. On the other hand, Rebecca's the one who gets up and shimmies on stage—I'd rather die, I really would.

I blamed Rebecca's resistance to becoming as besotted (B-sotted, if you prefer) with B as I was on innate feminine perversity. I knew such a thing didn't exist but teased her with the idea rather than graciously accept that her reservations about investing emotional capital in a house sparrow could possibly be valid. When she began spending time with B of her own accord it wasn't merely, as I at first believed, a gesture she was making to placate me—although that may have played a part in her thinking. Rebecca needs to be won over, not bowled over. She cites War Bird and the Trapped Sparrow Incident as pivotal events in her bonding process with B.

≡

WHAT REBECCA AND I CALL "WAR BIRD" DERIVES FROM A THING THAT happens in the wild when female house sparrows decline sex with their mates. Most town-dwelling Americans have probably witnessed these furious displays.

Female house sparrows have no qualms about initiating sex, but it's usually the male that opens negotiations by puffing and strutting in an attempt to arouse his partner. He bows and chirps, holds his wings out from his body with the tips almost touching the ground; this is Love Bird—a delicate and measured minuet danced by a male pleading his case. He seems to say, "Look, sweetheart, how can you resist my big black bib, my dashing white wing bars, my magnificent rump?" With one or two changes of detail, pretty much what I say to Rebecca.

The female flutters her wings and tail, chirps invitingly if she's in the mood. If not, she can be very assertive in defending her virtue, fending off a randy spouse by lunging at him and snapping. With one or two changes of detail, pretty much Rebecca's response to me. Sometimes the rebuffed male takes no for an answer; sometimes he doesn't and ratchets up the campaign. "Come hither" chirps become strident shrieks as his gestures broaden with his growing frustration. If the female thought her bobbing paramour overbearing before, she's convinced of it now. Alerted by the commotion, a solidarity bloc (I call them Marital Aides) of local males often swoops in at this point. These guys, most of whom have mates that keep them on fairly short leads, start courting the reluctant female—not because they expect or even want to have sex with her themselves but because of some curious house sparrow imperative that compels them to join in a combined effort to help a deserving neighbor arouse his mate. Seduction by committee, I suppose you could term it.

The beleaguered female finds such an onslaught unnerving and heads for cover followed by a chattering horde that bows, puffs, chirps, nips, and struts around her wherever she lands. You can almost hear a collective "Tallyho" shouted out as the mob begins pursuit. These winged boarding parties zoom past our house at least once a week during spring and summer. House sparrows are powerful flyers capable of speeds approaching fifty miles an hour, so I usually hear the ruckus more than I see it. By the time my brain wires me instructions to turn my head, the group is obscured in the middle of a tree. The interlude ends as quickly as it began, members of the delegation dispersing homeward to lie to their wives.

There is speculation but no proven explanation for this behavior. As pointed out by Calvin Simonds in his delightful little book *Private Lives of Garden Birds,* "Perhaps when a female is reluctant, the multiple courtship by a bunch of males is all she needs to bring her into readiness. One scientist has suggested that it is all part of a system that tends to make all females lay eggs at the same time so that breeding in the colony is synchronized." The idea, I gather, is that there is an adaptive advantage in having members of a new generation raised together into a ready-made flock. Regardless of why house sparrows behave this way, B and our other two males (albeit to a lesser degree) clearly inherited the predisposition.

B inaugurated War Bird in early spring the year after we found him. I was out of town but received a blow-by-blow account when I called Rebecca from my motel one evening. She reported a certain frostiness in B's dealings with her that she attributed to his being depressed and cranky because I was gone. She wondered if he blamed her for my disappearance, told me she kept denying the allegation in case he did. Whatever else he may have had on his mind, B was coming into sexual maturity, his sap rising as the days lengthened. It's neither here nor there, but the reproductive organs of many birds atrophy during the nonbreeding season in keeping with the avian policy of shedding superfluous weight by every possible means. In some cases, even their *brains* shrink seasonally. Male canaries, for example, temporarily scale back the neural wiring associated with song production—their primary method of attracting a mate.

Because she hoped to make a good impression beginning on the first morning of my absence, Rebecca visited B earlier than I normally do, entering the sanctum prior to having her own breakfast. As she described it, Akbar and Jeff were busy buggering one another (reminded me of Winston Churchill's comment on British naval traditions: "Rum, sodomy and the lash") and B was stationed on his mirror. He refused to acknowledge her existence both before and after she offered him Cheerios. As one who has experienced these snubs of his, I sympathized with how she felt. After B's glared at you for five minutes, you begin feeling foolish and unwanted. I get the impression he finds me painful to look at when I'm in disfavor. As if I've made myself feculent by sinning against him—tardiness and a gift for getting distracted being my principal transgressions.

Rebecca plodded down to the kitchen for coffee and oatmeal, returning with B's breakfast half an hour later. To appreciate the extraordinary effort she made on B's behalf, it must be understood that locating food is Rebecca's customary goal every morning upon waking. There's a lean and hungry look lighting her sleep-bleared eyes that, along with a couple of plangent grunts, expresses the anguish that rages in her famished gut. I didn't mean to obsess about this, it's just that I was incredulous when she claimed to have given B priority over her stomach. She then reminded me that she was a slim person who risked getting a headache if she didn't eat something first thing each day, her metabolism being funny that way.

B stood on his window perch when Rebecca entered with goop, spinach, apple, and bread arranged on a saucer. At this point in her story, I could tell that something remarkable had happened by how quickly she spoke and by all the third-person pronouns she began throwing around. "When I opened the screen door and started in, he turned and faced me and flicked his tail; I mean he really started to flick his tail—not like he usually does but faster and more pronounced. He was puffed, too. And he bowed. Wait. He didn't really bow; he did that later. He kind of nodded in slow motion and moved his head from side to side. *Then* he bowed, then he flew at my head, and that's when I dropped his plate."

After recovering from the surprise of B's simulated attack, Rebecca knelt to retrieve the saucer she'd let go of when raising her hands to protect her face—an understandable but unnecessary precaution inasmuch as B, who retreated to his mirror, has never shown any inclination to harm us when he flies against our cheeks in this way. I expected to hear that hundreds of ceramic shards had exploded across the room and that Rebecca hadn't been able to account for them all. But the saucer evidently bounced off the sofa in a complex, unrepeatable way before landing intact face down on the floor. The contents dispersed, of course, and as she herded bits of scattered goop together, a chirping B swooped down, nipping her hand as it moved back and forth like a whisk broom.

I returned home a few days later to find Rebecca thrilled with the novel activity she shared with B, flattered to be the focus of his amorous displays. I used to wonder if he actually viewed her as a viable mate, as someone he could count on to push out a clutch of eggs—a speculation tied to the more basic question of who or what B thinks we are relative to whatever image he has of himself. Even though attempting to describe the subjective and thus inherently private experience of another being is fraught with difficulty, trying to decipher B's thoughts has become an addiction with me. The whole enterprise is like trying to discover germs without the aid of a microscope, without even the possibility that such an instrument will ever exist. You end up working out inferences that aren't supported by direct observation. In his book *The Parrot's Lament*, which, as it happens, deals more with apes than with birds, Eugene Linden sums up the problem nicely: "Much of our own mental life never translates into actions and thus remains inaccessible to other humans, and so, barring some breakthrough in the mapping of how thoughts stimulate precise electrical events in the brain, the interior lives of animals will remain in the province of speculation."

Pet owners commonly declare that their cat or dog (or bird) "thinks he's people," an assessment meant as a compliment that unwittingly assumes the animal in question is improved by a cloak of humanity and is doltishly eager to fasten it on. A cat may be smart enough to act like a person but too stupid, deluded, or brainwashed to appreciate the obvious disparity between itself, a creature that bites the heads of mice, and human beings who, taken as a group, generally do not. When it comes to a bird who notices if I shift the cover on his house by an eighth of an inch, I think it's safe to say B doesn't labor under any illusions (sexual imprinting be damned) that by playing his cards right a human female is going to mate with him and be fertile. War Bird and the less frequent Love Bird are instinctual expressions of B's most basic drives performed as best he can in a setting with limited dating potential. Scoff if you must, but I think these rituals have fantasy value for him on par with the energy expended in acting them out. There's a distinct sporting quality to War Bird, a sense that B's improvised a game based on rules he found lying around his genetic code.

Months passed before B accepted me as a partner in War Bird. To this day he prefers Rebecca. He likes it best when I cheer from the sidelines as he subdues Rebecca's hand. He exults when both she and I extol his incomparable valor. Long after outside sparrows lay aside their libidinous pursuits in the off-season struggle to survive, the fire in B's belly still burns high. Molting is really the only period during which his appetite for a daily War Bird wanes—in deference, I guess, to feeling like crap. Most mornings, Rebecca is first to enter his room. While I'm brewing coffee and feeding the cats, B's battle cries echo down the stairwell. My first verbal exchange of the day with my wife generally goes like this:

"How's B?"

"He's good."

"Did he win?"

"He won."

"Was he fierce?"

"Fierce and brave."

There are mornings when B's spirit is willing but the flesh is weak. He'll flick his tail, take his preflight dump, execute preliminary strafing maneuvers, maybe even make one or two feints at his opponent's hand before petering out with the look of an impotent man exiting a brothel. When this happens, he often pickets for a War Bird later in the day, whisking from one high perch to another until either Rebecca or I say, "B, do you need a War Bird? Is that what this is about?" Voicing the rising "Chee-u" note he uses to confirm readiness for action, he expects us to move to the futon's broad expanse and open hostilities. Seldom lasting more than a minute, these contests represent a period of intense aerobic activity on B's part, a cardiovascular workout that leaves him heaving for breath through his parted beak. When he lands on my finger for a victory ride to the water dish, his feet are so amazingly warm they feel like tiny fireplace andirons, the heat of battle dissipating through them.

"Might there be love in the bird?" Rebecca coos in her most fetching voice. Black bibs are status symbols in male house sparrows, larger being better, and B responds to her words by thrusting his out as far as it will go. He's been making a slight, slow-motion bow in her direction as he stands between us on the couch. He gives her a sideways glance, bows deeply, turns his head and body from side to side, jumps to my leg, doubles his size by puffing out his feathers, hops on Rebecca's lap, and moves in stately circles around the finger she holds tip downward against her thigh—an ad hoc Maypole he nips with gentle sparrow kisses. As in War Bird, "Chee-u" announces intent. In this case, an odd inflection elongates the u syllable into a lover's languid plea and away from the clipped phrasing a warrior uses. I wonder if the word is an infinitive—to fight or to love, depending on context. Now come plaintive trills and "dweets" embellishing the ancient theme. On the farther window casement five finches sit listening as if they've found their bard.

I'm always a bridesmaid, never the bride in these drawn-out proceedings that sometimes last several minutes owing to B's penchant for inserting seemingly unrelated activities into the business at hand. He'll hit the cap, eat a seed. He'll fly to the window, the mirror, the sword, the gremlin, and the door before resuming a courtship not officially over until Rebecca says "B, I submit," her hand collapsing like a maiden with the vapors.

REBECCA STILL WEEPS WHEN REMEMBERING THE TRAPPED SPARROW incident, blames herself for its dismal finale. One evening a few weeks before the wedding, I noticed five house sparrows sitting along the edge of our roof, peering over the side and trying to look into the same eave out from which B had tumbled a little more than a year before. Having noticed a nesting pair flying in twigs and grass along with whatever else they could find—string, feathers, paper, gauze—I'd kept an eye on the spot since March. Given the mortality rate for house sparrows in the wild during winter, there's about a fifty-fifty chance these two were the previous year's tenants. This would have made them B's parents and, as such, of particular interest to me. Whoever they were, they'd fledged two broods so far that year, going in and out of the eave in an exhausting routine of nest maintenance and food delivery. The site is prime real estate from a house sparrow point of view, offering commanding elevation, a landing platform where the eave switches back at a forty-five-degree angle from the roof's edge, and a spacious recessed cavity with an opening too small for the occasional starling or marauding jay to enter. It's likely been used by generations of sparrows, and yet it wasn't until after finding B that I finally took notice of all the activity going on at the front of my house. Surprising, really, I haven't walked in front of a moving truck.

B's room lies directly below the place where he was born and from his nest untimely thrown. I find it fascinating that he'll pay strict attention to the chirping of his infant self when we play videos of his green time but ignore the cheeping of the hungry broods he can hear in his room even with the windows shut. I thought this had something to do with his making a distinction between sound from the eave that is outside versus sound from the television that obviously is not. But B is equally indifferent to recordings of our other three sparrows made when they were babies.

The birds on the roof stayed in place for at least an hour while I mowed the lawn, cleaned up debris, put tools away, and chatted with the neighbors. I was about ready to go inside for dinner when it occurred to me that those birds weren't necessarily hanging around for my entertainment. Two of the five looked like the resident adults, the other three their recently fledged children whose development I'd watched as they progressed from loud, invisible beggars to fluffy juveniles making awkward landings in our rhododendron bushes. I had a part-time job of a sort turning water on the calico cat from a couple of houses over that seemed to view our yard as her own private hunting preserve. She'd bust a gut scrambling over the fence to get away from the spray, invariably stopping on the sidewalk to look back at me as if she were saying, "You know what, man, you're fuckin' crazy. You know that? You're crazy."

I told Rebecca about the gathering on the roof when I went inside to find binoculars that, given the viewing angle and the camouflaging properties of a tree branch that partially covered the eave, were essentially useless. But after several minutes of observation and deduction we concluded that one of the sparrow siblings was trapped in the nest. The three juveniles seemed short on helpful suggestions. If nothing else, the binoculars enabled me to see the "Beats me" expression on their faces when they'd straighten up and look at one another after bending over the roof line to peer at the eave. The adults took turns flying off and returning a few minutes later with food for the prisoner. Rebecca noted the self-restraint with which the adolescents refrained from begging for a share of whatever the adults brought back. Although capable of feeding themselves, these three were still in that transitional phase during which young house sparrows take every opportunity to cadge food from their parents. Perhaps the gravity of the situation held their appetites in check.

I borrowed an extension ladder from the next-door neighbor that was about three feet too short, a fact not evident until I set it in place. Spectators drifted into the yard to see what was up. Rebecca handled public relations while I went off with a guy from the other end of the block who said he'd lend me a ladder that would reach the eave.

The upper half of our house is covered in cedar shakes painted gray. I noticed on my way up how the paint had worked its way into the striated texture of the wood; I wondered whether it had been sprayed on or applied with a brush. Had I been less distracted by trifles as I climbed, I might have considered the disconnect between going twenty-five feet up a rickety ladder to free a trapped bird and the caged finches opposite the glass of the window I was passing. The sparrow family shifted to the peak of the roof by the time I'd gotten halfway up, removing themselves to a nearby tree as I continued my ascent. I wondered if the parents might mob me the way crows badger hawks traversing their airspace. "What an odd death," I remember thinking, "to be pecked off a ladder by sparrows because I've crossed some territorial boundary relative to their nest." But other than chattered imprecations, they didn't interfere. It was as well they didn't. The farther I climbed, the less stable the ladder became as it shifted on the big divots of hardened clay that pass during summer for soil in our yard.

Rebecca trotted into the house for a flashlight after I discovered that sparrows don't install lighting in their homes. I could see the entrance well enough but nothing beyond a place in the soffit where the wood had separated enough for tenants to move in and out easily from what proved to be a spacious apartment beneath the roof's plywood under-layment. Even though it seemed unlikely that doing so would have much of a soothing effect under the circumstance, I made the same clicking noise I use to comfort B. The opening into the nesting area was too small for me to reach through, so I enlarged the hole by wrenching back a piece of molding, an action that produced brief shuffling within and a gash in my thumb when I brushed against a roofing nail. I could now make out the jumbled debris that house sparrows consider home. Much different from the elaborate and finely wrought nests built by other members of the weaver bird family whose nidification efforts (the ten-dollar word for nest building) produce structures that are strong, intricate, and beautiful. House sparrows compensate for their lax ar-chitectural standards by filling their nests to the point of nouveau riche excess. A "more is better" ethic prevails that may explain why these birds prosper in America. But whatever else can be said about their ap-proach to homesteading, it certainly created an efficient trap.

It's written in the Gospel of Saint Matthew, "Are not two sparrows sold for a farthing? and one of them shall not fall on the ground with-out your Father." As far as the creature that blinked and cowered in my flashlight beam was concerned, God had been sleeping at the switch when this particular sparrow got an eight-inch length of nylon fishing line wrapped around one of its legs. The tether formed the functional equivalent of a ball and chain since the opposite end was hopelessly knotted in a mass of twigs. There wasn't enough room for me to insert my hand without blocking the light. This made groping in that untidy chamber reminiscent of putting my hand into a bowl of ersatz brains during Halloween parties I attended as a kid. Not the slimy physical sensation, you understand, but the anxious hesitation.

For a bird that had spent its brief life unable to move more than an inch or two, it was in tolerably good shape: alert, well groomed, and fully as large as its more fortunate siblings. Rebecca snipped off as much of the line as she could with a pair of scissors that weren't pointed enough for the delicate operation of removing it completely from a leg that, inflamed and deformed, looked to me like a prime candidate for amputation. With proper care, however, it may have been salvageable. And yes, birds can survive with only one good leg; we have a canary to prove it.

The evening was well along by this time, daylight starting to circle the drain. B appeared on his window perch every few seconds (a sorry-looking paper tube, still in use today, around which Christmas wrapping had once been wound) belting out sharp "Get in here" chirps whenever he heard my voice. Since I was filthy, sweaty, and bleeding from the cut on my thumb, we decided I should take a shower and then tend to B while Rebecca drove the injured bird to an emergency vet clinic on the other side of town.

These events, made especially poignant because of the possibility that the birds involved were related to B, dominated my thoughts as I entered his room. I told him the story as if I were speaking to another person, "There's a good chance the bird I just pulled from the eave is one of your siblings, B. Your parents and the rest of the family were very upset." When Rebecca left for the vet, they were together again on the roof.

We tried games, but B's heart wasn't in it. He'd been a Cap-playing maniac all day and was tired. He yawned, rubbed his eyes on my finger, and went to sleep in my hand even before lights-down, barely acknowledged the irregularity of my turning the table lamp back on when I checked to see where I'd left my glasses. I decided to sit with him until Rebecca's car pulled up out front. I thought I might be able to tell whether the news from the vet was good or bad by how quickly she came into the house after parking, it usually being dark by the time she gets around to extracting items from her trunk (papers, gym bag, books, forgotten groceries) that are constantly waiting to be brought inside. Were it Rebecca instead of Charon who had the job of ferrying spirits of the dead across the river Styx into Hades, souls would have piled up on board until Pluto himself came out to complain.

As I sat in the dark with B in my hand, waves of anxiety broke through whatever barrier I'd erected over the previous months. The sad predicament of the bird in the eave probably breached the dam, but other things were shifting in ways I couldn't control. My father, who had been uncharacteristically depressed since returning with a pain in his side from a trip to Germany the previous March, had told me earlier in the week he didn't think he'd be able to make it to the wedding. His doctor, an idiot who'd have been out of his depth trying to man the wheel at a bloodmobile, diagnosed pleurisy—more a symptom than a disease—and did nothing. At least he didn't prescribe bleedings, colonic irrigation, or galvanic belts, which, considering this guy's diagnostic acumen, are probably favored items in his bag of tricks. My father, unfortunately, was of the generation that thought it unseemly to question decisions made by a physician or, in this case, by some clown who bumbled his way through medical school and as a practitioner simply didn't give a damn. My father's reticence dovetailed nicely with the fact that most symptoms remit of their own accord. Time was lost, treatment delayed. I can only assume that the quack in question slept through whatever course in differential diagnosis mentions that (hold on to your hats!) weight loss and pain can indicate illness. Insisting that my father was basically healthy, he doled out antidepressants and waited more than a year before referring him to a gastroenterologist who diagnosed the cancer.

Rebecca pulled up out front about twenty minutes later, the sound of her car contrasting with the "consistent little peeps" the finches uttered as they slept. Since B's house abuts one of the windows in the room, I could see Rebecca rooting around in her trunk as I nudged a groggy bird onto his sleeping perch. She didn't have much news to report beyond the admitting person's statement, "We'll have a look and call you when we know something." They, of course, euthanized the bird. I say "of course" because from the clinic's standpoint they didn't have resources to waste on a house sparrow, there being zillions more where that one came from. It's tempting to condemn their action with as much venom as I can muster, but doing so would be unfair. The clinic, a nonprofit organization, did the best it could under the circumstances; I sleep better knowing it's there.

Rebecca was, to use one of the more popular words in the lexicon of grief, devastated. She still blames herself for not emphasizing to the clinic staff that we wanted the bird back. That we would provide for it if its injuries left it permanently unsuited for life in the wild, that we were willing and able to pay for any treatment necessary to stabilize its condition until we could get it to our own veterinarian the following day. Accustomed as I am to dealing with vets who, aside from a compassionate dedication to the welfare of animals, have a vested interest in keeping alive what I bring them, I too would probably have failed to make clear that we didn't think of an injured sparrow as a throwaway, that it wasn't our intent to dump our problem on somebody else. If we'd have said, "This is our pet bird. Please fix. We have dollars," there'd likely be a one-legged sparrow with a name and a history living with us now.

Wind up believing an animal is meaningfully aware of its own life, and its death strikes you as something more than a cheap watch breaking. "I know she didn't have any reason to trust me," Rebecca said, "but she seemed to, you know? I kept promising that no one would hurt her—I don't know why, but I think it was female—and she looked at me when I handed her over, really made eye contact the way B does. Oh, God."

I'm having one of those visits with B during which we both mind our own business. As our relationship has matured, we've gotten to the point where we can spend time together without the necessity of constantly entertaining each other. In other words, we've gotten past the social awkwardness of sometimes being self-absorbed. I'm reading; he's messing around on the bookcase; the male finches are scavenging crap they can use to build nests. They treat the garbage bag as a hardware store that provides a reliable source of building material—paper towels in various configurations (shredded, wadded, whole), stripped millet twigs, mummified apple rinds, wilted spinach, and hardened bread crusts that, although they seem to have little practical application in finch construction projects, are coveted anyway. Me they regard as a specialty shop, the place to obtain hair and the much-sought-after fringe from my jeans. I've awakened from naps to the patter of little feet ranging over my body as three or four competing finches yank my ponytail and tug at my pants. Except that he didn't run the risk of winding up bald and naked, I feel the way Gulliver must have felt when he woke in bondage on a beach in Lilliput.

Bert's the second finch within the past year that's become fixated on what's known around here as the "air nest project." This insane effort seeks to establish a homestead on the room's overhead light—the circular fluorescent fixture already described, which has a brace about three-quarters of an inch wide running through its center. By doggedly flying millet twigs to the light, Bert follows a pattern of futility established by the late Akbar who became afflicted shortly before his death with the notion that gravity would grant him an exemption if he flew twigs to the light often enough. Lack of success never discouraged him, nor has it dampened Bert's belief in the concept. I no longer think that faith must be built on a nubbin of doubt.

Events have taken a dramatic turn as Monday tries to steal Bert's twig. B, attentive, stands on my knee watching the dispute. Monday's never been much of a nest builder nor popular with the females—despite his good looks. Today he's a prick. He has no more use for Bert's twig than I do. As confrontations go, finch battles are short on blood, long on restraint. There's a lot of "Oh, yeah" posturing and beak-fencing duels. My interest and, for that matter, B's interest in what's happening at the moment with Bert and Monday emphasize how much we take the finches for granted. B and his fellow sparrows are the headliners in the show, finches and canaries the supporting cast. But I'm gratified that our finches appear to lead interesting lives in such an artificial setting; I'm glad they're able to thrive in the background. It sometimes seems they are the background.

Over the years, seven zebra finches, including two that were born here, have died in this room. In each case without warning, each instance a wrenching reminder that birds are mortal. They always die overnight, a farewell turd stuck to their behinds when we find them in the morning, their toes curled as if death were a perch. We've mourned each blithe soul, wrapped each body in a paper towel shroud—I've no idea why. The human need for ritual, I guess. A gesture to shield them from the ravages of decay. They lie in the shade garden on the west side of the house, a green and fertile place that's pleasant to visit.

Without fanfare, Bert retains mastery of the twig while Monday brags about himself from atop the ficus tree, recounts his exploits in song like a Viking in a mead hall boasting to his friends. I've noted the same windbag characteristic in all the males, especially pronounced whenever one of them loses a contest. It's probably an attempt to salvage some dignity, but the lesson seems to be that while male zebra finches may be gracious winners, they make insufferable losers—one of their most human characteristics. For his part, B generally doesn't care what the finches do or how they settle their disputes. Today, however, the silliness with the twig continues to hold his attention. He's still on my knee, his beak parted slightly, and there's a look on his face suggesting he's had about all he can take of Bert's crackpot attempts to build castles in the air. This isn't idle speculation. We had a similar situation two months back that ended with

B confiscating Bert's twig, flying it into his own house, and dropping it there.

NEAR THE BEGINNING OF JOSEPH CONRAD'S STORY "THE SECRET sharer," he writes in reference to a ship's crew preparing for a voyage: "In this breathless pause at the threshold of a long passage we seemed to be measuring our fitness for a long and arduous enterprise." I hadn't read the story since my freshman year in college, but the gist of these lines floated back to me a few days before the wedding, on one of the few really warm nights we had that summer. I sat on the back porch drinking a beer, wired with the exhaustion of having worked all day on the house, getting it ready for our wedding guests. Rebecca's relatives mostly, but my sister up from Texas, my grown nephews, Marc and Eric, flying in from San Francisco and Denver, respectively.

Marlowe sauntered out to sit with me on the steps, his expanse of white chest fur catching shafts of light from the neighbor's windows. He was insulin dependent by then—two shots a day, one in the morning, another at night. Some of the time I spent with B had formerly belonged to Marlowe, but despite my faithlessness, our bond endured. I stroked his head, scratched his chin; a purr rippled his frame. I ran my hand along his back, found an aging cat's bony spine. He was not quite twelve then, an older cat, not an ancient one. Our years together had been better to me than to him. "So," I imagined him saying, "you're marrying that woman who dumped water on my head."

Adhering to the tradition that grooms not see their brides prior to the ceremony on the day of their wedding, Rebecca spent the night before it sequestered with her mother at a bed-and-breakfast. My best man, Scott Chisholm, and his wife, Linda—one of those fortunate people whose intelligence and physical attractiveness are surpassed only by sweetness of temperament—stayed at the house with me.

A week or so before the wedding, I decided I'd make a concerted effort to remember every detail of the experience. I reasoned that since, theoretically, you get married only once, you may as well make the most of it. With people and gifts arriving by the day, a festive air pervaded the house. Underneath it all flowed a gratifying sense of doing something very adult and proper, of being about to follow through publicly on a private commitment. It seemed to me that by concentrating on everything that happened, I'd be able to create a kind of unedited mental video viewable at will through the ensuing years. But by the day of the wedding itself, I was so sleep-deprived that most of what happened is hazy:

Linda ironing my shirt. Scott ducking out to a bookstore an hour before we left for the ceremony. The catch in my father's voice when we spoke on the phone. B made edgy by the change in routine and by strange voices filling the house; his dismay when the pet sitter arrived. Driving to Washington Park. The plump violinist we hired fiddling out a jig as our guests approached through the roses. Vows from the Book of Common Prayer in honor of my mother. Sixty people who would never again exist as a group. My bride (nothing I can say that wouldn't shortchange her beauty) dressed in a gown with a princess waist—a sufficient memory all by itself.

Rebecca mentioned again recently that she wants to have our wedding portrait taken. She feels the need, for some reason, to top off the scores of pictures we have that were shot on the day of the wedding itself. Two of these we had enlarged and framed. One hangs on a wall, another sits on a table. In my favorite of the two, Rebecca and I are standing in front of a background of roses. She's looking at me with a smile that's almost a laugh; my arm is around her shoulders, hers around my waist. She's filled with the joy of being thirty, stunning, and a bride of a few minutes' duration married to someone who isn't kidding himself that he actually deserves her. Our friend Mike Duncan acted as official photographer and took it along with all the others that Rebecca has since pasted into an album and captioned. He used a high-quality camera and knew what he was doing. The results are quite good, but Rebecca never got the kind of formal thing she had in mind.

This issue surfaces every year or so. I suppose if I showed enthusiasm for going into a studio dressed as I was the day we were married, Rebecca would take the initiative to dig out her wedding dress and make an appointment. After nearly seven years, I'm not sure this would be the smartest thing to do. We haven't aged appreciably but enough certainly to make it seem as if we'd be dressing in costumes from a bygone age. Who we were should remain in the past; let those two people who, as it's turned out, prepared well for their voyage into hard years since exist unchanged on that day when Avis came through with her set of lace curtains.

I've always liked the word "dawdle," which, by a strange coincidence, appears to derive from "dadel," the Middle English word for the chattering of birds. And even though I think "dawdle" sounds as if it should be the name of a rustic wind instrument rather than a term for wasting time, I find it pleasing to hear and a pleasure to pronounce. "I plucks the banjo a bit, but yew should oughta hear Clem blow on the dawdle." I was never more than a modestly talented dawdler. Having inherited a measure of my father's sometimes overbearing punctuality, I just can't fritter efficiently.

Zebra finches, however, are consummate dawdlers. This is being driven home to me at the moment by the fact that Rebecca and I have a dinner engagement, and I'm no closer than I was twenty minutes ago to switching off the remaining light. It seems they've made a collective decision to stay active long after they ordinarily take the hint that bedtime has arrived. They have last-minute preening to do, drinks of water to get, favored roosting places to inspect and settle into. These are their rituals, and I try to respect them. It's why our bird-room lights go down in stages, but my patience tonight is wearing thin.

B understands the routine. He's done a little feather maintenance of his own while standing on my shoulder and is now, with only his beak sticking out, nestled in my cupped hand waiting for the finches to stop being finches for the night. He'll probably give them a few more minutes before he gets restive and emerges from my hand to twirl in place and snap the air. I know how he feels, but there's nothing I can do except sit here fantasizing about how satisfying it would be to net each troublesome finch and, yes, cage it for the night. It's tempting to say "Screw 'em" and kill the light whether they're ready or not. A no-nonsense approach that appeals right now to the rising tide of latent sadism I'm feeling as five maddening pixies conduct their affairs as if it's the middle of the bloody day.

But B and I continue our vigil. The finches have no reason to concern themselves with our convenience. They do, for reasons of their own, what they need to do. Like wind or fire, they're elemental in this respect, a force over which I have no right of dominion. In the strict sense, of course, I have what it is I say I don't want. As with B, these creatures live in my house, depend upon me for food, are subject to my whim. I try to be a benevolent dictator. To plunge the room into darkness before each finch is settled would violate the feudal compact we live by here. Given their willingness to launch out into the void when dissatisfied with their perches, it could also be dangerous.

Zebra finches are fussy about sleeping arrangements and return each night to their chosen roosts. They're also particular, neurotically so, about positioning themselves once they arrive there. Bert, for example, will sleep on the windowsill tonight at the same coordinates as the night before, his body perfectly oriented within the borders of an imaginary chalk outline I've drawn around him. As long as no one deviates from habit, the system works well month after month—everyone goes to rest where they're supposed to, and I can gauge with precision when to turn out the light. Trouble ensues when one finch or another decides to change venue. Tonight it's Lisa.

Her decision ripples through the body politic, and everyone is aflutter. The last time this happened, Bart (perhaps tired of getting poked in the butt all night by a twig that jutted from the branch directly below him) dithered on and off his customary branch by making exploratory jaunts over to a nook on the bookcase he'd had his eye on. Back and forth he went between the two, B snapping like castanets in response.

When I turned out the light Bart was in his old spot but, if you see my point, no longer "of" his spot. He flew from the tree several minutes later headed for the bookshelf, missed his mark, and landed in a heap on the floor. Visual acuity in the average bird is conservatively estimated to be twice that of humans, thus making the avian eye one of the most highly evolved and efficient biological systems. Human vision is excellent, so even a mere doubling of its capability is remarkable. Just as a bird's rather superior auditory equipment picks up a richness of detail unheard by us, a bird sees more than we do in the images it scans. But in the cre-puscular dimness that descends after lights-off, the finches are liable to in-jury if they get themselves airborne and must fumble for their bearings.

Rebecca, dressed and ready to hit the road, enters the room for a status report. I tell her to go on ahead, that I'll follow when I can. B stops snapping and greets her with a rising chirp that acknowledges her presence and questions it. I hear the front door open and close, her car drive away. I'll have explaining to do when I get to the restaurant, and although the friends I'm meeting have never openly disparaged my deference to the needs of our birds, eyebrows will rise. If I didn't like these people as much as I do, I'd explain my tardiness in the kind of mind-numbing detail of which I'm capable.

B has stopped complaining and is back in my hand tucked and asleep; he doesn't stir when I nuzzle his head. I'm past being annoyed. All the finches are settled with the exception of Lisa, who's definitely choosing a new place to sleep. I'll give her as much time as she needs.

7 〰

FOUR DEATHS

There are years that ask questions and years that answer.
—Zora Neale Hurston, *Their Eyes Were Watching God*

"*T*HIS WON'T TAKE LONG," I INFORM B AS HE BEGINS MUTTERING COMPLAINTS
*when I pick up the telephone, punch in my father's old number, and
listen to the recorded message I expect to hear: "The number you have
dialed is no longer in service. There is no new number . . ." He died a year
ago today, and I suppose the anniversary of his passing is what prompts
me into making a call I've been contemplating for months. Why I should
have felt any suspense during the few seconds of ringing before the automated system picked up is difficult to say. Regardless, I get final confirmation that my father is dead.*

I always had an idea in the back of my mind, a belief many children
maintain regarding their parents, that my father would live forever.
After I grew up, I continued to think that losing him would be indefinitely postponed. He smoked heavily from the age of ten and hit the
whiskey hard enough for the better part of a decade following my
mother's death to qualify him as an apprentice alcoholic. He stopped
drinking after a very mild stroke gave him a whiff of aphasia; he never
parted with the cigarettes. It's hard to tell whether they or alcohol contributed most to his stomach cancer. Despite these two very bad habits,
he was always vibrantly healthy—leaving aside the two coronaries in

his early fifties from which he recovered so completely that more than one cardiac specialist viewed him as something of a medical oddity.

Although he often pointed out that "None of us get out of here alive," sheer longevity on the Chester side of the family seemed to imply otherwise. His mother bore seven children (the first DOA), and lived to be ninety-eight. She'd been a thin, to all appearances frail girl when, at the age of eighteen, she married my grandfather in 1892. His parents objected to the match on the grounds that such an apparently fragile young woman was unlikely to survive the rigors of childbirth. I used to wonder what my status would have been had my father, the youngest of the brood, succumbed to his bout with diphtheria in 1918. Very sobering to walk in old cemeteries and read the grave markers of entire families wiped out in the space of a few days during outbreaks of diseases that have since been largely eradicated.

A year after my mother died, I moved to Oregon permanently and was on the verge of the close relationship I had with my father for the next twenty years. Something about having a continent between us fostered a mateyness we never really had when I lived closer to home. We talked by phone once a week; he generally flew to Portland each summer for a monthlong visit. Twice, he rode back with me to Oregon those years I needed a road trip and had driven to Pennsylvania to see him. Since I did all the driving, I got to know his left profile exceedingly well. Often, when I think of him in a flash, it is that aspect of his face I see framed in the passenger-side window lit by indirect light from the north. His image swims into view against rivers, sky, prairie, and cultivated fields stretching away to houses and barns clustered near a distant tree line. "Beautiful, isn't it?" he'd say, pointing to some feature of the landscape that moved him to speak after a long reverie. Years later and desperately ill, he said to me, "I'm not as afraid of dying as I used to be." I wondered then in my circuitous way if I'd been wrong in assuming that my ordinarily talkative father had simply been bored during his periods of silence as we drove across Nebraska or the Dakotas or wherever it was we happened to be. I've since looked off into distances that have confronted me and seen the lineament of my own mortality rise in relief against a backdrop of the larger world.

Although George and I (somewhere along the line we ended up on a first-name basis) always got along well, my father wasn't a man who related easily to children. We never discussed it, but I imagine Lola, George's surviving child from his first marriage, probably found him as distant when she was a girl as I did when, as a boy, I'd often lose track of him for weeks at a time. Most of my early memories of him are tied to images of his working life: Scooped from the sidewalk at the age of three and placed in the big leather pouch he carried as he approached our house after finishing his mail route. Riding along in the car after he became a rural carrier—the job he held until retirement. Hanging around the composition room of our town's daily newspaper while rows of Linotype operators cranked out the slugs of lead type that my father set into pages for printing. He trained as a printer while in his early teens and moonlighted in the trade until well into his fifties. There were other night jobs as well: taxi driver, laundry supervisor. The man never slept.

My father's toil provided a middle-class life for my mother and me, a comfortable retirement for him. He was bright, skipped fourth grade and turned in a remarkable high school performance in an age when a student's marks were expressed in percentages. All while working full-time to assist the family and earn his spending money. A couple of years after he died, I was fascinated to discover in leafing through his senior class yearbook (*The Torch,* 1932) that he'd been president of the mathematics club and had taken an interest in astronomy. Other than passing references to the weather or to whatever the moon was doing at the time, I don't recall my father ever mentioning the sky.

When I returned in May 1995 for the family reunion George decided to host, I hadn't seen either my hometown or him in almost three years. He missed the wedding, of course, and then cancelled a second trip to Portland the following February when he was to have celebrated his eightieth birthday here with me and Rebecca. He decided at the last minute he couldn't face the flight. I should have been a lot less eager to conclude from our phone conversations that, all things considered, he was doing well. "I'm just not up to a long plane ride" is, however, as much as I could get out of him. It wasn't until after he died that I learned from his friend Gladys how anxious he'd become. "Chris," she said, "at the hour of your wedding, he sat at my kitchen table and cried." When he'd told me at the time how sorry he was to have missed it, I accepted the apology, assured him it was all right, even as a feeling of resentment flickered in a part of me that thinks I'm always entitled to get my own way. It's strange that a scene I didn't witness now links George more intimately to my wedding than his physical presence would likely have done.

Because of thunderstorms in Chicago, my plane was late into Harrisburg, one of my favorite airports—small, efficient, friendly. There was a problem with the rental car reservation, which is to say, my travel agent screwed up and logged it with a company that doesn't do business in that area of Pennsylvania. It's possible a car still awaits me at the airport in Pittsburgh.

When I stepped outside the terminal on that Tuesday evening, it was almost nine, and as I trudged along searching for the car I'd just rented at inflated prices from a nominally sympathetic clerk, I was struck, as I always am, by the difference in scent between the East and West Coasts. Broadly speaking, it's more that the West Coast doesn't have a scent whereas the East Coast clearly does. Leafy, with an overlay of old, wet rock—to my nose, at least. No doubt, there's a large psychological component in this, but I can't step off an airplane east of the Mississippi without having the urge to lay my head in the nearest field and inhale the bouquet of every formative event of my life. I stopped in the parking lot that night, turned my face to the breeze, and knew how absolutely possible it is to go home again if the wind is right.

I made good time. A couple of snatches of freeway and then forty miles north along the Susquehanna River on Routes 11 and 15, a nasty stretch of two- and three-lane highway that has probably seen as many head-on collisions as any road in America. Town after town with names familiar to me—Duncannon, Amity Hall, Port Treverton, Selinsgrove. Back across the Susquehanna and on into Sunbury where the north and west branches of the river meet for the run to Chesapeake Bay. I drove down Front Street to Market, along the retaining wall built by the Army Corps of Engineers after the infamous '36 flood that inundated the town and trapped my father on the second floor of the newspaper building. Riverfront photographs taken before the wall was erected show a park running the length of Front Street—shade trees with benches set beneath them, placid water a few feet away. All I've ever known is the sight of that tedious concrete structure. It proved its worth in 1972 by containing a crest significantly higher than in '36, but be-

cause I've come to believe that all naturally flowing water is a declamation, sometimes an elegy that evokes our beginnings while inviting
our blood back to the sea, I wonder if defeating a floodplain has been
worth the effort.

I drove up Market, around the town square—courthouse on the
right, Masonic Temple to my left, Herbie's ghost somewhere in the middle. I noticed a new historical marker in Cameron Park and was surprised to learn that: "Lorenzo da Ponte, Mozart's librettist in the 1780s
for *The Marriage of Figaro, Don Giovanni,* and *Cosi fan tutte* came to
America in 1805 and lived in Sunbury from June 1811 to August 1818.
Da Ponte wrote that on visiting Sunbury, the adopted home of his
wife's family, 'I grew so enamored of the town that I resolved to settle
there.'" Since a link to Mozart, however slight, seemed worth crowing
about, I was surprised George hadn't mentioned it to me. He often said
that if heaven existed, Mozart's music is what they would play there.

I continued out Market Street past buildings that housed thriving
businesses when I was a kid but were now mostly empty or fronting the
sorts of marginal enterprises—hobby shops, video game arcades, pizza
parlors—that populate small-town main streets after a mall comes to the
area and makes it all but impossible for anything else to compete. These
desperate efforts to continue earning a buck downtown are usually
brief, rarely surviving once the start-up capital is spent. You can almost
see winged dollar bills flying out through the roofs. I picked up speed
after the blinking traffic light at Fifth and headed up Market Street hill
near the base of which the Chester family mansion stood at one time.
My great-grandfather Theodore made a pile in real estate after the Civil
War but died more or less a pauper after inexplicably investing most of
what he had—the better part of a million dollars—in dubious mining
stock. As the story goes, he died cursing his broker.

When I pulled in front of my old home, I could see through low-
hanging sycamore leaves my father standing behind the living room
window. Before I was out of the car, the front door opened, and an old
man in shirtsleeves stepped onto the porch. This would be the last time
I'd arrive at George's door after a long absence and find him plausibly
connected to the world. But God, he was thin, much thinner than the
last time I'd seen him when remnants of wiry muscles still clung to his
bones. I walked into the house embarrassed to be so much taller and

stronger than he, wanting only a return to some rough parity of physique and age that would vex time, make us both more durable.

Regardless of these feelings, it was good to be a son who had found his way home. George, as excited as I'd ever seen him, padded about in old sheepskin slippers to show me things that had changed since my last visit and a good many that hadn't. He iterated details of the reunion I already knew—where it would be held, who would cater, the likelihood of rain. He told me that a bone in one of Lola's toes was still infected and asked if I'd please pick her up at the airport on Thursday.

While George searched for new pictures he wanted to show me, I called Rebecca. I'd phoned twice from Harrisburg, once when I got off the plane and again after dealing with the rental car fiasco, but the line was busy both times. I figured, correctly, that she'd been having one of her marathon chats with her mother. I wanted to find out how Marlowe had fared that afternoon at his vet appointment, and I craved an update on B. Although there's no one I trust more than Rebecca to take over in my absence, I'm vaguely apprehensive until I get confirmation that everything is fine.

B evidently spent most of the evening shrieking at the door or looking out the window. When Rebecca turned down the lights, he flew into his house and banged his mirror—a sure sign you've been dismissed. She sounded so harried that I regretted leaving when I did. Had I waited until Friday, we could have traveled together, and she wouldn't have been stuck with all the animal care while killing herself to meet a deadline at work. Knowing, however, that I wanted time with my father before everyone else arrived, she'd insisted I go to Pennsylvania early. Had we known Marlowe was seriously ill, neither of us would have made the trip. A decision that would have resulted, of course, in an entirely different line of regret.

The evening before I left, Marlowe went off his feed and began throwing up. Sometimes cats do this sort of thing; who knows why? Winnie has always had a touchy stomach. From the day I brought her home from the animal shelter seventeen years ago (she was sleeping in a recently cleaned litter box when I first laid eyes on her) she's been a recreational puker. The same holds true for Sammy, the big, elderly, mostly Siamese male we inherited from Rebecca's mother. Several times a week, I hear his distinctive retching as he pursues his hobby—

(1) Find an upholstered or carpeted surface and heave. Try to splatter. (2) Move forward several feet before releasing second volley. (3) Repeat until reservoir is emptied.

Employing a technique our vet refers to as "Scarf 'n Barf," Sammy and Winnie view food as ammunition to be downed quickly with water and then blown back up in a soupy melange garnished with fur. They trot off afterward with an improved opinion of themselves to await their next feeding.

As a rule, Marlowe threw up only on special occasions—after escaping outside and eating grass, for example. He rarely skipped meals. His overall health declined with the onset of diabetes, a hard disease to manage in cats. It's a pernicious, systemic condition that makes anything untoward a cause for concern. Although we took him to the vet periodically and had his blood glucose curve plotted as a means of helping us calculate an appropriate insulin dosage, deciding how much he needed was really more guesswork than science. Using the kind of automated test kit diabetic people use to monitor themselves, I could have plotted these curves at home had Marlowe not demonstrated such a marked antipathy to me drawing his blood. Beyond keeping an eye on his activity level and motor skills, the most analytical thing we could do was to use test strips to check for sugar in his urine. He'd be stable for some encouraging period—days, weeks—but the next thing you knew, he'd wobble around with dilated pupils because however many units of insulin we were giving him was suddenly too much. This was life-threatening and required a quick infusion of maple syrup or honey to balance him out. Maddening.

Rebecca returned home after dropping me at the airport, packed Marlowe in his carrier, and took him to the vet. Aside from a slightly elevated temperature, they couldn't find a problem, sent him home with antibiotics and an appetite stimulator. Rebecca called our sitter, Kera, to fill her in on Marlowe's condition and to confirm that she'd be at the house Friday morning before Rebecca left for the airport. Unfortunately, this superbly reliable caretaker has long since moved from the area and is no longer available to help us out when the need arises. Even B approved of her, becoming relatively chummy after we'd been gone a day. It was funny, though, the way he associated our absences with Kera's arrival and hid in his house whenever she dropped by for a visit.

Difficulty finding pet sitters with whom we feel comfortable is really the proximate reason Rebecca and I rarely travel together. It's virtually impossible to find someone who, in deference to our wishes, is willing to spend hours hanging out with a bird that may remain aloof. Or someone we can trust to stay in the house overnight without hosting a debauch. Someone who follows the lengthy instructions we provide and, most important, someone with an intuitive grasp of the B Consciousness concept. If it were merely a question of having a pulse stop in once or twice a day to distribute food and change water, we'd hire a pet-sitting service or a neighborhood kid.

By the time I drove down Friday afternoon to fetch Rebecca, I was pretty damn sick of returning to Harrisburg airport—technically, Middletown Airport. Until fairly recently, the terminal building was a Quonset hut. I liked this because it made it easy when you arrived there in winter with snow on the ground to imagine yourself landing at an Antarctic research post.

Seeing the tiny pink roses that formed the pattern on Rebecca's dress, I thought to myself how innocently and sweetly we adorn ourselves against miseries to come. I embraced her at the gate and told her I was feeling pretty maudlin. There wasn't any point in concealing my fears about George. Rebecca sees through my habit of repressing emotion as a means of coping with stress—if necessary, joking my way through it. She told me it looked, at least, as though Marlowe would be fine.

Rebecca hadn't been on the East Coast since childhood and was surprised to find that Pennsylvania had vegetation and breathable air. And the Susquehanna River impressed her, its surface dotted with lush islands along the section we passed as we headed north. The Alleghenies were bluer than usual beneath a heavy mist that hung in the air—one of those close days when the weather is like a sweaty acquaintance who follows you home and sleeps in your bed. "So this is where you're from," she said as we crossed the bridge into Sunbury.

When we phoned Kera the next day, B was shrieking in the background at a level nearly sufficient to drown out the finches. Marlowe, she said, was very ill. Friday night he had scarcely moved, had begun retching again—bile mostly, his stomach empty. There's an enormous mass curled around his liver. Inoperable, almost certainly malignant.

Tears were rolling down my face, and tears were rolling down Rebecca's face as she listened on the extension. I knew where the conversation was headed. I knew Marlowe's life was now mine to take. The vet told Kera my friend was in pain, that the kindest thing really . . . There's a veterinary oncologist we could see for a second opinion if we were willing to spend the money. I glanced at Rebecca who nodded her head and mouthed the word "Yes."

Kera said that each time a car stopped outside B flew to the window. I asked her to offer him cookie; I was curious whether he'd stand on principle. I was stalling, pretending, however briefly, that Marlowe was lying on our steps in late-morning sun rather than sedated and alone at the vet's. B sent me his regards by resisting the cookie.

We made arrangements with the oncologist who was particularly sympathetic to the fact that Rebecca and I were trying to manage this crisis from the other side of the country. He agreed to open his office and see Marlowe on Sunday morning. The news, of course, was bad. After talking with Kera on Saturday, Rebecca and I worked out a scenario that demolished Marlowe's tumor, that reduced his illness to something treatable—a diabetic complication was, I believe, the fantasy. Pretty thin, but it got us through the night.

"No question," said the oncologist. There was definitely a tumor surrounding Marlowe's liver, probably cancerous—inoperable, nonetheless. He said it was fairly common in cats, that chemo and radiation might buy a couple of months. "To be honest . . ." He spoke gently, accustomed to nudging people into accepting a reality their minds are working to convert into the polar opposite of what he's telling them. He said it would be fine if we took a little time and then called him back. I told Rebecca I didn't have the strength to order Marlowe's death, that having the power to do so struck me as obscene.

We sat in my father's kitchen at the old wrought-iron table my mother loved so much. My father, sister, and nephews had left for the reunion, and the house hadn't yet shaken off the peculiar silence that consumes a place after a crowd departs. Rebecca and I did the math over and over again, and each time it worked out the same: Let Marlowe go. We wouldn't fly back early, better under the circumstances to let Kera act as our proxy; at least Marlowe knew her. Rebecca talked of the maternal streak he'd shown the time Kera looked after things while

Rebecca and I honeymooned in Canada—napping with and grooming the abandoned five-week-old kitten Kera had been tending.

And so it went: Kera held the phone to Marlowe's ear while we said our good-byes, Marlowe purring at the sound of our voices. The vet depressed the syringe; Kera said, "He's gone."

IT HAD BEEN AN EXCEPTIONALLY RAINY MAY, THE RIVER ALMOST touching the broad lawn running down from the entrance to my father's club on the island between Sunbury and Northumberland. Before entering to join the reunion festivities, Rebecca and I walked through soggy grass to the water's edge, watched tree limbs and someone's brassiere rush by in the current. Near the opposite bank, two optimists fished from a punt. Hard to explain, but the familiarity of the scene made it seem to me like the set of a long-running play I didn't wish to sit through again. Grief redraws boundaries, sets you apart while undermining your ability to soldier on normally after each demonstration that you can't live unscathed. You long for a glimmer of other arrangements—for a different river, unseen and unheard. I've had, I think, a single glimpse:

Ashland, Oregon, is about three hundred miles south of Portland near the California border and is home to a world-class Shakespearean festival that's been running since the '30s. Friends and I used to go down together once a year, stay for a long weekend, and take in the plays. One night about fifteen years ago, we sat sipping drinks in a Polish restaurant, seven of us ranged around a big wooden table. During the conversational lull that fell after the waiter took our food orders, Adrianne (sitting diagonally across from me at the opposite end of the table) and I jumped suddenly as if we'd both been goosed in an elevator. Nothing amazing in this you might argue, one spastic jerk triggering the other. Fair enough, except that Adrianne and I both felt startled by what seemed to be an eighth presence sitting in our midst. And we both had the contradictory sensation that someone wasn't there who *should* have been there—we've no idea who. Of course, I take orders from a house sparrow, so my sanity, if not my veracity, is questionable. Adrianne, on the other hand, is not only a talented painter who loves salsa dancing and hosting costume parties but also a highly regarded physician. She's not given to concocting stories.

Considering that Rebecca and I had euthanized Marlowe less than an hour beforehand (murdered is really more what it felt like to me), the reunion was tolerable. As families go, mine is a dwindling clan. Thus, it was a fairly intimate gathering but with just enough kids on hand to prevent it from being sedate. It occurred to me that humanity's entire supply of cousins is made up of generic people who look as if they *could* be related to you—or just as easily not. The idea came to me as I stood outside during a sun break chatting with one of these so-called relatives I hadn't seen since childhood. I thought of asking this thoroughly pleasant person how many reunions he attended each year but lost interest in the project when I caught sight of my father fetching Wiffle ball and badminton sets from the trunk of his car—the most arresting visual memory I have of the day.

In retrospect, it's easy to view Marlowe's end as an omen, as an event that began and prefigured the two-year festival of loss that was then about to commence. The past is always filled with hints. We're desperate for symbols, especially where death is concerned. On our way home from the reunion, while Rebecca and I waited at O'Hare to catch our connecting flight to Portland, we walked outside the terminal and found an adolescent starling wobbling atop a "Tow away zone" signpost next to the curb. Its mien was that of Poe's raven—had that august bird been bibulous and liable momentarily to teeter from its perch into oncoming traffic. This silent apparition stepped onto Rebecca's arm when she offered it, stayed put as she moved back toward the terminal. After it climbed onto her shoulder and jettisoned a full load of intestinal baggage, I understood it to be delivering Marlowe's message of rebuke in the form of a joke—in the unlikely event, of course, it had any connection to Marlowe at all. After a little prodding, "Bowel" flew off to join the other fifteen or twenty starlings lined up along the girders supporting the covered walkway. After Rebecca and I left to board our plane, I imagine that he or she returned to its signpost and waited for the next gullible travelers to arrive.

It wasn't until after Rebecca and I returned home that we felt the full impact of having lost Marlowe who, contrary to long-established habit, wasn't poking his nose through the front-door mail slot when we set foot on the porch and fumbled with our keys. A few days later, I received a card from my close friend Barry Egener, a person whose views on self-awareness and cognitive ability in animals differ markedly from my own. He wrote, "I'll miss Marlowe, too. He had an amazing presence."

IT'S LABOR DAY 1995. TOMORROW AFTERNOON I LEAVE FOR TWO MONTHS IN England. I want to go and yet, in a way, I don't. Like a wind-damaged roof that's lost shingles, B is missing a few feathers on his chest, a few on his head; I've placed one in my wallet in hopes it will protect us both while I'm gone—me by having it and him by the primitive magic it allows me to perform on his behalf. He's resting on my knee, tiny beads of light reflect from his eyes as he looks at me, secure in his innocence that every day will be like today. Rebecca said to me this morning, "You'll probably look out your plane window and see B alongside flapping like hell to keep up." Knowing B as I do, I can almost believe he'd make the attempt.

For once in my life, I've finished packing ahead of time for a trip, instead of an hour before I leave for the airport. I took care of this chore last night while B slept so that I'd be free to spend most of today visiting with him. Rebecca has been moping around, saying she'll miss me terribly. The feeling is mutual, but I haven't said so yet. I'm trying to keep things as light as possible. I've told her I expect she'll have a parade of men through here the minute I'm out the door. Verbal revenge, you see. Before leaving in July for five weeks in Europe, she predicted I'd take advantage of her absence by reliving my bachelor days, which, in her mind, are a lot more exciting than they actually were.

B takes bites from the spinach leaf I'm holding and creates a pattern along the edge that looks like a child's drawing of a sawtooth mountain range with plenty of pointy peaks and equally pointy valleys. I'm thinking how easy it is to create personal superstitions and yet how much harder it is to dispel their power to make us uncomfortable. In the name of all that's irrational, it often seems simpler to just go along with whatever silly-assed thing they want us to do. Look what happened to Marlowe the last time I took a trip; am I not virtually killing B by going to England? The lazy, procrastinating side of my personality has always seized on such nonsense. Says, in effect, "Aside from the fact that traveling is work, why tempt fate? Here's a good, paranoid excuse to stay home." I'm not falling for it, but I fret that B will have forgotten me by the time I return.

If I had it to do over again, I would not have gone to England when I did. I'd take the time and spend it with my father. I went because Scott Chisholm and I had been planning it for some time and because George assured he was doing better. In fact, I was doing better. Several months had passed since Marlowe's death; Rebecca and I marked our first anniversary still confident we'd each married the right person; B was healthy and playful. You could say I was happy enough with my life to want to change it for a while. The prospect of spending a couple of months abroad with an old friend seemed to me like the right way to do it.

Since half my ancestry is British (Chester and Chambers), going to England for the first time felt like a homecoming of sorts. It's likely I still have relatives there clogging the judicial system. Anyway, I remember the trip with particular fondness because, other than missing Rebecca and B, I had a thoroughly good time, a thing that's hard to do if you're me. As far as I'm concerned, a journey has plenty to recommend it if I get to stare at a room full of Turners (the Tate Gallery), sit at Jane Austen's writing table at her house in Chawton, and live for a time in the English countryside. Considering how things played out during the following months, I view my time in England as a more innocent age.

I've known Scott for more than thirty years. I like him for many reasons, not the least of which is his eccentric taste in reading material. Looking through his impressive library, you'll find titles such as *Shack Technology in the Age of Enlightenment: A British Perspective* or the equally sparkling *A Social History of Holes*. Although he's lived most of his adult life in the United States, he retains Canadian citizenship out of respect, he says, for Loyalist forebears who fled north during the unpleasantness between the American colonies and Britain. We've traveled together through a good bit of the United States as well as in Canada—which, as I'm fond of telling him, is really a U.S. outpost where we lodge undesirables.

Scott looks like a somewhat less insane version of Ezra Pound and is not only a gifted writer but also one of the most skillful raconteurs I've ever known. This makes him an entertaining traveling companion once you're accustomed to the unique filtering process that goes on in his frequently preoccupied brain. I found it disturbing during the early years of our association when, for example, he'd charge off on foot before I'd finished parking the car. It's not so much that he forgets you're with him, but more a benign dismissal of the larger reality you try to represent. I started posing the following philosophical question: If Scott were the only one around, would a tree falling in the woods make a sound? Now in his early sixties, he still has the powerful legs of an ex-hockey player, is the only person I know who'd express a sudden desire to dress me in an old-time deep-sea diving suit—helmet, lead boots, lead belt—for our flight home from England, is the only person I know with whom I could have had a serious debate over whether or not the bison we were watching through binoculars in the North Dakota Badlands was a nicely rendered fake put out there on display by an image-conscious park service.

I don't, as a rule, sleep well on planes. We were somewhere over the North Atlantic by the time I worked myself into a mild doze by staring at moonlight playing across the water passing below us. I remember congratulating myself on finally not being awake, thinking, "I'm pretty much asleep; the next thing I know we'll either be approaching Heathrow or crashing." Scott, however, had taken a sleeping pill and become the world's busiest person. He spent what seemed like weeks searching his seat for a pocket comb that was undoubtedly home on his dresser. I'll admit in fairness to him that he tried to be circumspect. The problem is that if you're the one courting sleep, your mind will fix on and amplify the other guy's effort to be unobtrusive.

From Heathrow, we took the Tube into London and spent a few days with our friends the Knox-Peebles at their house in Kensington. Brian is a former publisher of *Punch,* and tall, elegant Rose looks as if she's wafted out of a Pre-Raphaelite painting. I wanted to call Rebecca straight off, but with the eight-hour time difference, I knew she'd still be in bed or at least rolling around with a pillow over her head trying to muffle the finch racket that had probably already begun. B, a relatively late riser, would be sitting in his house quietly preening. Scott said he was hungry and wanted a pint of Boddingtons, so the four of us headed off on foot to a nearby pub—an archetypically British establishment named something like "The Stalwart Buttocks" or "Crapulent Plowman," a hand-painted sign above the entrance announcing the fact.

Five or six genuine English house sparrows were working the sidewalk outside the pub as we entered; they looked as if pickings had been slim. I was tempted to introduce myself, "You don't know me, but I serve your emperor back in the States," but having just met Brian and Rose, I thought it best not to make a scene. When I ducked back outside to feed them pieces of a bun I swiped from a basket on the bar (bear in mind that I was pretty fatigued by this time), it occurred to me that house sparrows form a kind of universal society to which I could elect myself an honorary member. As a Catholic, Scott always finds a church when he travels; I can generally locate a flock.

"Yay, I hoped it would be you," Rebecca said, when I got her on the phone. "I'm just now giving B breakfast." I related the short version of the trip to that point, mentioning that I'd seen Scott's daughter, Caitlin, when she turned up at O'Hare to spend an hour with us before her father and I boarded our flight. Caitlin, a remarkably pretty young woman, had recently completed a master's degree in social work and was employed by a family services agency in Chicago that she described as more in need of therapy than the clients it served. She moved to Portland about six months later and, as fate would have it, became what Rebecca and I like to refer to as our second sparrow's biological mother.

Rebecca said B had been indifferent to her throughout the previous day and increasingly agitated as dusk approached. "I pleaded with him for ten minutes before he came down from the bookcase and let me put him to bed. So far today, he's been friendly. He just ate a hazelnut on my leg and is now hopping around on the bed." I knew his molt was about to commence in earnest and reminded Rebecca that he might soon be clinging to her the way he does to me. As an escape from the misery of losing and replacing feathers, he craves a hand to sleep in whenever he's not eating like crazy to fuel the process. Rebecca blames my absence for the fact that the molt of '95 turned out to be the most radical one B's had to date. In pictures Rebecca took he looks more or less plucked and ready for the pot.

The day Marlowe died had been the first and only time I'd spoken on the phone with one of my pets. Never saw much point in it, seeing as how the conversation would be a trifle one-sided. But suddenly curious to see how B would react to the sound of my disembodied voice,

I asked Rebecca to place the receiver down next to him on the bed. Since Rose was passing through the room at the time, I felt a tad foolish but said, "Hi, B. How's it going, little guy?"

"First," Rebecca said when she came back on, "he sort of flutter-hopped backward when you spoke." I knew exactly what she meant. It's a movement B makes that reminds me of Charlie Chaplin's "Little Tramp" character's reaction to being chased: turn to the camera; splay the legs, open the arms, and jump. "But," she continued, "just now as I picked up the phone, he flew down to the floor and looked under the bed. He's still there." Is it any wonder I think B's a genius?

After five days in London, Scott and I picked up our rental car and headed about sixty miles west to the village of Barton Stacey where we'd taken lodgings for the balance of our stay. Brian and Rose were gracious hosts, to the extent of pretending their lives would be mean-ingless without house guests underfoot waiting to be fed. Thanks to a continuous belch of hot, dry air wafting up from Africa, we had warm, clear weather our entire time in England. It was, claimed the newspa-pers, the warmest September and October on record for the British Isles since the 1650s.

There is a plethora of "Bartons" in England. Barton in Fabis, Barton Turf, Barton under Needwood, Barton under Scrotum, Barton on Sea, to name a few. According to the *Oxford Dictionary of English Place Names*, the appellation derives from an Old English word for barley farm or an "outlying grange where corn is stored." As a settled community, Barton Stacey predates the Norman Conquest by the better part of a century and hasn't, I think, grown much since. Its business district contains a pub, general store–cum–post office, and a tiny coin-op laundry.

We took up residence at Church Farm, a five-minute walk from Bar-ton Stacey's somnambulant center. Set on extensive, well-kept grounds, Church Farm consisted of Church Farm House, the primary structure on the property, and the nearby carriage house with an adjacent "groom's cottage" built on at a right angle to the latter. Church Farm House is a mostly Georgian accretion added to an older slate-floored tithe barn that dates to the fifteenth century. It probably served as one of the village's early "bartons." By 1995, it was being run as a bed-and-breakfast by the owners, John and Jean Talbot. Scott and I rented the carriage house at off-season rates and couldn't have been happier. We had, well, a house: two bedrooms, two bathrooms, kitchen, living room with a fieldstone fireplace, laundry facilities, and a set of French doors opening onto a backyard with an in-ground swimming pool where hedgehogs came at night to drown themselves. We also got breakfast with the deal, requiring only a fifty-foot walk over to the main house to get it. We'd return in the evenings from our excursions and find the covers on our beds turned down—no mint, though. About every third morning, I'd arrive at the breakfast table and find a card or letter from Rebecca propped next to my plate. I'd open the envelopes and mounds of B's feathers would flutter out.

I enjoyed seeing big, obvious things—Stonehenge, Winchester Cathedral, etc. But just living there appealed to me most. It's impossible to find a road sign in the English countryside that's pockmarked with bullet holes. I tromped over half the Hampshire sticks without once feeling I had a statistically significant chance of being shot at. Some nights, Scott and I cooked dinner in our kitchen (to the initial consternation of Mrs. Talbot, wary that two men could be trusted not to destroy her new stove), watched BBC television late in the evening, and ate cans of rice pudding from Sainsburys. We had a comfortable feeling of having settled in.

I'd sit on the davenport by the French windows in the mornings and read; I'd look up to see house sparrows eating seed I put out or ten or twelve of them splashing around in the bath I kept filled. They reminded me of B in their quick, familiar movements, and I'd imagine him speculating on what had become of me. There were fields with sheep close by and trees where rooks perched in my line of sight. On those afternoons when Scott and I hadn't gone somewhere for the day, we'd play croquet on Church House lawn—an expanse of closely cropped grass that became after dark an empire of rabbits. Too stupid as a rule to equip ourselves with a flashlight, we'd stumble into the village at night. We'd pass the jostled tombstones and churchyard yews that were adjacent to Barton Stacey's ancient church with its Saxon bell tower high and square behind its nave. After last call at the pub, we'd move unsteadily back up the murky lane. On moonless nights, the ember of Scott's cigar was the only available light. We'd sometimes ruminate on the bones of our ancestors lying on that island. I believe we discussed two prominent attributes of the young woman who kept horses in a paddock not far from Church Farm. An idyllic couple of months. By the seventh week I was ready to go home.

On the way back from England, my plane from Chicago to Portland was so old its engines were coal-fired. Grimy-faced stokers passed through the cabin periodically on their way to the boiler room. The flight attendants complained among themselves that the ground crew hadn't swabbed out the johns or restocked the larder. I wondered what chores the mechanics had neglected. We rattled up into a driving rain, the ground quickly obscured in low clouds that didn't disperse until we crossed the Rockies. Somewhere to the southwest, Scott's plane shot toward Salt Lake City; soon, I thought, he and his comb will be reunited. I ate a bag of peanuts and downed a cup of surprisingly good coffee that partially revived me. A woman in the seat behind me tried sculpting the cranky energy of her three- and four-year-old children into pleasant dreams of their father waiting to see them in Portland. Their day had started in Glasgow.

I'm up and over to B's door early, Rebecca hard on my heels to witness the reunion. She's told me that she and B have gotten close, that she's had a bird for two months and liked it, that I now seem less crazy to her. She acts guilty, as if about to confess to having had an affair. Before entering, I pull the curtain aside. It's dim in the room, finches hardly stirring, B tucked and asleep on his perch. I'm like a kid on Christmas morning who sneaks downstairs at dawn to stare at his gifts. Even from this distance, in this light, I can see that all B's feathers have come in; I wonder what variants in color he's added, what accents and flecks. I've tried to prepare myself for the prospect of B flying to Rebecca's shoulder instead of to mine. I will, I imagine, be a stranger that bears watching. He wakes at the touch of my hand on the knob, peers out, stretches his wings, and combs them with his toes. He jumps to his lower perch, from there to the entrance.

I'm concerned that the reality of B will clash in a moment with my memory of B. Our front door is a darker green than I remembered, there are five porch steps, not the four I'd have sworn to. By reestablishing old routines, I may be able to displace Rebecca and become B's primary human again. This is my plan unless he won't have it or Rebecca objects—I refuse to win by a putsch. I walk through B's doorway annoyed with myself for staying away so long. Two or three weeks would have done, left some chance that the same person and the same sparrow could resume their fiction that each one's identity is imperishable to the other. I should have had Rebecca go in first and saved myself the ignominy of B treating me as a goon that's barged into his room at an unreasonable hour.

"I don't believe it. I just don't believe it," Rebecca repeats with a wide-eyed look on her face. B looped the room as I entered, plastered himself to my chest, said, "Chi-arete, Chi-arete," a sound I haven't heard him make before. He stands on my palm, level with my face; he touches my nose with his beak, turns his back on Rebecca when she offers him a finger. She nearly cries but is fighting it. Were B female, I'd rename him Penelope.

The day after returning home, I took a medicinal soak in a hot bath. Our upstairs tub is deep and long and perfect for nursing the misery I had in my lower back, injured slightly while throwing a baseball with Scott and subsequently wrenched into the locus of debilitating agony after I hoisted my overloaded suitcase into the trunk of our rental car. Anyone who's ever had lower back problems understands in a way no one else can how relentlessly connected that part of our anatomy is to every other part of our bodies. Eye blinking is painful, rising from the toilet a test of endurance, exiting bed a burlesque of old age. Looking like someone who's mislaid part of his spine, I spent my last few days in England hobbling around Rose and Brian's vacation place at Hove.

Although my back still hurt, I'd gotten through the worst of it, a detail about which I remained vague with Rebecca. She seemed happy pampering me, and I saw no reason to deny her the pleasure. A marriage won't thrive without sacrifice. Reflecting on the fact that a steaming bathroom was a sort of upscale womb with good lighting and a place to set drinks, I'd been in the tub for more than an hour, turning the spigot with my foot every ten minutes to add more hot water. When Rebecca came in with my nephew on the phone, I'd just turned from opening my stack of accumulated mail to repeatedly releasing a bar of Ivory soap underwater. I enjoyed watching it breach the surface like some strange, rectangular fish. Marc told me that his mother did not have an infected toe per se but rather late-stage multiple myeloma. Prognosis: Grim.

THE REALIZATION THAT WE VOLUNTEER FOR MANY OF OUR SORROWS has helped me a good deal. We acquire them in seed form with each new attachment and shouldn't be surprised when they sprout one day. Speaking as a person whose biochemistry manufactures gloom as a matter of course, it's taken me years to understand that fate has never singled me out. The universe has better things to do than plague me with loss or go out of its way to make my life miserable. A perverse egotism is one of the problems with free-floating depression. It sits on your psyche calling attention to itself until you half-believe you're important enough and special enough for the gods to persecute. Give this delusion the least bit of credence, and your will to cope begins leeching away. Chemically based sadness is real sadness but never proves its case that existence itself is inherently depressing—even though it may be. But in any event, it's unlikely that you can have a world operating on unbiased principles of process and reason without audience members sometimes seeing an arbitrary reality that's seemingly run by malign caprice. If medication provides the essential self with a means of sorting out this mess, then I say, "Sign me up." Pretending that force of will can correct a mental astigmatism that blurs and benights one's views of good and bad, happy and sad, has long since lost its charm for me. Our tragedies should destroy us or fail to destroy us under their own power, allow us to mourn loss as purely and directly as possible, unaffected by a dismal haze of our own making or because the end of joy is inevitable.

I haven't perfected any of this; I still argue my conclusions, remaining too affected by who I am. Nor would I necessarily change the latter were it possible to do so. As I've said, I'm far luckier than those who struggle with depression and anxiety that is far more potent than mine, people for whom pills don't work. They drown; I stand up to my knees on the fringes of the undertow. Taken all in all, I've had it easy, and I find myself pushing fifty with a sense of equanimity only partially attributable to pharmaceutical company chemists. My mother always said, "It's a great life if we can endure." The Year of Four Deaths tested the adage.

B sits chirping in my hand. There's exuberance in these songs of his that seem as if they must be observations he thinks I'll find interesting. He lilts and murmurs and turns from side to side, performing for the walls as well as for me. I like watching the muscles in his throat move as he forms each sound; beak parted, neck feathers puffed with the effort; no soapbox orator warms to his topic with more vigor than he. Traditionally, the syrinx (literally, the pipes of Pan), a pair of small, taut membranes in the avian voice box, was thought to be a bird's principal organ for producing sound. Thanks to research by Franz Goller of Indiana University and Ole Larsen of Odense University in Denmark, it now seems that the syrinx is really more a support structure. Their findings, published in the December 1999 issue of the Proceedings of the National Academy of Sciences, *suggest that airflow is regulated by two relatively loose tissue formations—the lateral and medial labia—with sound issuing as air squeezes around them. Humans use a similar system for creating speech.*

These outbursts seldom last more than a couple of minutes before ending abruptly. B resumes whatever he was doing prior to delivering his comments, and I sit wondering if I've responded appropriately. He may have just explained to me the meaning of life in simple terms. After ending his lecture, he often looks at me as if he's thinking, "Well?"

Having displaced two finches when he landed, B is now at the seed dish. He scans the contents, searching, apparently, for one particular seed out of thousands, uses his beak to scatter the decoys. Something about the way (don't ask me what) a few of the rejects hit the floor and bounce reminds me of sitting here the day George died, my mind on everything and nothing, more focused on old deaths, not yet able to drape myself over the serrated edge of my father's passing.

Mam, my maternal grandmother, lived with us when I was small. She adored me, spoiled me, and taught me to read before I started school. I was seven when she died. I remember my mother coming through the front door when she returned from the hospital after Mam's death. She wore a heavy tweed coat flecked with red, and it's the first time I recall seeing dark circles under someone's eyes. I remember making a connection between the phrase "bad heart" I'd been hearing whispered around and the fact that Mam had died. I have a few of her things. A bureau and a blanket chest, a silver-handled looking glass, some amber beads. I wish I could say that just one of these things fetches a clear image of her face from wherever memories of the dead lie hidden. But they don't. The chest is just a chest, the mirror only a mirror. She'd been so dear to me, you'd think I'd be able to heave into consciousness a more flattering portrait than the one that usually comes to mind. She sits nodding in her bedroom chair, upper plate dangling from her mouth, thick-seamed old-lady stockings bunched around her swollen ankles, stockings the texture of burlap and silk.

If, as it appears, only survivors experience death, it occurs to me that such a mighty voyage has relatively little to do with a heart that's ceased beating. It becomes a process of forgetting that completes the decedent's journey into oblivion. Years pass until we're racking our brains one day to recall how someone really looked, really spoke—the substance of the person, as opposed to their tokens or the space where they'd been. You can cheat with photographs or tapes, but such things flicker or curl at the edges. Hollow.

When Lola called saying, "Oh, Chris, our daddy's gone," I'd been back in Portland only a few days after the month I'd spent nursing George in Pennsylvania. The word "daddy" concussed me nearly as much as the news itself, that long-obsolete term adding another layer of poignancy to the news. Rebecca booked us a flight, called Caitlin to ask if she could look after B, the cats, and the house while we were gone. My father, ever methodical, had made his own funeral arrangements years in advance, or at least the having-himself-cremated part of the deal.

Doctors diagnosed George's cancer in May '96, operated in June. "I'll be fine," he told me. "Don't visit until after the surgery." His appetite hadn't been good before they opened him up and after it, worse. By late afternoon on one of the last days I spent with him, he'd eaten a slice of peach and nibbled some toast. A half-drained glass of Ensure was still on the table that evening. "Inanition," medical obfuscation for "starved to death," is listed on the certificate as the primary cause of death. Not that his surgery had gone all that badly. A man of eighty-one having part of his stomach removed can expect complications. He couldn't remember babbling for some days after the operation of an apartment he'd lived in fifty years before or pantomiming in an eerie dumb-show performance a man smoking a cigarette. But that's what those who were there claimed he'd done.

"Gladys," he said, "I couldn't have acted that way."

"Well, George, by God, you did."

That settled that. If his old friend Gladys said that's what happened, then, as far as he was concerned, evidently it had. He found the idea more than a little disturbing. Contemplating it beleaguered the solidity of things, the reliability of having been utterly himself for so many years. As if the very table where he sat might, on the strength of inanimate whim, contort into a fish and swim out the door. A linchpin had slipped in the vast machinery that passes as reality. I don't imagine he ever read Robert Lowell's lines:

> Christ,
> May I die at night
> With the semblance of my senses
> Like the full moon that fails.

The day before George went back into the hospital started with a bout of diarrhea that I dealt with using towels and a sponge. The adult diapers I purchased when his bowels started erupting a few days earlier hadn't been effective. I did my best to get the right size, spent twenty minutes scanning different brands for the jauntiest ad copy. Shit seeped down his pant legs and onto his shoes while he teetered just short of the bathroom trying to steady himself on the doorjamb. Cancer, surgery, and looming decisions about chemo and radiation were jolly larks as measured against the "I am undone" look in his eyes. Not a look of fear but recognition that, yes, we unravel, and the coming apart can be monstrous.

I settled him on the couch, arranged pillows under his head. I smoothed his hair. Although I must have, I couldn't remember ever touching the top of his head before. I felt the contours of his skull beneath the scalp and recognized landscapes of white stone stretching to infinity, a terrain of bad dreams from which the living do not wake. It was difficult to speak without crying; almost from the minute I returned home to help, such had been the case. In the twenty years since my mother's death (who at least had morphine mitigating the indignities of her body's dissolution, creating a comfortable flatness the ego poured itself onto, a place where shitting one's pants was no better or worse than not shitting one's pants), I'd come to find that life's sustaining cycles eventually lay us low. An erosion evident in George's face. Why, I wondered, don't we all just continuously weep?

My father sat on the edge of a hospital bed the last time I saw him, looking better in many ways than he had during the entire month of my visit. It had taken some doing, but we persuaded his doctor to readmit him—largely on the strength of neurological irregularities that began surfacing due, in part, to George's nearly depleted potassium level. When I walked from his room, past the nurse's station, down the elevator, and outside into the smell of baking bread coming from the commercial bakery a few blocks away, I'd convinced myself that George would be waiting when I returned in six weeks—as surely as the smell of that bread would be filling the air as it had always done.

He died a week later, exhausted by cancer, bungled postoperative care, and days of hiccupping—a detail that probably struck him as absurdly funny if he awoke on the other side with his wits about him and a chance to review the particulars of his exit. I called the hospital and spoke with him about three hours before he died, our conversation cut short because nurses wheeled him off for a test of some kind. For all I know, a Hiccup Resonance and Frequency Scan. "But I just talked to him," I pleaded when Lola rang with the news. I guess I thought that participants in recent conversations were immune from death. Lola had a weariness in her voice that people with feet in two worlds have when they speak. A bone marrow transplant left her too weak and too sick to travel up from Texas for our father's funeral.

It was unfair of me, of course, but I found myself loathing my hometown during the weeks I spent there dealing with George's estate. I began thinking of myself as an unfortunate tourist stuck in a malarial backwater because the only available bridge has washed out. Fortunately, the breach healed itself, and by the time I returned a couple of years later when Scott and I stopped in Sunbury during one of our cross-country road trips, I was mostly pleased to be there again. After we made our way north to the Bruce Peninsula and Scott's hometown of Wiarton, Ontario, sitting prettily on the western side of Georgian Bay, our first stop was the graveyard, just as it had been when we arrived in Sunbury. Stand with a friend at the graves of his parents, and you accept the weather that built him and the sorrows that reshaped him, as certainly as celebrants in church accept wafers and wine.

George died in the middle of August, and I returned to Portland in the latter part of September shortly before Rebecca's mother called with the news that she, too, was terminally ill. She'd known since July but refrained from telling us because of the situation with my father. This is when I started having House of Atreus, wrath-of-God paranoia—father dead, sister dying, mother-in-law dying. All gone in less than a year. You get jumpy wondering who's next, begin to suspect the trajectory of your own life arcs back to earth like everyone else's.

Finding myself orphaned at the age of forty-four, I had a distinct sense of stepping forward in a queue I'd forgotten I was in. Like a cold, middle-aged Russian waiting to buy vodka or toilet paper or a lousy cut of beef who detaches from his reverie to find his feet frozen and the line shifting. But the line doesn't go anywhere, and there's no point in being in it because there's no reward, nothing to buy when you make it to the counter. Except, of course, the farm.

As difficult as it was to lose my father, at least it fit the typical pattern. Lola and my mother-in-law were still relatively young women. Since the old are supposed to give up raging at the dying of the light long before their daughters and sons, it feels like the system works when they do. Glom onto the "He was old and had a good life" cliché, and the script practically writes itself. Then there's cancer. Why, the word itself is a tapestry. Throw it into the mix, and you save yourself time when describing a death. No two syllables in the language are as eloquent—as evocative of pain, degradation, and fear. The body turning on itself, tumors sprouting at night as we sleep. It's code for how frail we really are, and everyone understands because it's terrifying and rampant. Egyptian peasants probably derive a similar advantage when their family members are bitten by cobras.

I'm packed for the flight I'll be taking to Fort Worth this afternoon on an open-ended ticket. I'll return sometime after Lola makes her leap. B has been lying in my hand for the past half hour. Except by turning his head periodically to scan the area of the room where the latest finch insurrection is taking place, he follows my lead and stares into space without moving. That he is this subdued in May, always a high-energy month for him when play tops his agenda, I attribute to his ability to empathize with my moods. He knows I'll soon be leaving, infers it somehow from changes in routine that precede my absences. He sees and hears better than I do, and I credit him with the ability to make good use of that enhanced stream of data. Pants being placed in a suitcase make, I suppose, a distinctive sound; my face is different when I clench my jaw.

B has been with us for almost four years. Less than a week ago, I thought I'd killed him. Rebecca was in California with her mother, who is now, I think, losing her battle with leiomyosarcoma. She tires easily, and her breathing has started to become problematic. Rebecca will return for the duration as soon as I get home from whatever awaits me in Texas. I held B's seemingly lifeless body in my hand after picking him up from the bed. For the ten or fifteen seconds it took him to revive, I was convinced that I'd crushed him. Shaking, sobbing, faint with shock and relief, barely able to tell the story, I called Rebecca at her mother's. I've reviewed the scene countless times in my mind, but I still don't understand precisely what happened.

It was late evening and dusky outside, nearly B's bedtime. He'd played all day with a purple cap I'd given him that morning, bringing it to me every time I entered his room. I ate a sandwich, made a couple of phone calls, went back upstairs to wrap things up for the night. B greeted me with his toy, rattled it around in my hand as I walked over and sat on the edge of the bed. Because he was still enthusiastic about playing, I decided to give him ten more minutes of Fetch before turning down the lights.

B bolted after the cap when I threw it. Because I overshot my mark, it bounced off the sofa and landed on the floor. What I absolutely cannot grasp is how he ended up behind me. I saw him dive after the cap and disappear between the sofa and the wall. Never, as far as I remember, did I take my eyes off him or the spot where he vanished. I waited a few seconds, expecting him to emerge flying toward me, prey in his mouth. Nothing.

Figuring he was hesitating because he didn't like the lay of the land, I raised my ass far enough off the bed so I could get a view of the canyon into which cap and bird had dropped. The cap lay in the corner but no sign of B. Calling for him, I sat back puzzled, reasoning that he must have skirted under the sofa. Not like him to do so, but what other explanation could there possibly be? I assumed he was now biding his time because he heard a trace of alarm in my voice, and it's always fun to make me sweat. He'd pulled disappearing acts before that had me frantic. I walked over and looked under the sofa—no B. I'm thinking, "Christ, where the hell did he go?" I'm saying, "Come on, B, this isn't funny."

I turn around, and there he is on his back, lying on the bed in the approximate place I'd just been sitting. You see a bird motionless on its back and you think, "Dead bird." Of course, this wasn't just any bird. I start wailing, literally wailing, "Oh, B—oh, my God—oh, my God." His eyes were closed, his toes limp; no reaction when I picked him up, stroked him, kissed him. He lolled from side to side when I rocked him in my hand. I knew then that I'd crushed him, that I'd somehow violated the unbreakable rule of never shifting my weight unless I knew exactly where he was—a rule I believed I'd internalized to such a degree that obeying it was as automatic as breathing. It's one thing to lose your dearest friend, quite another to believe yourself the cause. Absurdly, inevitably, you work on a way to undo what you know in your agony cannot be undone.

Half a minute later, B stood up in my hand, as dapper and lively as ever. Relief and amazement vied for control as I confronted what seemed to me a genuine miracle. I blew out neurons as if I had them to spare. At first, I favored a supernatural explanation for B's resurrection, vetted it thoroughly with Rebecca when we spoke. As far as I was concerned, Lazarus had nothing on our bird. Then I remembered an occasion when B had displayed a similar catatonia. In other words, played dead. I'd been in the process of lifting him to his perch for the night when I accidentally rammed my foot into the bilge bucket, which, having been emptied that afternoon, went skittering across the floor. B froze in my hand, and I thought he'd had a heart attack. But his eyes were open, and he gingerly clasped my finger when I slid it under his toes—much different from the state he was in when I found him on the bed.

I'll never know whether or not my descending buttocks had anything to do with what happened that night. Maybe my posterior grazed and frightened B, my screech then pushing him deeper into an eerie quiescence where death was aped with convincing fidelity. I'm more troubled by how he got on the bed without my seeing him do it. Had I been so preoccupied with Lola and my mother-in-law that my attention strayed from him? Had my mind trotted off somewhere and left in place what amounted to a looped videotape replaying a faithful image of what I believed I was seeing? Or maybe B's faster and wilier than I thought.

I will never say, "I can't imagine what it would be like not to have B." I can imagine it graphically. He wouldn't be warming my hand as I sit here pondering the approaching weeks and months during which sadness over

my sister will merge with grief for my father and Rebecca will grieve for
her mother—as will I.

IT WOULD HAVE BEEN NICE, I THOUGHT, HAD SOMETHING LUMINOUS
remained, hovering, perhaps, before floating away to join forces with
the wind. In the muted light, an inert form beneath a winding sheet, the
summoned undertaker probably finishing his toilet, sipping his coffee,
looking for hearse keys, starting his day. The morphine pump had
stopped; silence piled upon silence, Lola an hour dead. We prayed
for this, to whatever deity snips finally the threads of suffering—God,
how Lola suffered; multiple myeloma more aptly named vicious,
adamant myeloma. A hospice nurse moved on the periphery; folded
this, stowed that, with polished deference stepped between boundaries, smiled once and moved from the room. Did she ever, I wondered,
meet Death after hours? For a drink, say, the way coworkers do? When
he shoulders his scythe and returns to work, do the Reaper's balls swell
with desire?

Or rather, Death as a beautiful thing, marvelously natural. If not
quite Shakespeare's "consummation devoutly to be wished," then certainly a proper, albeit forced, rounding out of one's life. Why argue?
May as well set out to improve the stars. At least Lola had been released, as our father had been nine months before. Released, as if the
dead are let off their tethers. Pen door opens, the chain's removed, and
off we bound on an eternal frolic. One idiotic image after another. Truth
is one dies, and the mind coughs itself out. Your atoms simply find
other work. No wispy heaven, no campy hell, no shifting to a higher
plane, no white light beckoning, no Zen-like merging with the fucking
cosmos. Christ, the things we tell ourselves.

I averted my gaze from my sister's body, looked at my feet or out
into the escape provided by the hallway behind me. This was my time
with her—private, final. I could have lifted the sheet if doing so would
have served any purpose, but it would have only embarrassed us both.
Her outline was enough to throttle my belief that cynics prosper on the
strength of their doubts.

I joined my nephews waiting in the kitchen for the funeral-home people to arrive. We poked words at the ineffable, tried killing off the little vipers of guilt that coil around one's sense of relief. Sunlight fleshed out details in the yard—a single running shoe, a pecan tree. "I wanted them to let me go," Lola told me on the phone a few weeks prior when I asked why she'd gone home early from the hospital. The double entendre had been obvious, the weariness in her voice an entity born of a never-ending series of pointless procedures.

The day before my birthday, she surprised me with a party—sang "Happy Birthday," and gave me a present. She ate a smidgen of cake and a spoonful of ice cream. It was easy to recall how stunning she'd been, her undimmed radiance trumping the ruined exterior. How could that be? For that matter, how could any of it be? Not only that she was dying but that enough time had been squandered to put her end within reach. The simple, daily act of living having brought everyone in the room to an event no longer grimly hypothetical. The kind of circumstance we're bayoneted into returning to who knows how many times over the course of our lives, right down to our own last hours. Lola died two days later.

I'm digging up part of our lawn. I like that the weather's uncomfortably warm, that boots, shorts, and a pair of work gloves are all I've got on. Besides a shovel and hoe, I have no mechanical advantage helping me with this project; I like that too. B sits on his window perch and chirps at me through the screen. He'd enjoy riding on my shoulder as I work out here if, that is, I could guarantee no disturbing noises, no light glinting off cars, no hawks, of which there's at least one in the neighborhood that considers this area its pantry. Our next-door neighbor tells me he recently saw a squirrel plucked from the power lines across the street. B quicksteps back and forth along the perch as he tries to keep me in view. If I disappear for more than a few seconds, he shrieks. He's edgy because I'm edgy, because Rebecca's away again at her mother's, because I'm visible but out of reach.

I'm surprised and gratified by the amount of work this project entails. Weeks without rain has left the ground not so much hard as impenetrable; I have fantasies of blasting it with dynamite I'd detonate using a traditional red box and plunger apparatus with wires running out of it. I've never liked this four-by-twelve-foot chunk of lawn. Too small to mow, too large not to mow, it consists of a few blades of actual grass plaited together with the far more numerous strands of something that hasn't yet evolved to the sophistication of crabgrass. It's what bark would be if it grew in thin stalks rooted in clumps. Amazing that anything grows in this Sahara of clay boulders I'm working to dislodge. I plan on removing enough dirt to bring the level down below the concrete walkway that leads to the front steps. I went yesterday and bought sand, paving stones, and bags of good soil. Half the area I'll plant with rose bushes, the other half I'll make into a rest stop for the neighborhood birds, a place where they can bathe and eat protected by our fence. My idea is to lay the stones over a layer of sand, edge them with a scalloped border. I'll buy a concrete birdbath and pedestal from the place over on Burnside that specializes in cut-rate yard accoutrements. I'd like Rebecca to see something pretty and useful in this space when she finally comes home.

B's been absent from his window perch for the past few minutes, off attending to other interests—secret bird things, or SBTs as Rebecca and I call them. I should quit playing in the dirt, take a shower, and rejoin him. It's Saturday, but he hasn't seen much of me today; I've been too restless to stay put and feel like a cat that's tired of being held. I've been milling around missing Rebecca, thinking how bad these months have been for her. We talk every night. She tells me about her day and what new sign there is that miracles don't happen. Leiomyosarcoma, pretty goddamned tenacious disease. Avoid it. You start thinking shark cartilage, shamans, concentrated moon beams, turpentine enemas. Anything. And you think, if anyone (fill in a name) can beat this disease, this person can. But they can't, and they don't, and you end up where we are now. Too early to tell if busting sod is cathartic, but I'm happy this ground is as unyielding as it is, that blisters are rising underneath my gloves. B probably appreciated the month of lethargy that beset me after Lola's death. Although boring, I must have seemed a sedentary marvel, inordinately attentive to his need for companionship. Indeed, all I wanted was to sit with him, soothed by the reality of his continuing existence.

When Rebecca went back to California poised for the long haul, hoping somehow for mercy from a god she doesn't believe in, I thought it unlikely the divine finger would be lifted in anything other than an obscene gesture. She returned to her mother's already guilty she wasn't doing enough, worried she was failing in her duty, failing in her love. I saw myself, a year earlier, going off in a similar frame of mind to be with my father. I told Rebecca, "Whatever you do, you'll come to regret it, and most likely you shouldn't. These situations have bad endings. No matter what we do, the result is the same." It took time for me to appreciate the wisdom of my own advice. George died, and I can only hope that the fact of me, as much as anything else, made it easier for him to do so. I knew that Rebecca would do whatever was right and necessary, but I worried about her.

I knew what the aftermath would be. Sorting through someone's life, so much of which turns out to be heartbreaking debris. Stuff and more stuff; some of it you remember from childhood, some of it you don't. Dismantling my father's home seemed to me a desecration. I was at once my grieving self and my own barbarian horde plundering my past, robbing in their absence my mother and my father. I expected their ghosts to turn up wailing, "Chris, what have you done?" For months afterward, I'd wake at night replaying the weeks I spent chipping away at what constituted the material strata of my parents' lives: Furniture and utensils and photographs and books and clothing and bedding. Washcloths, towels, bric-a-brac, doodads, shoes (God, the shoes got to me. Something to do with how forlorn they looked emptied of feet that could walk them out into the world), outdated medicines, a hot-water bottle so old the rubber shattered when I touched it, my mother's jewelry box, my father's Masonic apron. I'd wake striking the set again and again; everything dispersed, siphoned off into realities I cannot track. I'd stand in the middle of it. Things piled up—pulled from places in cabinets and drawers, strewn at first into rough categories of this I keep, this I sell, this gets thrown away. For days, I wanted it all, even the least scrap of paper having connection to those who were, to what had been. After a while, though, you become ruthless, able to part, at least, with the obvious junk—the plastic flowers, the wax fruit displays, those specimens of oddly poignant matter that clutter our lives and seem so pathetically, tenderly human. Betraying in their tacky, fading colors those lapses into bad taste that bind us together as vulnerable creatures. You'll understand when I tell you I pitied those things as I threw them away.

You sell the house, close the bank accounts, cancel the credit cards, settle the bills. You step out that last time, shutting the door on a place to which you could always return. Rebecca's time for all that had come. Never easy, but in this case, far too soon. Her mother was barely fifty-four.

As with my sister's death, Beverly's demise felt like a scam. Two women who should have had time to relax, grow out of their bodies in a serene decline twenty or thirty years from now. That this was denied them stuck in my craw, seemed to justify my anger at the universe's plan or amoral randomness. I accepted because I was forced to accept what was not only an embezzlement of these women's time but a lynching by natural causes as well.

The way I see it, Beverly wanted tea. More precisely, she hoped to retire from her phone company job and live out her days in unstressed civility. She went through a brutal divorce from Rebecca's father while in her early thirties. Her childhood had been rougher—alcoholic parents, on her own from the age of fifteen. During the last few years of her life, she began collecting tablecloths and delicate china. I think she hoped to pour Darjeeling from an elegant service while seated at a table in a blossoming garden. I like putting Rebecca and her sister in the frame, wisteria or some such scent in the air. No conversation, just the three of them together enjoying the day.

After slipping into a coma, Beverly died in her apartment on the last day of July 1997, a year to the day after they diagnosed her cancer. Rebecca, having left to run errands, returned an hour later to find her sister, Jenny, sitting in the living room. "Mom died while you were gone," she said. It took Rebecca a long time to accept that leaving for an hour was not an act of treason, nor were the uncharitable thoughts, unexpressed but real enough, that she sometimes had during the weeks she spent at her mother's trying to cope with the inevitable. Because I was spared the worst aspects of a protracted death with George—he didn't linger on the cusp, and by the time I got back to Pennsylvania was ash inside a mahogany box—I'm unqualified to comment on what Rebecca and her sister faced with their mother. But, it seems to me, you can't spend week after week dealing with what goes in and out of a dying parent without resentment and anger flitting through your mind. Indifference would have been the real sin. "The wind never stops here. I feel like I'm smothering," Rebecca told me each night when we spoke.

B IS CLEANING HIS KNICKERS, THE FEATHERED BREECHES THAT STOP ABOVE HIS knees. Not to be confused with knickers, as in the British sense of "underpants." When he preens that part of his anatomy, we refer to the process as "cleaning under his kilt." Which is exactly what it looks like, given the way he puffs out his belly feathers into a kind of skirt while attending to the chore. When I came in here twenty minutes ago talking to Rebecca on the cordless phone, B waited until I was almost to the sofa before he swept down from the sword to a landing on my shoulder. Rebecca could hear the breaking whoosh of his wings as he did so. She spent a few days in Portland after her mother's death but returned yesterday to California to finish preparations for Beverly's memorial service. I'll fly down Friday evening, return Sunday. Caitlin has agreed to stay in the house and look after B while I'm gone. I'm thankful she's available and willing to help us. I could do without another funeral to attend, but I can't miss this service, nor would I want to. That B knows and likes Caitlin removes a whopping big parcel of stress from the necessity of leaving him. Ever since Kera moved away, Rebecca and I have relied on the generosity of friends to take up the slack in our absence. I think we're both superstitiously afraid that B is now at risk from our rampaging karma. The prospect of hauling in a mercenary stranger to care for him these days strikes us as foolish.

Before we hung up, Rebecca asked me if I'd speak at her mother's funeral. I'm ill-prepared for the task but willing to do it. When I rose in St. Matthew's Church to eulogize my father, I did so for Lola as well as for myself. It was strange, I can tell you, to stand at the lectern and look out at the pews where I sat as a child with my parents, to look out at so many of my father's friends, at Rebecca, my nephews and aunt sitting up front, at the center aisle down which my mother's and grandmother's coffins once rolled, to see the stone font near the door where I was dipped and named. In a few days I'll stand in an unfamiliar place and, as I tried to do with my father, welcome Beverly officially into everyone's past.

B keeps listening at the heating grate, appears incredulous that Rebecca is once again gone. She spent half her time in here while she was home, much of it alone. Except when he's shoving a cap in your face or demanding acknowledgment, B's the most nondirective of therapists. There were times when I'd part the curtain on his outside door, see Rebecca sitting with tears dripping from her chin, B perched on her *finger. I told her she looked like Snow White evicted by a unanimous vote of the Dwarves.*

A crash downstairs sends B circling the room—three loops ending in one of his phenomenal sideways landings on the screen. He hopes it's Rebecca banging around in the kitchen and thus ostensibly available for games. The smart money says one of the cats (Thea, likely) is patrolling the counters, knocking things over. If I weren't seated comfortably with B looking up my nostrils, I'd go downstairs to assess the damage.

The phone rang as I got out of the shower a little after seven on the Thursday evening before I flew to California for Beverly's funeral. I recognized Caitlin's voice as soon as she spoke and thought, "Something's come up. She's calling to cancel." I was expecting her to drop by about nine to pick up a house key and get an updated list of bird instructions, maybe hang out with me while I put B to bed. One of the great things about Caitlin is that she doesn't find it odd that Rebecca and I live in an aviary.

"Listen, I just got back from jogging, and I found a baby bird lying on the grass next to the sidewalk—it's really tiny—I'm holding it right now—I don't know what kind it is—I don't know what to feed it—can I bring it to you right away?" I told her to stop en route and pick up puppy food.

8

BAD BABY

I have been versed in the reasonings of men
but Fate is stronger than anything I have known.
　　—Euripides

RAISING A SECOND HOUSE SPARROW WAS A POSSIBILITY REBECCA and I discussed from time to time. These purely speculative conversations revolved around questions of how B would react to having a mistress. Would he mate with her, fight with her, be indifferent to her? We agreed that should we ever run across someone with a female sparrow they needed to unload, we'd consider adopting her. Almost from the time we found B, rumors began surfacing about other people in town who lived with tame house sparrows. These individuals, if they exist, have consistently fallen into the "friend of a friend" category the way characters in urban myths always do. We've never seen one in the flesh.

As soon as I got off the phone with Caitlin, I located B's old heating pad and rummaged in the basement for a suitable box. The cellar was littered by then with so many odds and ends from my father's house that going down there felt like stepping into a cubist painting of my childhood. Along with a clean white towel, I installed the former in the latter, plugged it in, set the dial on low. I checked our toothpick supply and made certain I had a bottle of isopropyl alcohol in the medicine chest. Not wanting to risk transmitting disease to B, I'd need to sterilize my hands after handling a bird whose health and parasite status would be indeterminate. As an afterthought, I searched through closets until I found the adjustable window screen past which B had slipped on his maiden flight. I didn't really expect Caitlin's bird would be in any condition to fly, but our brief conversation hadn't specifically ruled out the possibility. The "really tiny" baby bird she mentioned could, I reasoned, include one already fledged.

"Actually, I ran right past without registering what it was. I don't know why, but I turned around and went back," Caitlin explained when I asked for the particulars of how she found what proved to be a baby house sparrow at the same stage of development (one or two days old) that B had been when he dropped from our eave. As with B, there was no evidence of injury, nor did he (I arbitrarily settled on a gender-specific pronoun because I hate referring to an animal as "it") make any sound. I've wondered with each of our sparrows at what point intervention would have come too late—in three of the four cases, whatever heat they departed their nests with had long since drained away.

By the time I opened one of the cans of puppy food Caitlin brought with her, it was nearly dark outside. Winnie and Thea yowled in the basement; B wanted games and called for me to return to his room. Since there's a bit of an art to getting the proper amount of puppy food on a toothpick without using your fingers, I was pleased to find that my skills hadn't deteriorated. I had a good-size morsel ready to go in one deft stroke. The trick is to roll the toothpick between thumb and forefinger while simultaneously rotating your wrist. I developed the technique as a means of countering my tendency to end up with large, messy globs that got smeared on top of B's beak rather than in it. I've now had four what could be called "initial feeding moments," each more suspenseful than the last. I didn't know it at the time, but I was dealing with Bad Baby—Rebecca's bird. Since we've batted a thousand so far, I understand what we'd have lost had any one of our four sparrows refused or been unable to eat.

It took longer than with B, but Baby eventually opened his mouth and accepted a helping. Although relieved that he was eating, I wondered what sort of weapon Rebecca would use to kill me for bringing another bird into the house. I planned to lay as much blame as possible on Caitlin, who, in my opinion, was clearly the guilty party. Bad form to run about picking up baby sparrows you're not in a position to keep because you live in a tiny house with a roommate, two cats, and a dog, because you work long hours and commute fifty miles to work every day.

"Are you handling this bird and talking to it?" Rebecca asked when I called her that night.

"Not as such."

"I love B, you know that, and I'm glad he's with us, but we really can't take on another bird. What happens if the new one's male, what would we do then? Won't they fight all the time? What would we do if we had to separate them? We've given up one room; we're out of space."

These were the same reasonable concerns I had. I wasn't by any means convinced I wanted the responsibility of having another sparrow to look after—even one that by my reckoning stood a 50 percent chance of being female. When I'd mentioned to our vet that we were considering taking in a female house sparrow if the opportunity arose, she pointed out that doing so carried the risk of altering the current human-bird dynamic in a way that might not be to my liking. How would I feel, she asked me, if B bonded with an avian mate? I'd be like the old college buddy it's fun to see from time to time with whom you no longer have much in common. Someone tolerable in small doses but pretty much a yutz. I'm selfish enough to have been troubled by the idea of B constantly glancing at his watch whenever we met over a beer to rehash old times, parting after an hour with empty promises to get together more often.

I assured Rebecca that my interest in the new bird was purely humanitarian. What I didn't mention was Baby's lame foot—the kind of imperfection that strict Darwinist parents would use as their excuse for dumping him onto the parking strip where Caitlin found him. A congenital defect, the front toes on Baby's left foot lie on their side and can't grip properly; the back toe is normal. As disabilities go, it's slight, but how much of a handicap it would have been for him in the wild is hard for me to say. Other than the fact that it makes scratching himself problematic, it doesn't slow him down. The scratching issue is funny, though. For us, at least.

If, for example, Baby has an itch on the right side of his head, he can't address it properly because doing so requires him to stand on his left leg while the right one deals with whatever's eating him. This is difficult since he can't stand solely on his left leg without losing balance. One or two swipes with his right foot is about all he gets in before toppling to starboard as if he's one toke over the line. An itch on the left is easier to treat because he's stable when standing on the right leg only. The difficulty here is that the toes on the left aren't flexible enough to get the job done. It's rather as if you tried scratching your head with a lightly clenched fist.

Spike Milligan once wrote, "Gradually the sun came up. There was no way of stopping it." Exactly how I felt at six-thirty Friday morning when Baby shrieked for his breakfast. I'd put him in the back bedroom, about six feet from my bed as the crow flies. B was still tucked on his perch when I peeked in on my way to the kitchen to retrieve puppy food from the refrigerator. The finches were quiet but beginning to stir. When I lifted the towel from Baby's end of the box (in the early morning light, an excellent facsimile of B's old digs), he lay on his side struggling to right himself into feeding position. With my help, he retreated into his corner after only two helpings—a far more subdued performance than the one B turned in the morning after we found him. Aside from the fact that Baby was alive and somewhat interested in eating, the presence of a fresh evacuation near the entrance to his tent was the most encouraging part of the visit. I wasn't sanguine about his chances when I left that evening for the airport. Although he chirped for food every twenty or thirty minutes, he never ate much at one sitting. He seemed to lack B's will to survive. Finding him on his back or side whenever I lifted his towel did not inspire confidence. I left Caitlin a note detailing my concerns, along with permission to bankrupt me at the vet's if Baby's condition worsened.

I slept most of the way to southern California, coming to when the plane touched down at Ontario, a quaint, gaslit airport forty miles east of Los Angeles with horse-drawn planes and the anachronistic necessity of walking across tarmac to enter the terminal. I immediately called Caitlin and received a good report—B, grumpy but well; Baby, holding his own.

Rebecca was completing her third orbit through the passenger pickup lane when I stepped outside and flagged her down. She looked like someone planning a funeral, which, of course, she was. She was chatty and incongruously upbeat; the same as I had been the day before my father's sendoff. Although she doesn't like driving at night and was by then on her second trip back from the airport that day, she declined my offer to take the wheel for the fifty-mile drive northeast on I-15 over the San Bernardino Mountains to Victorville—essentially a truck stop that's afflicted with elephantiasis. The only reason I can think of why a town would exist there is because it's the last place anyone would look. Of course, if you staggered in off the neighboring Mojave Desert, you might be happy to run across Victorville—conceivably.

Aside from the Roy Rogers Museum and the fact that nothing lasts forever, Victorville has little to recommend it. I was keen to know why Roy located there until I remembered that he'd stuffed Trigger—two decisions linked by a common thread of dementia. After a two-day stay, I can assure you that Victorville is a place that only its Booster Club members could love. A ceaseless wind blows unending garbage through strip-mall parking lots and into the desert where, if I were a resident, I'd cast my gaze and hope for salvation in the oblivion it offers.

"So, have you named the new bird yet?" Rebecca inquired after we were seated on the couch in her mother's apartment. Other than asking about B when we met at the airport, she hadn't mentioned birds. We'd talked about Beverly's service—who was coming from where and what food would be served at the reception. She told me again how much Beverly loved the dozen yellow roses I sent her a week before she died. I could see by the ransacked condition of the apartment that Rebecca and her sister had begun to sift through their mother's belongings. Closets and drawers were open, and half-filled boxes littered the floor. Beverly's cat, Sammy (which we inherited and moved to Portland), walked in and out looking bewildered, his universe unraveling. Whenever he passed beneath Rebecca's legs, she'd stroke him absently like someone dipping their fingers in flowing water.

"No, I haven't named the bird yet," I said. "To be honest, I'm not even sure he'll survive." Death had become such a common occurrence by then that I might have been stating my belief that the weather was seasonal. "He doesn't have a lot of fight in him, not like B had."

"Maybe his personality is different from B's, more subdued or something. But, we can't keep him if he makes it. OK? Promise me you won't try to tame him."

I didn't buy the different personality theory. It seemed to me that Baby had simply been further gone than B had been when we found him. And despite my respect for house sparrow abilities, I doubted that birds of the same species would differ markedly when it came down to basic survival. I told Rebecca I wasn't scheming to keep the new bird, that I didn't feel the immediate affinity with him that I had with B. I'd do anything necessary to pull Baby through, but beyond that I had no agenda. All I wanted from the future was a break.

"He has a lame foot, you know," I said later that night after we'd gone to bed, neither of us able to sleep, unwilling, I think, to surrender ourselves to the predatory wind.

B's fed up with the way I pop in and of here whenever Baby squawks for food. He knows there's a demanding interloper nearby, spends a good bit of time clinging on the screen-covered heating grate straining to catch a glimpse through the slats of whatever it is I'm hiding next door. Seeing to Baby's needs while placating B makes for long days. I return to my office tomorrow after a week off—a diversion I'm looking forward to despite the backlog of work that awaits me. I'll pack Baby in his box and take him along the way I once did with B.

A week has passed since Beverly's funeral. I'm remembering my time in Victorville much better as the days pass. It's the recovering amnesiac feeling I had after George and Lola died. A sense of detail coming back into consciousness as the initial stress of the situation wears off. My memory was quite good at one time—a genetic link with my father, I suppose. He could see a license plate once and never forget the number. Today, the face of each person who attended Beverly's service is clear to me. I can tell you what they wore, where and with whom they sat as I faced them from the podium. A much younger crowd overall than the one I addressed in St. Matthew's Church, not as ready to imagine themselves as the guest of honor.

B, I've discovered, is right-handed—winged, sided, or however you'd describe such a preference in birds. He's been exceptionally playful today because he'd like me to ignore Baby. Whenever I rise to answer the summons, B shows up with a bribe—caps, paper, sticks, a pushpin that held one corner of the wall calendar in place. I'm amazed that I've never noticed before that B arcs to the left when he pounces on a cap. If he's holding one in his beak and flicks it toward me, he does so right to left. I'm fascinated enough by this that I keep throwing caps all over the room to see if he'll make an exception. So far, out of twenty throws, he has not. How vanishingly small the probability that at some point in my life I'd be sitting in this particular room in this particular city at this particular time throwing a plastic cap in order to see in which direction a house sparrow turns his body when landing to retrieve it.

Rebecca estimates she'll be home in a week or ten days, depending on how quickly she and her sister wrap up Beverly's affairs. The relative normalcy we enjoyed before the events of the past year intervened seems like a gentle fantasy we indulged ourselves in, a hiatus from the hyperreality that has descended since. In response to Baby's now indignant chirps, B stands on my arm flicking his tail, defying me to leave again after another short, unsatisfying visit. I don't know what I'm going to tell Rebecca when she gets home and finds Baby sitting in my hand while I stroke his head.

BY THE MIDDLE OF OCTOBER, REBECCA, WITH MY CONCURRENCE, HAD made serious plans to send Baby to live in San Francisco with her friend Lorraine Grassano. I was fond of Baby by then but agreed with Rebecca that he'd have a wonderful life with Lorraine, the only person we could think of who'd be as dedicated to him as we were to B. In the first place, she'd sooner cut off a limb than cage any creature. By setting up a feeding station at an open window in her kitchen, Lorraine has put her apartment at the disposal of wild birds living in her neighborhood. Her customers hang around inside like regulars in a coffeehouse.

A slim woman in her forties, Lorraine speaks with the thick New Jersey accent of her youth, sits on the board of the Whooping Crane Conservation Association, and works as an urban park ranger in Golden Gate Park. If you've gotten a ticket there within the past ten or fifteen years, Lorraine may have written it since she reluctantly accepts parking patrol as one of her duties. She draws the line, however, at shooing out the homeless. The thing I find most endearing about her is that she coined the phrase "Feed two birds with one seed." While a brace of avians might very well encounter difficulty pursuing such a strategy, the sentiment is preferable to that expressed in the original aphorism.

Thanks to Baby's foot problem, Rebecca didn't file for divorce when she returned from Victorville to find a young, very tame house sparrow flapping around in our bedroom. Counter to my initial pessimism about his chances, Baby rallied after the first week, fledged rapidly, and took to the air every bit as quickly as B had done. Because I couldn't think of a lie exempting me from responsibility for Baby's conspicuous fondness for humans, I decided to chance it and gamble on the truth.

I explained that I was a weak man who couldn't resist holding Baby and talking to him even though I'd made efforts at first to feed him unobtrusively and then leave the room. I pointed out to Rebecca that she could see for herself how appealing he was and that it was pointless to pretend that his lame foot didn't make releasing him a bad idea. There had, we agreed, to be an alternative.

In the first place, we had no reason to assume without proof that B and Baby wouldn't get along. If Baby turned out to be female, there was a chance B would accept her as a boarder, possibly as a mate. If Baby were male, we had the Jeff and Akbar precedent to consider. I thought it would be ideal if B and Baby developed a civil, workaday relationship that allowed me and B to continue as before. If they didn't get along, the issue really boiled down to a question of space allocation—in retrospect, a charmingly antiquated concern. The idea that we worried about keeping two out of three bedrooms bird-free (desirable in many ways, I must admit) is now a middle-class pipe dream the elusiveness of which troubles us about as much anxiety as the threat posed by Sputnik. Carrying him in the tiny cage we use for trips to the vet, we moved Baby into B's room the following morning.

B recognized Baby as something other than a finch. He landed on my shoulder before I'd even set the cage on the bed, did so without any tail-flicking prelude or any time spent cogitating from the highest perch in the room. He hopped midway down my arm, stood in the crook of my elbow looking back and forth between Baby and me. I could almost hear him thinking, "So this is the little shit you've been running off to feed for the past three weeks." Baby gripped the bars with his one good foot and slid to the bottom of the cage.

My respect for B increased over the next several weeks because he refrained from murdering Baby, who spent most of his time imitating everything B did. It was as if Baby wanted to occupy the same physical space as his idol. If B went for a drink of water, Baby went for a drink of water; if B sat on Hugh's house preening, Baby joined him; if B tried settling in my hand, Baby was right behind him; if B retreated to his gremlin, Baby, like Mary's lamb, was sure to follow—and believe me, the seating capacity of that gremlin is limited. Rebecca found Baby's behavior endearing. "Isn't that adorable?" she'd say. "He wants to learn from the master." I sympathized with B. He must have felt like a celebrity being stalked by a deranged fan. His life wasn't his own anymore. Even cap games were ruined as Baby, with the subtlety of a bulldozer at a cricket match, blundered his way into the middle of the action. Trailing Baby in his wake, B would fly away to sulk. Benjamin Franklin noted, "Fish and visitors smell in three days." B would argue that the stench sets in sooner.

By saying, "No, baby." "Stop that, baby." "You're a very bad baby . . . ," we tried to discourage Baby's fixation on B. After hundreds of repetitions, Baby had his name. Tensions eased by mid-September. Both birds were molting heavily, and their activity levels dropped off sharply. Baby, an August hatchling, was constructing his second set of feathers in less than a month. He ate, slept, and forgot about B. Rebecca wishes she had pictures of me stretched out on the bed with B asleep on one side of my neck, Baby asleep on the other. I'd put on a CD of nature sounds—flowing water, crashing surf, twittering birds—and doze for an hour in a peaceable kingdom. This must seem a poor substitute to someone with time to spend napping in the woods, but at least I had sparrows asleep near my face.

With pronounced white eyebrows contributing to the mad-scientist look he has going for him whenever his inability to scratch his head properly leaves him with a series of spiky cowlicks, Baby emerged from his molt a sleek, handsome adult. Had tiny black bib feathers not sprouted on his chest halfway through the process, I'd have had more faith that his truce with B would endure. But after three weeks of calm, their premolt skirmishing escalated into feather-pulling spats. Although B remained tolerant, he no longer viewed Baby as a child and began resorting to force when provoked—Baby's attempts to displace him by worming his way under my chin when B was already there, for example. To his credit, B's responses were always measured, even over the central issue of who owned me and despite the fact that he could have injured Baby had he really wanted to. I thought it unlikely, however, that B's restraint would last into spring when hormones came on line.

I understood Baby's side of things, too. I'd pulled him through a tough infancy, and it was to me he took his first flight. My promise to

Rebecca notwithstanding, I'd been, if anything, more physically demonstrative with Baby than I had been with B when B was a nestling. That Baby ended up more or less bonded with me therefore came as no surprise. I say "more or less" because he was also enamored of Rebecca, appearing torn between which of us to go to when she and I were together in the room. He shows, actually, a slight preference for women. Perhaps because a woman saved him. It was, after all, Caitlin who found him, warmed him, soothed him. It was her toothpick skills that kept him alive while I was in Victorville.

These were still dark days around here, especially for Rebecca, whose loss was more recent than mine. I, at least, began waking in the morning without thinking right away of my father or sister. Rebecca's outlook remained grim, and it seemed to me that Baby's affectionate interest in her provided a healthy diversion. After going through what she had, you're relieved to be home even as you find yourself a fugitive in it. You're kicked from room to room by grief, ambushed by the most prosaic things conspiring to remind you of what it is you've lost. I call this the "peach syndrome," so named after I opened a bag of what turned out to be four ripening peaches on the evening I returned to Portland after settling my father's estate. And suddenly there's George leaning over the kitchen sink the way he always did while eating a gushing peach that he's opened and quartered with a bone-handled paring knife.

"You'll say I'm nuts . . . ," Rebecca said to me one evening during a break in sparrow hostilities, B on my shoulder, Baby on hers. "You'll say I'm nuts, but have you ever thought how weird it is that Baby showed up when he did? He's like a consolation prize I've gotten for having lost my mother."

"Maybe he's her envoy," I suggested. "Maybe you get to appoint one after you die." I wish I understood why people strain to graft deeper meaning onto this kind of stuff. Dostoyevsky wrote, "I am well-educated enough not to be superstitious, but I am superstitious," so maybe *he* knew. I still think after almost four years that there's more to Baby than he's at liberty to divulge.

"Thanks. Now I feel even more guilty that we're sending him to Lorraine. By the way, she called me at work today and said she's definitely decided to take him."

Despite, if you will, a certain understated bravado on her part, I think Rebecca was nursing doubts about giving up Baby. Had I really been intent on keeping him at that point, I could have manipulated her already fragile emotional state by floating the mawkish image of a young house sparrow with a lame foot and a bindle over his shoulder heading out into a cold world as Rebecca and I showed him the door— even though he'd be going to a good home with a trusted friend. But for once in my life, my better judgment prevailed. Baby made B's life miserable and we were out of space. And it was only a matter of time until someone got injured—Baby, probably. Not only was Lorraine the ideal person to adopt him, but the logistical problem of transferring him to San Francisco was made simple by the fact that Rebecca's company was sending her there on a business trip near the end of October.

As the days passed and the time drew near when Baby, as carry-on luggage, would board a plane with Rebecca, we began regretting the necessity of giving him up. We'd started to appreciate Baby's distinctiveness, what I suppose you could call his emerging personality—or avian-ality, to stretch a point. Rebecca has often said that B descended from nobility, Baby from hearty peasant stock. Certainly the idea holds up in light of the differences between them in regard to sleeping and waking. B views sundown as the beginning of a soiree; for Baby it's his signal to go to bed. And regardless of how much sleep they've had the night before, B's still at his toilet in the morning while Baby's fixing to hitch up the plow.

Nor has Baby ever been interested in the elaborate bedtime ritual B considers his due. The first night he spent in B's room, he flew at dusk to a spot on the bookcase I'd noticed him investigating earlier in the day. Taking his cue from whatever the onset of dusk told him to do, he scuttled into his makeshift roost, tucked his head, and went to sleep. I found an old shoe box the next morning, cut a sparrow-size entryway in one end, draped a cloth over it for extra privacy, and placed it on top of the bookcase. B buzzed me a few times while I set this up but quickly lost interest in a rag-covered box. Baby, however, inspected it at intervals throughout the day and flew to it that evening as if sleeping inside it were a long-standing habit. And so it went for the remainder of the time the two birds roomed together. After Baby retired, the balance of the evening would proceed normally until lights-down half an hour later, at which time he always grew restive. I'd be sitting with B in the darkened room, and Baby would wake up with what sounded like a hankering to move furniture. Because I know for a fact his shoe box wasn't furnished, how he made those noises is anybody's guess.

A few days before Baby's scheduled departure, Lorraine called to tell us she'd changed her mind after deciding that her work schedule was such that there'd be far too many days when Baby would scarcely see her at all. We weren't caught unawares by this development. Lorraine agonized over her decision to take Baby even after she'd made it. During a number of long phone conversations with Rebecca, she tried to prepare herself for adopting Baby by absorbing every detail of our experience with B. Rebecca's lengthy description of the obligations our bond with him entails doesn't speak well for her sales technique—if you accept, as Lorraine did, that such a bond involves an emotional and moral commitment that shouldn't be taken lightly. I admire Lorraine for having put Baby's needs ahead of her own strong desire to adopt him. Rebecca is thankful, and so am I.

The morning after Lorraine made her final decision, we purchased a relatively large cage (the sort usually associated with parakeets or canaries) so Baby would have a housing arrangement similar to B's. "I don't know about this . . . ," Rebecca said as we set it up in the back room, which is where she and I were sleeping at the time, having turned the large middle room into a communal study and a place to lodge guests. "It's temporary," I remember saying. "I'm sure we'll soon find him a home." Neither of us sensed how perilously close we were to ceding half the house to birds. I don't imagine we could have then envisioned any contingency that would compel us to do so.

Priorities change, however, and sensibilities evolve along with events until the thought of reverting to a more conventional arrangement strikes you as odd. Reverting to normal would require the removal of not only the tangible, omnipresent evidence of birds, but the birds themselves—an unacceptable alternative. Opening up a second sparrow room was good for B, good for Baby, and, depending on your level of estrangement from the social compact, either the real beginning of our descent into madness or our liberating embrace of the adult prerogative of doing what we pleased. Of course, this isn't to say that a thought balloon containing a larger house divided into relatively discrete bird zones and human zones doesn't form above my head on a regular basis. But since even handyman specials in Portland are incredibly expensive, we won't be moving anytime soon.

Our new setup required additional screen doors—one for our bedroom, one for the middle room, another at the top of the stairs to prevent Baby from going down, cats from coming up. With the latter door in place, Baby gained safe passage down the hallway to the middle bedroom, into which he followed Rebecca every chance he got. He took to sitting on her shoulder in the mornings while she curled her hair and applied makeup at her vanity. Two or three days after Baby started bunking with us, Rebecca saw her first Marx Brothers movie after I insisted on renting *Duck Soup* as an antidote to the general funk under which we both still labored. When Rebecca nicknamed Baby "Chicolini," in honor of Chico Marx's character in the movie, I knew he'd found his permanent home.

B's beak is long again. Specifically, the upper mandible has grown out past the lower. This gives him a fierce, curved overbite, the look of a pint-size bird of prey. It must be genetic with him, as opposed to a dietary deficiency of some kind. B's eating habits are the most well rounded of all our birds, and yet he's the only one with a beak that grows faster than its owner's ability to trim it.

It's curious how beak length affects B's energy level and mood. He's perched on my thumb at the moment, and even without my glasses, I can see the wicked hook he's been fussing with all morning. At this point in the cycle (about every six weeks), he takes frequent naps in what I assume is an effort to escape the irritation of having a beak he's unable to manicure. He behaves as if eating and preening are laborious tasks. I could intervene with clippers, but this involves holding him against his will—something I'm loath to do unless a life-threatening situation leaves me no choice. The first time B's beak grew to such a length, I took him to the vet and had her snip it. I vowed never to do so again. It wasn't that she did anything wrong or that B was upset with riding in the car to a strange place. It was how frightened he looked restrained in the vet's hand, his head clamped between her fingers—I damn near fainted, would have been more at ease being publicly circumcised. I've since learned that the beak problem resolves itself. Once a certain length is reached, the tip snaps off cleanly of its own accord.

Baby is outside looking in, a habit he developed three years ago after he got his own room. He hangs on the curtain that covers the window on B's outside door and taps on the glass to get our attention. If Rebecca's in here, he's very persistent. His obsession with B has lessened but not disappeared; he swoops in every chance he gets and clings to the screen until we shoo him away. The last time he and B had direct contact, Baby slipped past us as Rebecca and I were exiting. The two met midair, grappled, and spiraled to the floor where B got Baby by the throat and attempted to throttle him. I pried them apart, cupped Baby in my hands, and carried him out—no damage done. Were they to meet today, I'm not certain which bird would prevail in a fight. Baby's burlier and four years younger, but B has hundreds of War Birds under his belt. He's poised, seasoned, and quick.

Baby's provocative face pressed against the glass always looks to me like that of a thirsty speakeasy patron who's forgotten the password. B sits on the screen door's center brace preening wing feathers and wiping his bill across the brass curtain rod I placed there as a perch. B's studied composure drives Baby mad—he seems to understand that being ignored is the sincerest form of contempt.

OUR INTENTIONS HAD BEEN GOOD WHEN WE ACQUIRED A FINCH, equally so when we bought a canary. If Baby had been B's cross to bear, Clive was Baby's comeuppance. With Rebecca back at work full-time and my off-hours devoted primarily to B, Baby wasn't getting the social time we felt he deserved. Fortunately, he was adept at entertaining himself by decorating his house with whatever oddments he could find that were light enough to be airlifted to it. He still plays with a piece of silver-threaded material about two feet long and slightly wider than a boot lace that escaped long ago from one of Rebecca's costume-making disasters. Then there's "Get the Bird," a game he enjoys that involves sparring with his image in mirrors, brass light-switch covers, metal picture frames, and other shiny surfaces. Rebecca says, "Get the bird, Baby," and off he wings to find his reflection. She often gets ready for work while Baby bangs at the vanity's mirror. As does B, Baby craves an audience, stops periodically to look up at Rebecca whenever she thinks her attention has wandered. Were I blind, I could find my way into the middle bedroom simply by following the rat-a-tat-tat.

Early in the new year we dropped all pretense that Baby was up for adoption. There'd been a nibble or two, but our standards had become so impossibly high that I'd have run a background check on Buddha himself before giving him Baby. The canary idea issued, I'm pleased to say, from Rebecca's brain—a fact I delight in reminding her about whenever Clive is bursting with song. The din the finches produce pales beside Clive's ear-splitting solos. Please note that I don't use the term "ear-splitting" because I'm too lazy to think of something less hackneyed; Clive can send you running from the room with vaporized eardrums and blood running down the sides of your head. Consider the following snippet from the entry on canaries as it appeared in the illustrious eleventh edition of the *Encyclopedia Britannica*, published in 1910 (the italics are mine): "The natural song of the canary is loud and clear; and in their native groves the males, especially during the pairing season, pour forth their song with such ardor as sometimes to *burst the delicate vessels of the throat*."

If you'll excuse the expression, Clive's an odd duck. Burnt-orange in color, he doesn't fit most people's image of what a canary should look like—in other words, canary yellow. Turns out there's a wide color distribution in these birds resulting from years of hybridization and selective breeding. In the wild they tend to be grayish brown. A head taller than Baby, Clive's the more willowy bird by far and often stands in a way that emphasizes a kind of stoop-shouldered thinness that makes him look like a particularly avaricious nineteenth-century undertaker. Dress him in a black suit and put a top hat on him and he'd be in context sitting at the reins of an old-fashioned hearse.

He and Baby hit it off well, often sang duets together in late afternoon, Baby croaking along as best he could while standing wing-to-wing with an avian Caruso. Things changed when we acquired Daphne (full name, Daphne the Plump), the classically yellow female that Rebecca insisted we buy as a mate for Clive—an arrangement I favored because it seemed the best way to moderate Clive's incessant singing that, although beautiful and varied, was (and remains) too much of a good thing. Male canaries sing to claim territory and to attract unattached females, announcing via the intricacy and robustness of their song what virile providers they promise to be. Daphne fell for it after several days of playing coy. Of course, under the circumstances, she had little choice. Clive then acted as if his old singing partner reminded him of a past he wished to forget.

He began following Baby and glaring at him—amusing considering Baby's history of tailing B. Nonplussed rather than threatened, Baby shrugged Clive off in the way you might duck out of interviews with a crazy but harmless relative wandering around your home. We granted Baby unlimited access to the middle room after we discovered Clive in a Bates Motel kind of moment standing on top of Baby's house staring at him while he napped on his perch. This defused the nascent hostilities until Clive decided that all areas of the upstairs (excluding B's room) were legitimate parts of his realm. His attempts to annex the middle bedroom as part of his Canaryland vision pushed Baby's patience to its limit. As a result, Clive got his clock cleaned several times a day and returned to Daphne with fewer feathers than the last time she saw him.

I was so taken with the fact that people we knew had stopped dying that I'd say to Rebecca, "Guess who isn't dead." Morbid, of course, but it's an amazing thing to be able to say that someone you know is free of that predicament. It makes them accessible. My outlook improved further after I decided that years of tightfisted money management plus the windfall from my father entitled me to blow off working full-time more or less indefinitely. More hours a day spent with B seemed a far better use of my time than repairing computer equipment that wasn't long from the landfill anyway. As did seeing more of Rebecca, who usually worked from home three days a week. There are people out there referring to software documentation written by a woman with a sparrow in her hair.

B insinuates himself into my hand before I have a chance to sit down. Even if there weren't drops of water on the floor and splashed around the rim of his dish or, for that matter, suspiciously moist finches in a line on the windowsill, B's eagerness to lie fluffed in my palm makes it a safe bet that he's bathed within the past half hour. Except for a damp spot on his belly, his feathers are dry but not yet lying as smoothly as they will after his definitive postbath preen. On a day as hot as this one is, it seems unlikely he wants in my hand for the warmth. It's more as if the relaxed mood induced by bathing is something B seeks to amplify by lounging in the one place that's synonymous in his mind with a feeling of contentment. If he owned slippers and a smoking jacket, he'd be wearing them now.

The way B shows up in my hand is often inexplicable. In the present instance, the process was obvious: after zooming onto my wrist as I walked in the door, he ducked under my thumb and settled in my palm—voilà, bird in hand. Other times he simply materializes, as if his desire to be on me is so immediate that he's able to bypass the customary ways in which matter moves from place to place. But I suppose it has more to do with my being caught up in my own thoughts and not consciously noting his arrival. It's a neat trick however it's done, appropriate for a familiar—a guileless sort of magic that succeeds not because of B's intent to deceive but because of my frequent failure to observe. Alerted by a curious paddling motion he makes with his feet as he settles, I find him occupying a hand I'd have sworn was empty. A phantom sense of him doing this very thing has come to me at times when I've been far away from his room: waking in a shabby Nebraska motel, vague for a moment about where I was; while sitting through a program of twelve-tone rubbish at a recent chamber music recital; shopping for pants.

B flies to his seed dish, extracts a specimen, and returns with it to my hand—an expedition that burned more calories than it netted. I fancy him saying, "I'm hungry, but I can't tear myself away from you long enough to deal with it properly." It wouldn't surprise me if I'm hit one day with the disturbing epiphany that not once in all these years have I responded appropriately to these gestures of his. He doesn't bat an eye when I reach in and remove a cat hair that's lying across his beak.

Rebecca is moving around next door changing Baby's water, talking to him as she goes through the motions of cleaning his dish after emptying its contents in the bathroom sink. Baby's on her shoulder, burbling along in the argot he uses only with her; a vocabulary different from B's—more vowels drifting in the stream. Earlier they had "Battle Baby," a bastardized version of War Bird that B finds vulgar. He clung to the heating grate listening as Rebecca said, "Oh, no, it's a fierce Battle Baby. I'm under attack . . ." Other than a single generic chirp before returning to me with a "That was pathetic" look on his face, he listened without comment, his head next to the screen, beak in the air.

BECAUSE WE CONTINUE TO INDULGE OUR CATS IN THEIR ANCIENT privilege of sleeping with us on the bed, we lock Baby in his house overnight. Contrary to B, who prefers a perch, Baby sleeps in a store-bought nest fashioned of reeds—a sort of enclosed oval with a hole in front like the opening to a cave. He usually stirs when I tiptoe through the darkened room on my way to bed; Rebecca, much harder to disturb, is oblivious. In the light leaking in from the street, I can see Baby's white eyebrows topping his face, the tip of his beak resting near the entrance to his den. He waits until I say, "Sorry I disturbed you, Baby," before withdrawing inside for the night. He'll rise early to begin work rousing Rebecca, who, prior to releasing him, must escort Sammy and Winston out to the stairwell. Shortly after sunrise, I relocate to the living room couch, hoping to salvage another hour of sleep before B requires my presence in his room.

Baby understands crescendo. The amount of noise he makes in the mornings escalates until Rebecca gets up, dispenses with the cats, and lifts the little portcullis-like door on his cage—because he's locked in, the "house" euphemism seems inappropriate here. He begins badgering her with chirps and shrieks but soon moves on to exploiting the acoustic properties of the metal that surrounds him. Light tapping on the rungs is followed by an increasingly vigorous jiggling of the door; an annoying strumming then ensues as he swipes his beak across the bars like a convict with a tin cup. If this doesn't get a rise out of her, it's time for resounding leaps from the top of his nest to the metal grate below. With or without a pillow over her head, not even Rebecca sleeps through this.

Baby's racket in the morning is a small price to pay for having him with us. I feel, actually, that I'm in his debt. In ways I could not, he helped Rebecca cope with the loss of her mother—far better at flying off with an earring plucked from her lobe, at grooming her eyebrows, at standing his ground when she might have thought she preferred the exclusive company of her grief. He made my madness for B understandable to her.

For two years after Baby's arrival, things were balanced nicely. I had my sparrow, Rebecca had hers; our middle bedroom was comparatively birdless. The canaries showed genuine affection for one another despite Clive's desire for a harem. He's a randy old bastard who doesn't shoot blanks. Nor, as it turned out, did the male house sparrow who took up residence in B's old eave.

9

PEE WEE AND SEVEN

"Immature female of the species."

"*What* species?"

Passer domesticus, Morse. Can't you recognize a bloody house sparrow when you see one?"

— Colin Dexter, *The Remorseful Day*

PEE WEE, NICKNAMED "BUDDHA BIRD," EMBODIES THE MOST PERFECT serenity I've ever encountered. Such statements tend to ring hollow in a hyperbolic age, but I assure you it isn't possible to overstate the essential calmness of Pee Wee's nature. I say, "Up, Pee Wee," and she steps, not hops, onto my finger and reposes—the only word for it. You get the feeling she sees beyond time. You get the feeling she sees the ragged edges of your soul where it broke away from the greater whole. Perfectly at rest, perfectly alert, she's also one tough cookie. She was covered with ants when we found her.

B's natal eave went unoccupied for three years. It was still the attractive nesting spot it had always been—high, recessed, equipped with a convenient landing area. Maybe rumors were abroad that the place was haunted. The only activity came from disappointed starlings poking around and squawking over the diminutive size of the entrance. After the Trapped Sparrow Incident, Rebecca wanted me to board up the opening; I intended to do it too, but since I'm like Sherlock

Holmes's description of himself as "the most incurably lazy devil that ever stood in shoe leather," the job went begging.

A claimant arrived in the middle of May, broadcasting his status as a property owner. In what sounded like a series of Hyde Park political tirades, he puffed and shrieked on his "porch" for the better part of a week. In fact, all over the neighborhood lascivious male house sparrows were singing for mates. Assuming that such advertising is more than just passionate noise, I'd love to know whether it's lyric poetry I'm hearing— or the recitation of a proud lineage or embellished accomplishments à la padding a résumé. If good diet and the right genes have endowed you with a larger-than-average black bib, your prospects soar. Confers, as I understand it, an elevated social position you don't have to earn.

I couldn't remember any of the previous eave barons taking possession without a mate already in tow and mention the fact because the incessant singing of the latest tenant made B uneasy. He stood at the window every so often and craned his neck trying to catch sight of the exuberant presence perched less than seven feet away on the other side of the intervening wall. Since B rarely pays attention to outside birds, it was interesting to hear him reply in bursts of profanity-laced invective that I translated as, "Move along, shithead; this place is taken."

In addition to being covered with ants and very cold, Pee Wee was at the same Play-Doh stage of development as B and Baby had been when we entered their lives. A moment of reckoning must come a day or so after house sparrows hatch when the parent birds decide which, if any, members of their broods they're going to jettison. Either that or nestlings are strong enough by then to wiggle themselves into trouble. In any event, it was lucky for Pee Wee that I was out gathering yard debris for our twice-monthly pickup the following morning. She lay next to a pile of weeds I'd pulled earlier in the week, a few inches away from where B had lain six years before. I thought she was dead.

Rebecca stopped planting marigolds and trotted over when I gasped at what seemed a grisly déjà vu. Rebecca's eyes being sharper than mine allowed her to see in the fading light and shadows cast by the arborvitae that my discovery was still breathing. "Goddamned ants," she exploded with more ferocity than I'd have thought her capable. "Goddamned ants," she repeated as she ran into the house with Pee Wee cupped in her hands. "Goddamned ants," she muttered as she rinsed Pee Wee in the sink under a stream of tepid water. I salute those readers now thinking to themselves, "Heating pad, box, puppy food, toothpick."

Pee Wee came around almost immediately due in part, I suspect, to the rejuvenating effects of the water. It took very little prodding to get her to eat—three or four helpings after which she settled in my hand, already displaying her signature placidity. Both B and Baby struggled to move under cover after feeding, flailing their ungainly limbs in an effort to push themselves somewhere, anywhere, out of the light. "That's incredible," Rebecca said after we'd finished the now familiar emergency drill. "I thought for sure that this would be the one we'd lose. God, I hate ants."

"I know you do, dear," I said. Rebecca had her reasons.

TWO DAYS AFTER FINDING PEE WEE, I EMBARKED ON A TEN-DAY TRIP I'd had planned for months. I hated leaving Rebecca with the extra chores a baby bird generates, but she was between projects at work and said it was, all things considered, a good time for me to be gone. I think she looked forward to being Pee Wee's primary caregiver, to being the first person Pee Wee saw when her eyes opened for the first time. Rebecca's chance, however brief, to be the unchallenged focal point in the life of one of our birds. Other than minor grumbling over the issue of space, vis-à-vis our growing lack thereof, she remained silent on the topics I assumed we'd discuss at that point. I wondered if the pleasure she took in thwarting ants had somehow addled her brain.

Pee Wee was, for all practical purposes, a bird I'd never seen before by the time I returned from my trip. I regretted missing the transformation she underwent during my time away. Every night on the phone, Rebecca described new feathers, fluttering wings, a beak less broad and yellow. Confirming that we had, indeed, another tame house sparrow, Pee Wee flew to Rebecca's shoulder a couple of days after I got home. While Rebecca insisted that we'd surely find ourselves saddled with a third territory-loving male, I felt certain that Pee Wee was female.

I gloated two months later when Pee Wee acquired her adult plumage without black feathers appearing at her throat. Along with reassembling our dryer in working condition after replacing a bearing, the gender thing with Pee Wee is one of my two prized "I told you so" triumphs. Rebecca, ever gracious, admits that Pee Wee had a different sense about her from the beginning and that I'd been quick to interpret what that difference meant. Suffice it to say that Pee Wee has a kind of *femaleness* about her that's distinct from the males. I know it's unwise to generalize from such a limited sampling—experience with one female house sparrow certainly qualifying as limited—but until further examples come my way, I'll base my conclusions on what I have.

To begin with, there's the tail fluttering. This characteristic, absent in the males, is something Pee Wee's done since she first lay in my hand after fledging. She spreads the feathers and quivers them like a co-quette's fan at a ball. This is not exclusively a response to tactile stimulation. "Sweet, beautiful Pee Wee" said in my most bewitching tone is enough to set her in motion when she's open to flattery. There's probably an underlying sexual component to this behavior, but it isn't for me to say. Both the male and the female finches perform lots of monkey business with their tails as a manifestation of their frequent—all right, permanent—state of arousal. Sit in B's room when they're mounting one another and the breeze is palpable. If that popular metaphor for the interconnectedness of things known as "the butterfly effect" is correct in pointing out that a butterfly flapping its wings in China affects weather distantly elsewhere, our finches are probably responsible for meteorological upheavals in any number of places. Monsoons in India, twisters in Arkansas wiping out trailer parks. All I know is that Pee Wee's already elevated level of bliss seems a notch or two higher when she flutters her tail.

The other thing about her adolescence I considered suggestive of gender was how conspicuously uninterested she was in Baby's activities. A far cry from the latter's juvenile compulsion to follow B ad nauseam. While the prospect of Pee Wee giving Baby a taste of his own medicine had a certain karma-balancing appeal, Rebecca and I felt short on options (meaning rooms and lack of time) in the event that Baby and Pee Wee didn't get along. If you considered nothing more than the screen doors and the ever present seed casings crackling underfoot, it was already evident that Rebecca and I had strayed pretty far from the domestic values with which we were raised. My mother, who would have autoclaved bleach, waged an endless war against germs and clutter. It would trouble her to know that I work for the enemy.

Excepting, however, what you might call an occasional exchange of pleasantries, Pee Wee and Baby ignored one another. He probably knew prior to her first molt that she was female and therefore posed no territorial threat. House sparrow fights are infrequent and, unless the combatants are a mated pair, tend to be male-to-male or female-to-female affairs. Even Clive started behaving himself. I think it dawned on him that since he hadn't much luck bullying one house sparrow, his odds against two were bleaker still.

Beyond looking askance when Pee Wee landed on Rebecca, Baby minded his own business or flew to me if I happened to be present. This is around the time he developed his penchant for hair baths, one of only a couple of things he'll do with me but not with Rebecca. He paddles on top of my head the way outside sparrows wallow in dust. Rebecca's hair may be too straight or flat for bathing (or whatever it is he thinks he's doing up there), whereas mine stands up in interesting ways because it's thick and untamable. I'm nearly a foot taller than Rebecca and provide a better view. And yes, he now and then leaves mementos of his visit.

In any event, we never seriously considered giving up Pee Wee. It isn't every day a creature embodying supreme contentment falls, as it were, in your lap. Look at her when she sits on your finger blinking in that glacially slow way she has and you realize that your heart rate, blood pressure, and respiration have dropped and that the plaque in your arteries is dissolving away. I think I speak for Rebecca when I say that we'd have deeded the middle room to Baby if doing so had been our only means of keeping the peace. In that event, Pee Wee, who seems happy wherever she is, would have been stuck living with canaries. Daphne took no notice of her, and Clive, as I've said, was being civil. Now, of course, all this is moot. Avian hegemony over our upstairs is long since complete. "This worked out better than I thought it would," Rebecca remarked at the time. "We've absorbed a third sparrow into the house and still have one bedroom left as discretionary space."

Spring doesn't arrive officially for another two weeks, but every year about this time, B's hormone levels rise and he's a handful for several days until he adjusts psychically to the changes in his chemistry. Whatever juices are flowing make him dissatisfied and more than usually dictatorial.

He preens frequently. His neck itches. He nips my chin when I don't pay attention—even when he's only sitting on me or being otherwise unremarkable. Without any real interest in games, he brings me caps, including ones I'd forgotten we had. Odd ones dredged up from the bottom of his toy basket. He's nipping me now with enough pressure to make it painful but not excruciating. He's frustrated today and trying his damnedest to apprise me of the fact.

This is always a difficult time. B's unhappy, and I confront my limitations as a surrogate universe. He takes no interest in Pee Wee when she visits. They sit apart and look at their feet like awkward kids at a dance. The price B pays for never being cold, hungry, or stalked (aside from Baby's abortive attempts) is desire without an object—a harder lot in some ways than being jilted or spurned. Rebecca will be home soon and can seduce him into Love Bird. There's a good one-word pun in "sublimate" I must remember to mention. We'll add it to our B-related wordplay collection. Because he likes when I talk to him, I decide to be topical. I describe an advertisement in today's newspaper announcing a special on parakeets, a species that holds the record for having the largest avian vocabulary—more than twenty-five hundred words. At least according to the pet bird literature I picked up at the vet's. The ad says they make great "starter birds." I find this unsettling—as if these creatures were the commercial equivalent of a training bra. I look at B and shiver at the thought of him sitting in a store as a salable commodity.

After yanking on a day-old whisker, B zooms toward his wall mirror as I wince and curse, turns back in midflight when I mention corn—a word I've experimented with just to prove to myself that he really knows what it means. Careful never to vary the intonation, I've asked him if he'd like born, torn, morn, horn, worn—all to no effect. He's now stretched full length on my shoulder trying to see around my head as I grope for the plastic baggy containing treats that I slid behind the couch cushion so it wouldn't be pilfered. I think of Sir James Frazer's passage in The Golden Bough, "Amongst the Saxons of Transylvania, in order to keep sparrows from the corn, the sower begins by throwing the first handful of seed backwards over his head, saying, `That is for you, sparrows.'"

HERE'S A STATISTIC: WITH THE ADVENT OF BABY FOLLOWED BY PEE WEE, we were acquiring house sparrows at an average rate of one every three years. I mentioned this to Rebecca with the observation that the influx amounted to a regular deluge, considering that the first forty-one years of my life and the first twenty-nine of hers had passed without hatchlings pelting us from the eaves. Four weeks to the day after we found Pee Wee, sparrow number four (minus the ants but featherless, of course) arrived one evening in the usual spot. Pee Wee's younger brother from a subsequent brood is our guess. He lay quite still but was warm to the touch. In the brilliant evening light we had that day, his breathing was obvious even to me.

There's a food-burning tradition in Rebecca's family that's genetic. I watched her father carbonize three consecutive loaves of bread he intended to serve with the scarcely charred dinner he cooked for us one night when Rebecca and I visited him in Montana. I mention this because I was about to head inside with my find when Rebecca bustled onto the front porch carrying the blackened remains of a saucepan in which she'd been boiling what had been beans. "You do understand," I asked, "that with sufficient heat and time, water in a pan will boil away?"

"Oh, yes, but I got distracted," came the standard reply. "What have you got in your hand?"

"A big surprise."

"You're kidding me. You've got to be kidding me. Tell me you didn't find another sparrow."

"I didn't find another sparrow."

"Really?"

"No."

Had there been time, I would have liked to talk with her more about the smoldering pan cooling on the sidewalk. Vapors innocuous to us can be fatal to birds, their tiny respiratory systems being extremely fragile in this regard. We don't use aerosols; we don't burn incense. Kera, our erstwhile pet sitter, came within a deuce of losing her parrot to fumes he inhaled from a spray-on deodorant used in her house by a guest. When found, he lay on the bottom of his cage gasping for breath. Excepting Rebecca's lapses with the stove, we're fanatically careful.

Reviving Seven (you'd think in naming him after a number we'd have chosen Four, but Rebecca wanted Seven, as in Lucky Seven) went according to form except for the unusually long time it took us to get him eating—maybe, I hoped, his parents had given him a farewell dinner before kicking him out. Half an hour passed before he'd open up on his own. At one point, Rebecca slipped a fingernail between his beak and managed to insert a tiny bit of food, but he sat holding it in his mouth and refused to swallow. I worried he had internal injuries as a result of the fall. It continues to baffle me how birds survive these drops unscathed.

As a hatchling, B was feisty; Baby, spastic; Pee Wee, tranquil; Seven, grumpy. He's the easiest of the four to identify in baby photos because he's the one that appears to be frowning. The sides of his beak turned slightly downward at that stage and gave him the look of someone who's just found out his luggage is missing. That Seven's infant personality was reflected in a dour visage was a little bit eerie, but for whatever it's worth in the nurture-versus-nature debate, I must emphasize that although Rebecca and I had neither hoped for nor expected another sparrow to arrive within a month of Pee Wee having checked in, Seven was as well-provided-for and fawned over as any one of the other three. Rebecca doted on him shamelessly. "Because," she said, "he looked so burdened by the world."

Although Seven may be wired to the anxious side of normal and therefore easily frightened, he's as tame in his way as the rest of our sparrows. Perhaps parental rejection destroyed his faith in the reliability of others. If, indeed, he was banished from his nest, I'd like to know on what grounds. He seemed then and seems now a healthy, well-formed specimen to me. Rebecca thinks the fall traumatized him. No doubt it's terribly frightening to find yourself snug against your siblings one minute, slamming into the ground the next. Seven would blossom as an only bird. But B monopolizes me, and despite changes in their relationship, Rebecca and Baby are still very much an item. Pee Wee, always happy to see whomever whenever, thrives because she's willing to share. Of course, any attempt to psychoanalyze Seven must take into account his unfortunate run-in with a scrambled chicken egg—a story that brings me back to the canaries.

Not long before Pee Wee arrived, we started finding canary eggs. This wasn't surprising since, with the arrival of spring, Daphne and Clive discovered an activity they could do together; did so with an avidity that rivaled the finches' dedication to the craft. Results followed in the form of bluish, mottled eggs dropping out of Daphne's backside, a turn of events about which she seemed genuinely puzzled. Freshly laid eggs showed up everywhere—on the bed, the floor, in the sink. One rolled off the ceiling fan motor and hit me on the head. Rebecca said it was a good thing we weren't trying to support ourselves as canary breeders. Daphne's approach to egg laying was certainly an effective, if clumsy, method of birth control.

Presently, however, we noticed Clive hanging around as Daphne pulled threads out of an old towel we had a water dish sitting on. As the days passed, it became evident that cloth destruction was more than a passing fad with Daphne, more an addiction. If we stood a respectable distance away from her, she'd cast wary glances in our direction but continue demolishing the towel. She'd pull out one strand at a time in that quietly methodical way you associate with people who sit in the activity rooms of places that have the word "sanitarium" in their names. Removing threads seemed to be an end in itself. After tugging one free, she'd set it aside in a little pile and then begin on another. Quite hypnotizing, actually. I should have asked myself the big question: "What happens to the pile?"

It turns out that female canaries attend to all the nest-building chores. Clive's job involved staying out of Daphne's way and signaling our approach with a rising, elongated "Peep." In our absence, she moved hundreds of painstakingly acquired strands up to an unused plastic seed dish that had been sitting for months in a corner of the big cage she and Clive still use as a house.

The canaries were so secretive that they could have been building ICBMs in our bedroom during the day, and we wouldn't have known it. Except while sleeping, Rebecca and I spent little time in the back room. We'd get up in the morning, throw what amounted to a tarp over our bed, usher out the cats, and release the birds. Making it clear that they had no intention of spending their days cooped up with canaries, the sparrows clamored shortly after dawn to be let into the middle room. They'd head straight for the two ceiling-to-floor bookcases in that room, which they, with their innate predisposition to disport in cubbyholes, find endlessly compelling. We thought of finding a new home for the canaries, but the possibility of them ending their days caged somewhere is not a risk we're willing to take. And besides, Clive and Daphne grow on you after a while. For all the bitching I do about Clive's melodic excesses, his singing is so much a part of home life now as to be quite indispensable.

Daphne's egg-laying binge made her hungrier than usual and bold enough to take corn from my fingers when I distributed food every morning and evening. She'd sidle over to me in that jerky, tentative way animals have when struggling between hunger and fear. Rebecca started scrambling chicken eggs with powdered calcium mixed in—a big hit with Daphne. With Clive, too, when he began feeding the chick that hatched from one of the eggs Daphne incubated on the sly in her upholstered seed dish.

We named the new bird Timmy after Tiny Tim in *A Christmas Carol*. His right leg is tweaked and sticks out at a right angle from his body. Our vet tried remedying the problem by folding Timmy's leg into its proper position and placing him inside a paper tube that would hold him motionless while the leg readjusted. We were instructed to keep him that way for at least a week. He looked like a circus performer about to be shot from a cannon (he was inside an abbreviated toilet paper roll), and Clive stopped feeding him. We released him after a day.

As an adult, Timmy's leg makes for a few minor problems, mostly by throwing him off balance and sometimes causing him to skid on his belly when landing. All things considered, I think we were correct in discontinuing the physical therapy; I doubt he'd have survived it. Although incapable of the hell-for-leather flight of the sparrows or even the somewhat less powerful locomotion of his parents, he moves with a daffy, endearing grace and has adapted well.

My favorite image of Timmy is of him motoring down the hall one morning, entering the middle room, and circumnavigating me as I stood with Pee Wee in my right hand, Seven in my left, Baby on top of my head. He made two complete orbits before puttering back to the canary room. Had he worn an old-fashioned aviator's helmet, his performance would have been flawless.

Seven, a month younger, learned to feed himself more quickly than Timmy and was flying even before Timmy's primary flight feathers had finished growing in. Clive and Daphne were indulgent parents that seemed to realize their son was a "special needs" child progressing at a slower pace than the hot-shot sparrows. For months, Clive gobbled up and transferred to Timmy a good bit of the egg and corn we supplied in abundance. Competition for the egg was stiff because Seven favored it then above all other foods. Baby and Pee Wee liked it well enough (B is indifferent to egg), but ate only dignified amounts from the share we placed each morning in the middle room. Seven's policy was to abstract the canaries' portion after polishing off his own allotment—petty larceny that exacted a penalty.

It was mid-September, Rebecca was out of town on a business trip, and I'd gone upstairs to hand out cookie before leaving the house to run errands. I found an agitated Seven trailing a hair behind him in the canary room. He flitted from perch to perch, stopping every few seconds to wipe his beak. Rebecca's hair is long, mine even longer, and because we shed, we're a menace. Every six months or so one of the birds gets a leg snarled in a strand we've dropped, and I resolve to either get a crew cut or begin daubing my locks with an industrial fixative. This wouldn't neutralize the threat Rebecca poses, but at least I could claim moral superiority. My good intentions wane after I forget what a pain in the ass it is to catch and restrain whichever bird has gotten entangled. The sparrows more or less cooperate, but the procedure becomes a career when the victim's a finch or canary that thinks Rebecca and I are pursuing our lunch.

After ten minutes of coaxing, Seven landed in my hand long enough for me to see that he didn't have a hair around his foot. He'd swallowed one. I cupped him in my free hand, pinning his head between my middle and index fingers in such a way that he was lying on his back in the palm of the hand that had covered him from above but an instant before.

Apologizing like crazy for restraining him, I tugged gently and without success on a strand that extended ten inches or more from Seven's mouth. I had visions of it wound in an unyielding mare's nest around every one of his organs. A simplified schematic of damaged bird anatomy kept popping into my head along with Rebecca's description of a girlhood dog her family owned that ate a pair of pantyhose. Their pet's nonconformist choice of entrée came to light when Rebecca observed her squatting and yelping in the yard, an odd mass dangling from "Emily's" rectum. Rebecca's mother donned a pair of latex gloves and made the supreme sacrifice by holding on to the now extremely used undergarment while Emily struggled forward and completed the extraction. As disgusting as this was to contemplate, the story offered hope: Emily survived to eat other inedibles. I snipped off all but about two inches of Seven's hair, put him in a travel cage, and called the vet.

"Hi. I'd like to bring my bird in right away."

"Is it sick?"

"Swallowed a hair."

"How do you know?"

"I can see it."

"Have you tried pulling it out?"

"Yes."

"And . . . ?"

"Seems to be stuck."

Escorted by a vet tech who weighed Seven and confirmed my diagnosis, they put me in an exam room as soon as I got there. No doubt they get lots of people fabricating swallowed-hair stories so they can skip to the front of the line. When the doctor arrived, she held Seven as I had done, tugged on the hair and failed to remove it as I had done. I must reiterate that I'm a coward in these situations, absolutely craven. I hate being out of control when the stakes are high. Even though I don't know the first thing about piloting an airplane, I'd be far more comfortable traveling by air if they'd hand me the stick when I board. You can't live with house sparrows as I have done without developing a profound empathy for their feelings. The sight of Seven pinioned in a big human mitt with his beak pried open made me weak in the knees.

The vet said that if all else failed, she'd crop the hair as short as possible and rely on Seven to pass the rest. "All else" consisted of clamping a small pair of forceps onto the hair and pulling again from inside Seven's mouth. My head swam. Why the forceps ploy worked when fingers did not is between the vet and Seven. He looked decidedly uncomfortable as the strand, the nether end of which was embedded in a piece of scrambled egg, slid slowly upwards and emerged without breaking. The hair wasn't wavy, so I looked forward to teasing Rebecca that evening when she called to check in.

"Oh, my God, you mean they actually had to operate?"

"Yep, laid him open from stem to stern. Used special glasses so they could see to untie all the little knots."

BABY HELD A GRUDGE FOR THREE MONTHS, AND REBECCA ADMITS making a mistake when she changed her itinerary so she could visit her sister in Laguna Beach rather than come straight home after the conference she'd attended was over. Since she hadn't seen Jenny in more than a year, I encouraged her to do so. The sparrows were molting and easy to manage. Except for the incident with Seven, I was having a peaceful time running things solo. When Rebecca called each night from her sister's, I understated Baby's reaction to her absence. A truthful answer when she asked, "Does Baby miss me?" would have had her on the first Portland-bound plane out of L.A.

Baby spent most of the day sitting on Rebecca's vanity making sad, mewing chirps. The only time he'd play Get the Bird is when he'd hear Rebecca's voice coming out of the phone when she and I spoke. He'd fly to the mirror in his house (because of the way it reverberates off the bars when struck, I'd wager) and dash off a series of staccato pecks as if he were sending Rebecca a coded message. Afternoon servings of grape perked him up, but he'd then revert to singin' the blues. He lost hope after two days that noise from downstairs meant Rebecca had come home. He gave up plastering himself on the screen in expectation of seeing her walk up the stairs. His songs became more plaintive by the day, notes drifting higher into the treble clef—an interesting contrast to B's deepening silence as his molt progressed.

B resented it, but I spent extra time with Baby that week. I'd go in, sit in the rocker, and wait for his descent to my shoulder from the little fort he'd built earlier in the year on one of the upper bookcase shelves. It's a property he ferries stuff to, jealously maintains, and guards against Seven. "Chez Baby" is the first place Rebecca looks whenever she's missing her bus pass, earrings, photographs, or one of her precious lists; twenty-dollar bills have ended up in there. Baby watches in silent horror as Rebecca sifts through his collection of precisely arranged junk. Were he a little old man, he'd have the collected newspapers of a lifetime bundled and stacked in accordance with an arcane inventory system that had meaning only to him. I sat in the rocker with Baby in hand, listened to the barely audible sounds B's feet and wings made next door when he changed his listening position on the heating vent.

Rebecca's cab pulled up out front late Sunday afternoon. From B's window, I could see her digging in her handbag. Since she loses something important about once a week, I felt chances were good I'd be paying off the balding Pakistani chap who'd driven her home from the airport. By the time I made it downstairs, however, she was on the front porch rummaging through luggage, searching in vain for her house key. As regards our respective relationship to our possessions, Rebecca and I are closed books to one another. In her mind, she doesn't spend any more time hunting things down when they're needed than I do keeping track of them to begin with. The dazzling illogic of her approach is offset, as far as I'm concerned, by the stunning fact that she's never misplaced any of our birds. And birds were on her mind when she swept through the door: "Hi, sweetie," she said, "follow me upstairs, I'm dying to see Baby." I felt like a butler with an unfortunate last name.

I assumed their reunion would reprise the "love conquers all" theme of my post-England return to B. Rebecca, anticipating same, was visibly disappointed to not find Baby clinging to the screen door when we got upstairs. When she sang out "Where's my Chicolini?" there was an absence of Baby racing to her shoulder. Other than a couple of greeting chirps from B, all was silence—as if the other birds were eavesdropping. It took Rebecca several minutes to locate Baby hunkered on the bookshelf, obscured in plain view. He looked as though he expected a siege.

In the old screwball comedy *Twentieth Century*, John Barrymore's character says, "I close the iron gate on you" whenever he dismisses friends and associates who've displeased him. While I can't honestly tell you that Baby said anything of the kind, you don't often see body language more expressive of the sentiment. He stood and turned his back when Rebecca offered her hand by reaching up to where he sat near the entrance to his cluttered estate. When she tried again, he sidestepped away. He put himself to bed early that evening, forgoing his customary nightcap of apple and millet—an eloquent gesture of pique on the part of a molting bird whose appetite was keen. Late the next afternoon, Baby landed on Rebecca long enough to confirm, as it seemed, that she was actually there and not an illusion.

I have no certain explanation for his behavior; Rebecca had been away before, albeit for much shorter periods. If B had set a precedent by shunning me after one of my lengthy disappearances, I might have concluded, "Well, that's just the way house sparrows are." I suggested to Rebecca that Baby had gotten it into his head that she'd been off somewhere having sex with other birds. "But what does he *want* from me?" she kept asking as weeks passed and Baby's refusal to accept her penance became, if anything, more resolute. She'd sit being ignored by him for hours on end. But when she left the room, he'd shriek. He had her in tears. Except in Rebecca's presence when he'd pay me excessive, showy attention, my relationship with him remained as even-keeled as ever. He knew all about twisting the knife.

Rebecca was showering one morning in mid-December when Baby relented. He flew into the bathroom through the half-opened door, landed on the hook holding her towel, began chirping in the concerned, interrogative way sparrows have when confronting nude people. Rebecca dripped her way back to the middle room with Baby riding atop the towel she'd wrapped around her hair. Within minutes, the sound of "Get the Bird" echoed through the house again—for Rebecca, the most joyous carol she heard that season. Baby acted as if the whole era of bad feeling between them had been a misunderstanding he didn't wish to discuss. "Typical man," Rebecca observed, cocking an eyebrow in my direction.

Initially, I viewed Rebecca as a wronged woman in her long imbroglio with Baby. Although hesitant, naturally, to anthropomorphize the situation, I speculated that Baby indulged himself in a protracted sulk because he hadn't gotten his way for ten days. Rebecca and I joked that he'd heard rumors that she'd been feeding croissants in the morning to birds outside her hotel. Rebecca followed him around the room asking, "Is that what all this is about?" Later, I decided that Baby had a less frivolous (at least to him) reason for behaving as he did.

I think Rebecca's return upset Baby more than her absence. House sparrows must understand loss, I imagine; embrace the grim optimism of a "Here today, gone tomorrow" philosophy in order to cope with the reality of being prey. You may argue that coping doesn't enter into it, that sparrows have no more foreknowledge of death than a stone has of erosion, but I don't believe it. Humans once thought themselves the only tool-using animals, a belief now known to be patently false. House sparrows are too bright and, in my opinion, too emotionally complex not to have an inkling that the bell eventually tolls for them. How they visualize the concept is anyone's guess—a plunge that wings are powerless to reverse, unhearable silence, a cat's gaping mouth.

Rebecca disappears, is presumed dead; Rebecca returns without an explanation that Baby can fathom. Maybe he bursts with joy but can't get past his outrage that she faked her own death. "Don't ever do that to me again" could have been the message he tried driving home to her each day of their estrangement. A fanciful hypothesis that fails to explain why B never closed the iron door on me.

It's four in the morning, and B blinks in the flashlight beam I'm shining into his house. We had an earth tremor a few minutes ago that woke Rebecca and sent Pee Wee diving under the bed. I assume it was little more than a blip on the Richter scale but a reminder, nonetheless, that Portland straddles a number of restive faults and lies close to where the North American and Pacific plates grind against each other to form one of the world's livelier earthquake zones. The geologic record indicates that this area gets a "Big One" once every two hundred years or so. We're due.

I woke with Rebecca crawling over me on her way to Baby who was thrashing about, desperate to escape whatever invisible force had jiggled him out of a sound sleep inside his nest. While Rebecca worked to calm him, I rode the crest of my adrenaline rush out into the hallway and found the flashlight that, for once, was on top of the blanket chest where it's supposed to be. Poking my head into B's room, I determined with a sweep of the beam that he was safe on his perch. A head count of finches showed all five in their customary places—Bert and Lisa on the air nest, Bart and Kess on the belled whirligig that hangs in a corner, Monday asleep in the dead ficus tree. Saying, "I'll be back in a minute, B," I headed off to check on Pee Wee and Seven, known to us in plural as The Kids.

Birds now own the back room. With Clive striking up the band at dawn and the sparrows campaigning to be let out to join Baby in the middle room, sleeping there became unprofitable—its comfortable snugness a thing of the past. Although the sparrows flit in and out, the canaries have the room to themselves pretty much all day. At night, The Kids go to roost by burrowing beneath the towel on top of Clive and Daphne's house—the large cage sitting on a shelf I installed above the sink. Flattening themselves against the bars like feathered patties, Seven sleeps on the left, Pee Wee on the right. Timmy roosts on top of the towel, somewhere in the middle.

We keep the closet light burning for just such contingencies as this when, because it's been frightened, a bird might launch out into what would otherwise be unnavigable darkness. Unlike in B's room, little outside light finds its way in.

As missing-bird incidents go, this one was anticlimactic. Before I could panic over my discovery that Pee Wee wasn't in her place, a flutter of wings directed me to her. I nudged the closet door open with my foot and let enough light into the room that the birds could have done barrel rolls had they felt a need to do so. Pee Wee stood under the bed, a few inches back from the throw rug next to it. Saying "Up, Pee Wee," I lay out prone and offered her my finger. Rebecca wandered in at this point to report that Baby was back in his nest. She told him the earthquake was my fault and that she'd make it a point to strip me of my powers. I handed off Pee Wee and returned to B.

I'm seated in my usual spot on B's couch, flashlight off. B, silhouetted against the cloth that covers the side of his house where he sleeps, has reversed heading on his perch four or five times since I came in, looks like a tiny, disgruntled man tossing around on a vertical bed. Lately, I've been good about not drifting in here at night. Doing so wakes B and serves no purpose other than to allay the irrational fears for his safety that I've harbored since his first night in this house. But having survived an earthquake together seems a decent enough excuse to sit a few minutes watching him hint that what he'd really like is for me to go away. Unable to resist the pun, I tell B how proud I am that he remained unflappable during the tremor. I'd have bet Pee Wee would have been the one to stand her ground, that she'd have used some mystical technique to convince herself that quivering walls were only an illusion.

Rebecca opens the outside door, asks in a whisper if everything's OK. She says she's wide awake, too. I tell her everything's fine, that I'll be right out. I hope she wasn't sucking around for an invitation—she can be maddeningly indirect. B changes direction again, and by giving his mirror a couple of short taps calls for more silence and less talk.

The finches peep and rustle when I exit while B, in this way he has of making you feel as if he suspects you're stealing from him, leans around his canopy and watches me go. Rebecca's probably correct in believing that if he owned silverware, he'd spend hours counting it.

WHAT WE NEED IS ANOTHER FEMALE HOUSE SPARROW. AS IT STANDS, Baby and The Kids live together with a certain amount of friction—the inevitable consequence of our having run out of bedrooms. They form a tenuous ménage à trois in the traditional (and accurate) sense of the term. Which is to say, a permanent household or living arrangement made up of three members, rather than three participants having an ad hoc sexual encounter in a room with scarlet carpet and mirrored ceilings. It seems to me that two males paired with two females (at least nominally) might neutralize some of the competitive tension that derives from the gender imbalance we currently have. Instead of squabbling, the couples could play canasta all day.

Baby and Seven don't necessarily loathe one another, but a mutual antipathy smolders between them that peaks in spring when they're strutting around with their gonads on fire. Sometimes they end up in a clinch and pull each other's feathers. The balance of the year they bicker. It's mostly a property dispute. Seven covets Baby's shelf despite the existence of an identical bookcase on the other side of the big double window in the center of the room. A bookcase with identical shelves filled, as far as Seven is likely concerned, with identical books. Baby, forced by circumstance to protect his property, spends hours parading back and forth in front of his fort. I'm thinking of giving him a little toy rifle with a rubber bayonet.

Baby is clearly the injured party. Any fair adjudication of the case would award him damages—and a restraining order. After all, he staked his claim and made improvements to the property long before Seven's arrival. On the other hand, a skilled advocate for Seven's position could argue that his client provides a healthy diversion that keeps Baby on his toes.

Our middle bedroom is a lively place when Baby and The Kids are excited and three canaries are sailing in for visits. It's like a busy airport without traffic controllers. To stand without flinching while a high-speed chase brings three sparrows careening toward your head takes some getting used to. The thing to remember is that bird reflexes are better than yours. Much better. Chances of them colliding with you are extremely small if you simply stand still, far greater if you move. Don't, in other words, zig when they zag.

Everywhere you look there's a bird passing through—especially in the mornings when they're filled with an infectious compulsion to be up and about. Nothing is sacrosanct, not even the bathroom. One or more sparrows escort us to the can; we bathe with an audience. I often have three of them squawking on the shower enclosure as I lather the torso. Pee Wee will sit on Rebecca's head while she stands in the spray.

A downside to all this hilarity is that Pee Wee is in constant demand from early spring until late in the summer. Because she and Seven were raised together, Seven assumes that life has provided him with a built-in mate. He's obsessed with making more sparrows, or at least with his part in the process. Baby originally paid little attention to these erotic (and very public) interludes, preferring Rebecca's company and his shelf-guarding activities to involving himself in anything carnal. Seven's cupidity seemed to strike him as the sort of crude behavior that well-bred gentlemen affected to ignore.

Pee Wee herself isn't all that enthused. Her attitude toward sex actually seems somewhat Victorian, as if the best she can hope for from the process is to close her eyes and think of England. The ferocity with which she'll often fight off Seven's advances stands in marked contrast to her usual even-tempered acceptance of whatever comes along. Sometimes she clings to us for protection, hoping we'll shoo her pursuer away—a thing I hate doing to Seven, especially since the contretemps with the hair made his innate jumpiness worse. Of the four, he might most easily have overcome a pampered infancy and been happy in the wild. But it's hard to send your children to war.

Pee Wee is happiest when sitting in our hands or helping Baby expand his collection of junk (assistance Baby could do without) or cooperating with Seven in the wholesome activity of building a nest. She's shown no interest in incubating any of the numerous eggs she's laid. She hunkers down, pushes one out, and then deliberately rolls it off a ledge with her beak; I suspect Daphne has given her pointers. After what must have been a rough delivery, we found her groggy and unsteady on the bed one morning, a freshly laid egg smashed in the sink.

We'd have been out of our minds with worry had not our female finches displayed similar symptoms on occasion. They'd remain grounded (but damn hard to catch) for an hour or two and then rebound as if nothing at all unusual had happened. A potentially lethal condition occurs when an egg binds and can't be pushed out; the victim squats, straining to no avail. Cockatiels are prone to it. This wasn't the case with Pee Wee, but she lolled on her side and could barely stand. While I dug out the travel cage, Rebecca phoned the vet.

Perhaps the car ride bucked her up. All we had to show for our trouble was a radiant, healthy bird that flew to my shoulder when we entered the exam room and I opened the cage. We left feeling, however, that the trip had not been wasted. After describing our concerns about the egg-laying toll Seven's attentions were inflicting on Pee Wee, the vet informed us that science had an answer in the form of human chorionic gonadotropin, or HCG. Levels of this hormone rise during the first trimester of pregnancy in human females; it's the substance tested for in urine to confirm pregnancy. Injected into birds, it works to inhibit egg production. Except, of course, in Pee Wee.

Last year near the end of July, Rebecca's work-at-home days ended for a period of weeks owing to the start of a new project that required her daily presence in the office. Either in response to her more frequent absence or coincidental with it, Baby began heeding his instinctual obligation to rally around and help Seven seduce Pee Wee—that male house sparrow solidarity thing. But he soon realized that forming his own alliance with Pee Wee promised anatomical and strategic returns that Rebecca couldn't provide. He acted for a time like an adolescent who suddenly finds his mother a lot less interesting than the girl next door. And Pee Wee, adroit at playing two suitors against one another, soon turned this development to her advantage. By not saying yes and not saying no, she kept two beaus but no lovers. She stopped laying eggs. The boys quarreled, but they did that anyway.

Thanks to Pee Wee's skill at dividing her attention between Baby and Seven, a tenuous equilibrium now prevails. It even fosters a spirit of cooperation when the need arises. This was in evidence recently as I sat in B's room reading, B on my shoulder, both of us drowsy. The crash when it came sent B to the heating vent and me to my feet.

Baby and The Kids were lined up on the top shelf of the bookcase; a framed picture of Rebecca's father lay on the floor. I'd noticed the three of them earlier in the day fooling around with the felt-covered flap that propped the picture in place. It never occurred to me they'd have the strength or inclination to dump it on the floor. They stayed in place when I hustled in from B's room, watched calmly as I approached their shelf. Three bird heads tilted downward as I knelt and picked the picture up. "All right," I said, turning back to the bookcase, "who's responsible for this?" I spoke in a normal conversational tone, but they took my question as a preamble to ass-kicking, bolted as if composed of one body and mind fleeing for its life. They disassembled an impossibly short time later into three separate birds sitting atop the canary-room screen door. It was like witnessing a bizarre, cutting-edge physics experiment in which an effect appears to precede its cause.

B TURNS EIGHT IN ANOTHER TWO MONTHS. REBECCA DRAWS A DEEP breath every year at this time as we head into the long days of summer when it often seems there are too few hours strictly our own. But, as Rebecca says, "Any day's a good day when our birds are healthy and happy." A simple philosophy that expresses a fundamental truth about our lives. Unfortunately, it's of limited value in helping us cope with one of the consequences of daily life inside this cuckoo clock that is our home: life breeds more life.

I thought about this fact while walking home from the grocery store one day last August. As I approached the corner where our old gray house sits, it occurred to me how pretty and well tended our domicile looks from the outside. This isn't to say we'd win landscaping awards, only that strangers passing by might very well conclude that the people who live here make an effort to keep up their property. We've made improvements: the shade garden with a privacy fence around it; new steps and porches both front and back; bushes and small trees—some potted, some in-ground. Inside, I've tiled the entryway, laid a parquet floor in the kitchen, replaced the old sink, installed better fixtures. We have a new gas furnace, that sort of thing. Other touches here and there. There's also evidence of projects I've started but never completed. The downstairs bathroom is a case in point. Every morning I glance up from the newspaper and am reminded by the unfinished paint job on the kitchen ceiling that spending my free time with birds is a lot more fun than screwing around with rollers and ladders.

What you don't see from the street, or even necessarily notice after coming inside on a brief social call, is how teeming this place is with insects and vermin—creatures that to a greater or lesser extent are as much a result of having uncaged birds in residence as is the metabolized output of our avian friends. The latter, of course, is abundantly evident throughout our upstairs.

I suppose I should be thankful for the various four- and six-legged beasties that conduct their business here. I suppose I should value bird shit as well. It's a given, after all, that every story needs forces in opposition to the protagonists, a clash of competing interests on which to hang a plot. Rebecca and I have struggled for a long time against what crawls, scurries, and splats in our midst. But from a dramatic standpoint, the action hasn't gotten us anywhere: the plot hasn't thickened; nothing's been resolved. After years of contention, we've battled to a draw. Our real difficulty relates less to the specifics of dealing with unwanted life forms infesting the premises, or to cleaning up after our birds, than it does to maintaining a measure of sanity in spite of it all.

An absurdist approach works best for us. We haven't joined the Dada camp, but we've been in touch with the membership committee. Our solution has been to redefine sanity, to laugh off what our peers consider a highly questionable way to live. To a certain extent, Rebecca and I lead double lives. Like spies at large in the outer world, we work hard to maintain our cover. And we manage to blend in. If you ran across us at the symphony, you'd think, "There's a respectable couple. The guy's a bit scraggly but seems decent enough." At home, though, we're really in our element. As Rebecca puts it, "We're married. What do we care? May as well let ourselves go."

10

DON'T TRY THIS AT HOME

We were walking on, surrounded, enclosed, enveloped, being
eaten alive by *ants*.
—Barbara Kingsolver, *The Poisonwood Bible*

Look, look, a mouse!
—William Shakespeare, *King Lear*

My bowels boiled, and rested not. (Job)

"I ATE ANTS," REBECCA ANNOUNCED AS SHE STOOD AT THE FOOT OF
our bed wiping her tongue with a paper towel.

"Excuse me?"

"I ate ants!"

"Why?" I asked, fixing on the question of motive.

"What do you mean 'Why?' They're in the raisin bran; that's *why*."

"Sorry," I replied, stifling a yawn, "I thought you were bragging."
She threw her paper towel at me and stomped out.

I joined her in the kitchen a few minutes later prepared to apologize
for having been flippant, or at least pretend to apologize for having
been flippant. Someone who wakes you from a sound sleep first thing
in the morning by declaring they've eaten ants pretty much forfeits
their right to be taken seriously. This line of reasoning had evidently

occurred to Rebecca. "Sorry I woke you," she said without sarcasm after I'd seated myself at the table and she'd placed before me a bowl that contained twenty or thirty ant corpses floating in milk.

Having risen early and gone downstairs for her morning feeding, she'd poured herself a big helping of raisin bran instead of cooking oatmeal, her usual fare. So far, so good; easy to visualize the sequence of events. It's harder to credit that she downed an entire portion of cereal despite noticing after a single mouthful that it "tasted funny." Hard to credit until you recall that Rebecca is never meaningfully awake until after breakfast, by which time her circuits have warmed up like so many vacuum tubes in an old radio set. It's not that she's sleepwalking, more a dreamy twilight fugue wherein her brain's happy to go along with anything related to food as long as her hands continue shoveling it in.

"You think that's gross," Rebecca continued, pointing at the bowl, "have a look at this." She slid over the cereal box inside of which the contents milled in a mildly swarming sort of way. We keep cereal in a cabinet above the stove, out from which and into which two lanes of ants flowed like bumper-to-bumper traffic on a beach highway over Labor Day weekend. Single-file columns disappeared into a crack between baseboard and floor. This was the state of our pest problem three months before we discovered B.

"How'd they taste?"

"Terrible. The way they smell when you crush them. I think we should call an exterminator."

That smell, of course, was formic acid—a colorless irritant central to the quality of being an ant. It's why anthills are called formicaria and why our house is one big formicarium. Birds of many species take "ant baths" periodically, a practice that has never caught on here. Some squat on anthills and pick up passengers by ruffling their feathers. Others crush ants in their beaks, preening themselves with the resulting puree. Formic acid discourages feather mites.

We're hosting a party this evening. It's a little surprising that we know as many people as we do who are not only willing to attend but seem eager to do so. They probably expect Rebecca and I will be announcing a decision to have ourselves surgically altered so we'll look like birds. I'm sorry to disappoint them. We just thought it would be nice to celebrate the social flexibility we've gained recently with the ending of daylight saving time—the annual beginning of lights-down early for B and the others. I have every confidence this gathering will be pleasant. The day augurs well because I woke this morning to find bananas on the hood of every car in our neighborhood within a two-block radius. A similar thing happened last year, but in that case it was pears. Maybe this time around there's a philanthropic chimp on the loose.

B, of course, is pissed off, his posture suggesting that he's a bird that knows a traitor when he sees one. He sits on my toes glaring at me, avoiding my eyes when I glance his way. Having people in means getting the house ready, which means Rebecca and I have been busy most of the afternoon working downstairs. The perpetually pregnant young woman who fumigates things for us every couple of weeks phoned up last night with a hacking cough she caught from her two-year-old. You don't realize what an inconvenience germs are until someone you're relying on gets sick and bows out. I'd finished scrubbing the bathroom, when Rebecca passed through saying, "I'm having serious bird guilt. I'm on my way upstairs to visit Baby and The Kids." Since I needed a break and wanted to see B, this confluence of sentiment worked out fine.

"Bird guilt" isn't as loony or onerous as it sounds. It's shorthand for the feeling Rebecca and I get whenever circumstances are such that we've been unable to give our sparrows the kind of attention they need and expect. Of course, we profit from the arrangement as much as they do. To my mind, B dissecting me with a frosty eye is a damn sight more interesting than, for example, any television program I could expect to see.

I'm thinking out loud about this stuff, trying to mollify a disgruntled bird by keeping things chatty. He leaves a turd on my toe and flies to his mirror, appears at the moment to be debating his next move. Rebecca would say, "How sweet. B gave you a present he made himself." I flick my gift into the garbage bag and tell B his options are dwindling. I'm willing to sit here another five minutes before returning to my labors downstairs. It's late afternoon, and there's lots left to do.

Contrary to popular belief, I like a clean house. And although she tends to generate clutter (the detritus, as she tells it, of an active mind in an active body), so does Rebecca. We're attempting to create an illusion today, one that will convince guests that we live with more gentility than we actually do. We seek to fool the eye, trompe l'oeil as the French would say.

We're practiced magicians who know how to combine the hard work of cleaning with the prestidigitation of the right kind of lighting. Rebecca usually sets an array of candles across the mantle and at other strategic locations that will light up the high dining and living room ceilings, leave in shadow what needs to remain there. The only evidence of birds this evening will come from the various statues of them that punctuate our decor. Although not the best rendered of the lot, I suppose my favorite is the replica sitting on a bookcase of the eponymous object that Bogart chased in the movie version of The Maltese Falcon. *It was, after all, "The stuff that dreams are made of."*

B is now on my shoulder, daring me to leave when I said I would. It's time for me to confront the kitchen—our primary source of embarrassment when people visit whom we don't know very well. Some will be on hand tonight. Our close friends understand that there's life beneath the surface here, that the sound of movement in the walls is no cause for concern. Rebecca has instructed me to act surprised, to say, "Now that shouldn't be" if neophyte guests mention ants, moths, or mice they've just seen.

I'll state for the record that in my opinion, ants, once acquired, are a permanent fixture. Short of going to the nuisance of detonating a homemade hydrogen bomb (you can't buy one—I've checked), nothing gets rid of them. I honestly believe ants would survive here even if I torched our house and salted the ground where it stood. There will be brown sugar ants on this location until after the next glacier passes through. Let me be clear on this: nothing gets rid of them. Certainly not the "ant traps" one buys after being suckered in by the outrageous fiction that entire ant colonies will perish when the poison the traps contain is carried by workers back to their nests. Ants avoid them—assiduously. Sprinkling cinnamon on ant trails doesn't work, nor does mint or any of the other "earth-friendly" remedies that people who've never actually had ants often recommend. Professional exterminators I've talked with have never come right out and said, "Good luck, chump," but I recognize their temptation to do so by the way they shake their heads.

Oh, you can kill an individual ant, or hundreds, or thousands; makes no difference, there are always more. I used to pour stuff called Terro, a clear, viscous poison—active ingredient Borax—onto little cardboard squares that came with the bottle. I believed it to be the ultimate weapon. Ants gathered in droves to lap it up, circling like cattle at a watering hole. This resulted in dead ants everywhere, but headquarters sent reinforcements, and overall, their numbers increased. I began to admire them. They're a hell of a lot more numerous and a damn sight better organized than people; possibly smarter. Ants will be annoying whatever supplants mammals once the inevitable extinction of our line is complete. I recall reading that if you gathered up and weighed all animal life on earth, ants would make up 10 to 15 percent of the total. As you can see, we're well on our way to being replaced. As far as I'm concerned, ant ascendancy is a foregone conclusion.

I believe the ants in this house are descended from those in residence when I bought the place in 1989. They were well behaved, relatively scarce. Now and then I'd see a pair of them in the kitchen moving at a brisk pace as though late for a meeting where they were expected to speak. They didn't bother me, I didn't bother them. Détente ended a few weeks before Rebecca's astonishing raisin bran performance when I discovered a roiling knot of the little monsters ravishing a LifeSaver in my top dresser drawer. Eight years later, dresser long removed to a different location, ants still monitor the place where it stood. I infer from this that ants archive data on every food discovery a colony ever makes. Even during winter when they seem to more or less hibernate, lone scouts keep tabs on all the places—countertops, for example—where their records indicate that vigilance was rewarded.

I don't know why ants burst forth as an inescapable presence here. We've always been cluttered but not what you'd call completely unhygienic. Which is to say, we're not in the habit of leaving decomposing food lying about. But we're not perfect. The cats strew kibble in their wakes, Rebecca has mishaps with sugar, and I forget to rinse my plate. For one thing, ants like water and will congregate around sinks to obtain it. With food we leave out for our birds added to the equation, any chance we had of starving the ants into submission pretty much vanished. And because we have birds, out went the thought of paying to have the house sprayed with carcinogens. I remember listening to an interview on NPR with a Harvard entomologist who specialized in ants. Here, I thought, is a guy whose brain I'd like to pick. I didn't listen long before I wanted to get his tenure revoked. It's all very well to spend one's life enthralled by ants, quite another thing to recommend that people plagued with them in their homes merely sit back and "enjoy the prehistoric splendor of their guests." In the long run, of course, you don't have a choice. The professor sounded delighted about it.

We're not without defenses. Stopgap measures, I admit, but anything helps. I'm proudest of Garbage Island. Applied technology that impedes the ants in their quest for edible trash while symbolizing the human capacity to win a battle, if not the war. It commemorates an era. Guests love its sleek postmodernist lines dominating one corner of our kitchen, my eclectic use of adhesives and plastic—the optional tour. The thing is simplicity itself: garbage can stands atop an upside-down storage bin that's been ant-proofed with a band of duct tape encircling it with the sticky side out. You're thinking, "Why not simply wrap tape around the can and be done with it? Your pedestal, sir, is superfluous." In the first place, the garbage can's design makes it difficult to apply tape without leaving gaps under which ants could easily crawl. And on purely aesthetic grounds, I like the inverted post-and-lintel aspect of the thing. Makes me feel I have a connection with early cathedral builders. If I could work in flying buttresses, I would. Originally, we employed a moat with the can standing in about four inches of water inside the bin. While effective, it was also swampy. Rebecca and I got tired of coming down with malaria and yellow fever, of having to add water before the level dwindled enough for the ants to find portage. As it is now, the only necessary maintenance is to replace the tape after it attracts a traversable pelt of cat fur and dust.

B flies into Hugh's old house whenever I come into his room. I gather he finds me tiresome this morning. I'm in the second day of a head cold and explode periodically in torrents of snot. My father was a robust sneezer, and having listened to him blow through walls when I was a kid predisposes me to do the same. I've heard it said that a person's heart stops beating during a sneeze, so maybe B's telling me he's a little squeamish about sitting on the shoulder of an intermittent corpse. As far as I can tell, birds don't sneeze. The closest B comes to clearing his pipes in this way is to fling into the air a beak-full of spit.

With B leaning down and forward on his perch while eyeing me intently, I'm too self-conscious to get very far in the book I'm reading. He's probably waiting for my next blowout but looks like a bird that can't remember whether flight begins with jumping or flapping. It makes me self-conscious when he stares at me in such a disapproving way; I feel as though he's looking over my shoulder to see if my lips move while I read. Three tandem sneezes convulse me. Each one loud enough to send a bird as nervous as Seven ducking for cover in a parallel universe. Unfazed by the noise and spray, B flies over with a piece of fringe he seems to have plucked from thin air. I know what he's thinking, "The old boy looks gruesome today; I'll shove this string up his nose—should make him as right as rain."

Their winter hiatus over, ants trickle in under the closed window. It's a sure bet that whenever I glance at the sill at least one ant will be either coming or going. The idea that ants "trickle" is apt. An image of seeping water is essential to understanding their genius as trespassers. If you'd care to examine my window casements, you'll find indications of failed containment efforts involving tape, spackle, and caulk. There's a well-known D. H. Lawrence poem called "Snake" in which he describes an encounter he has with the title character at a watering trough in Sicily. "The voice of my education," the poet says, warns him that the snake is venomous and should be killed. But he confesses liking the visitor, finds himself glad it "had come like a guest in quiet, to drink at my water trough." It's only after the snake has slaked its thirst and begun to retreat into a "dreadful hole" that Lawrence is compelled to action by his horror of the blackness into which the snake pours itself. He throws a log after the slowly retreating form—an action immediately regretted as "paltry" and "vulgar," and by the end of the poem, "something to expiate; A pettiness."

I'm not enough of a visionary to claim that I've learned to like ants. I can't say that observing their quiet persistence endows me with some deeper appreciation of the natural world that only invading insects can provide. When, however, my fingers aren't reeking of formic acid because I've reflexively dabbed at a tickling on my cheek, I'll admit that living with ants could be worse. So what if they pick through my garbage? They're not poisonous, they don't burrow into your brain as you sleep, don't transmit parasites that turn people's bowels into rioting tenements. They do bite sometimes, but this always strikes me as an act of desperation rather than policy. Our likelihood of eating ants decreased markedly after we started keeping our vittles inside plastic bins. Ultimately, it's the sheer ubiquity of these insects that makes a person crazy and mean. About the only place *they haven't found their way into is the refrigerator. I expect they will if they can ever find parkas that fit.*

B stands on my knee watching a lone ant circle the rim of his water dish. I too have been pondering this same ant as it's marched around and around for the past several minutes. They're usually more agenda driven than this one seems to be, and I wonder if it's trying to make a statement about futility. There was a time when I'd have killed it out of hand. I'm unpredictable. Earlier this morning I washed an entire regiment into eternity that had assembled inside an unrinsed juice glass in our kitchen sink. I cackled at the time, but I'm not proud of it now. There's something about a horde that brings out the executioner in me. And yet, I pity one ant going in circles and another moving a crumb across the floor.

MOTHS, I MUST SAY, ARE A LOT MORE WHIMSICAL THAN ANTS, EVERY one of which strikes me as a Calvinist overachiever that's one more picnic away from a heart attack. I feel as though these creatures (little tan bits of life of the type my mother referred to as "miller moths") would be happy to join me for a drink despite their propensity to inadvertently drown themselves in any available body of liquid. I'm forever fishing them out of water dishes and toilet bowls where they float with outspread wings, their legs unsuited for paddling to shore. It's a kind of catch-and-release program. Since moths are capable of floating for several hours before they succumb, the survival rate is high.

Whereas ants came with the house, moths are directly related to the fact we keep birds. Or, to be precise, are a by-product of seed we scoop out of big wooden bins at the pet store. Anyone who buys bulk flour or grain probably knows they're also getting larvae and insect eggs along with a lot of other unadvertised crap that wasn't filtered out during processing. Consumption of insects, bits of insects, or insects to be doesn't usually present a health threat, and if it weren't that most people have a psychological aversion to downing creatures possessed of six legs, we'd probably be charged for what we now get for free.

I've often sifted the contents of a newly purchased batch of seed through my fingers and come up with pendants held together with the sticky, weblike secretions that moths use to swaddle their eggs. These baubles are pretty and impart an organic respectability lacking in the relatively sterile prepackaged seed mixtures we occasionally buy. Pet store clerks insist that freezing bulk seed for a few days eliminates moths by killing stowaways before they hatch. I don't honestly think it makes a damn bit of difference. Bugs may be cold-blooded, but they're good at wintering over.

Picture Rebecca on tippy-toes in a blizzard of moths. She stands in the canary room holding a portable vacuum cleaner in her left hand, the nozzle in her right. I suspect there's a glint in her eye as she sucks moths from the air, the ceiling, the walls. From atop Clive and Daphne's house, the canaries wait for the storm to abate. Clive sings; Daphne and Timmy observe the show with what passes as indifference. Having seen it all before, they understand Rebecca's tendency to snap in the face of sudden surges in the moth population, numbers that wax and wane in accordance with actuarial trends we've never been able to quantify. Truth is, Rebecca's conflicted over the moths. Especially so since I pointed out that they're essentially butterflies, there being scant differences between the two lines that, taken together, form the order Lepidoptera. Butterflies are active during the day, whereas moths are usually nocturnal. Resting butterflies hold their wings in a raised position; moths at rest do not. Butterflies have knob-tipped antennae; a moth's antennae are plumes—extraordinarily sensitive ones capable of detecting tiny amounts of pheromones, the source of which may be a mile away.

Years before I met Rebecca, I worked through my own moth-infestation demons while living in a big house with an assortment of roommates, one of whom stashed in the cellar (I've no idea why, and no one ever admitted guilt) a large bag of moldering walnuts pregnant with miller moths that resulted in a fluttering multitude numbering in the billions. Well, it seemed like billions. They were certainly numerous enough to affect visibility in our kitchen. Like unskilled rustics leaving the farm in search of better lives in a city, moths drifted one at a time up from the basement in a silent, invisible exodus into the land of light, water, and food. Had they traveled instead as huddled masses yearning to breathe free, it might have taken a lot less time to figure out where the hell they were coming from. For several months, passing through the kitchen (to say nothing of cooking or eating there) involved plowing through moths, inhaling moths, swallowing moths.

Other than wave them away from our faces when absolutely necessary in order to impress dates, we took no initiative in addressing the
bug problem. Everyone opposed using insecticides, while less drastic
measures required levels of gumption and creativity beyond the means
of seven educated adults living together in a ramshackle old pile that
featured cheap rent. My tolerant facade crumbled in a burst of violence
that commenced after I sat back down to the bowl of ice cream I'd been
savoring before going to the refrigerator for another glass of milk. Two
moths plastered on a ledge of vanilla I'd carved into a passable likeness
of the Matterhorn looked as if they were injured skiers waiting for a
tiny St. Bernard to pant to their rescue with a firkin of brandy. I went
berserk.

If God turns out to be a moth, I don't suppose I'll find eternity a particularly pleasant place. My rampage couldn't have lasted more than
two or three minutes, but it seemed to continue for hours as, drunk on
blood lust, I strode about the kitchen smashing every moth that caught
my eye—airborne moths, stationary moths, moths dithering on one surface or another the way they often do. With an almost postorgasmic
sense of satisfaction (a petit mal afterglow, if you'll excuse an interlin-
gual pun), I finally stopped swatting and stood surveying the carnage
I'd wreaked in the form of a couple of hundred small deaths. The scene
reminded me of something out of a Revolutionary War painting by John
Trumbull, except there weren't any smoke-filled skies or shattered can-
nons; no sabers, no toppled horses, no expiring generals or fallen regi-
mental standards. Only dead and dying moths everywhere I looked, my
hands stained with the pulverized remains, tan blotches of smeared
moth on the deeper tan of the walls and standing in relief on the dark
brown of the cabinets. I went around with a paper towel wiping up the
mess, executing the injured. Some were partially crushed, trying with
one quavering wing to fly themselves free from the ruined half of their
bodies. I didn't much enjoy the rest of my ice cream.

The problem with feeling guilty about killing insects is that it's hard
to know why, exactly, it is that you do—feel guilty, that is. They're a nuisance when they're around, plus, it's hard to think of them as individuals with riveting biographies. Beyond the heart-stopping ugliness of
some of the spiders I've met, they don't offer much in the way of personality. (I know, spiders are arachnids, not insects, but you get my

point.) Excluding vegetables and bacteria, few living things play it closer to the vest than bugs; rashes are often more interactive. Should it turn out that insects are self-aware, I imagine they spend a good bit of time wishing they weren't. Unless, of course, living in crevices is an underrated Eden.

Anger got the better of me when I massacred those moths, just as it gets the better of Rebecca when she plugs in the vacuum cleaner and fulfills whatever doomsday scenario moth scripture prophesies. "They'd have died anyway, right?" she asks after subsiding back into Dr. Jekyll, as it were. Her question isn't rhetorical. More as if my confirmation of moth mortality soothes her conscience with the idea that all she's really done is save them valuable time on their way to the grave. I know how she feels: Disappointed with herself for allowing anger to triumph over compassion. Sorrow over the mass destruction of lives that, when you breathe deeply and think about it, haven't been more than a minor irritation.

At least when you annihilate ants, it seems like self-defense. Because of the weeks of dining pleasure you'd provide, you can tell yourself they'd prefer you dead. Since their wild cousins in the tropics actually do attack large vertebrates, to think of "domesticated" ants moving against you with murderous intent doesn't seem that far-fetched. Miller moths, on the other hand, might not mourn your passing, but neither would they celebrate high feast days if you keeled over with your eyes x-ed out. They're so indecisive and gormless I doubt they know whether they're drawn to the flame or the flame to them—attributes that render them pathetically inoffensive. It troubles me that I'm unable to adopt a governing ethic in my response to them. I wish I could rise above the whims of my own volatility, eliminate the subjective sense of being annoyed from how I decide when and what I'll live and let live.

I watched an ant toil across the floor recently carrying a damaged moth that had gone to ground beneath the windows in B's room. The two formed an odd contraption that looked, until I intervened and deprived the ant of its meal, like a jeep with an airplane lashed across its hood. My respect for the natural order falters when it comes to something being eaten alive. In this case, a creature with a shredded wing that one way or another had taken its last flight. I crushed it between my forefinger and thumb, thinking how reluctant I'd be to destroy such an exquisite thing had I made it myself.

Finches are dismantling the dead ficus tree. They were instrumental in killing it so I guess they're entitled to whatever lumber they can scavenge in the form of small branches and twigs snapped off from the desiccated trunk. Bert's attempting to shove a forked stick ten inches long into a covered seed dish that has a three-inch opening. Not since the ill-fated Air Nest Project have I seen anything more destined to end in failure. The dish in question sits on top of Hugh's old digs, helping to hold in place a towel that forms a canopy similar to the one draped over B's house. Thrums and pings the stick makes when dragged against the bars attract B's attention, prompt him to fly over and inspect Bert's work, toil he suspends because he's now being watched. He looks like a pupil expecting to have his knuckles rapped because he can't do sums or conjugate verbs. I hear B thinking, "Why don't you just get a smaller stick there, Sport?" B is logical when it comes to matter, brings to problem solving a sort of house sparrow sangfroid that contrasts sharply with the impressionistic approach to manipulating objects that I believe is responsible for most of Bert's engineering blunders.

Until they tugged and shat it to death, the dead ficus was the only plant Rebecca brought from San Francisco that flourished here, growing about as lush and stately (it currently looks like it belongs on the set of a stage play about witches in a graveyard) as something could be that lived in a plastic tub with rising levels of nitrogen in the soil. I used to bring in what I thought would make first-rate nesting material—dryer lint, shredded newspaper, excelsior from a gift pack of imported cheese someone gave me as a Christmas present—without having the slightest effect on the finches' leaf-stripping proclivities. Their motto appears to be, "Things not stolen aren't worth having."

Pestilence is about the only indignity this tree hasn't suffered. Given the damage wrought by the finches, I suppose this is a semantic quibble rather than a meaningful distinction. But I'm thinking along the lines of blight or fungus or insatiable locusts. I'm also thinking of the Eastern tent caterpillars (the larval stage of moths, naturally) that built huge, silky cocoons in shade trees and orchards every summer when I was a child—still do, I imagine. Unfortunately, tent caterpillars eat leaves. Do-it-yourself types burned them out using poles topped with flaming kerosene rags, an annual exercise in bad judgment that resulted in guys igniting themselves, the trees, or adjacent garages. Occasionally, all of the above. At least

Rebecca and I have been spared whatever level of desperation builds up before you go off half-cocked, leaving destruction in your wake.

When moths first emerged from our bags of seed, I assured Rebecca that B, Akbar, and Jeff would eliminate whatever invaded their airspace, an assertion based on my poor understanding of subtleties in the food chain. Birds getting as much free grub as ours do have little incentive to hunt. Rebecca evidently inferred from my pompous "Don't worry, the birds will prey on moths" declamation that I'd conducted an exhaustive study of the topic, consulted the best minds. The omnipresence of uneaten moths reminds me of my error, as do Rebecca's now tiresome witticisms at my expense—"I think our birds are getting fat; must be all those moths they're eating," or "Ooh, there's a brave moth. You'd think it would be worried about all these hungry birds. Ooh, there's another brave moth . . ." One flutters a few inches from my face, barely above stall speed. B, back from inspecting Bert's latest bout with reality, stands on my shoulder evaluating a flapping technique I'm certain makes no sense to him. The thing bobs in front of me suspended, it would seem, from strings pulled by a novice puppeteer. With the exception of an incident some years ago in which B lashed out from my finger and dispatched a passing moth as if to prove to me he could do it, he's remained as uninterested in pest control as every other bird in the house. In a veritable blink of an eye, he transformed that one unfortunate insect into two cleanly snipped halves that spiraled downward the way seed casings from maple trees do. "B," I say as he watches the current moth drift past— off, most likely, to a watery suicide—"if I offer a bounty, would you consider hunting insects?"

"THEY'RE NOT RABID" IS ABOUT THE ONLY COMPLIMENTARY THING I can say about living with the armies of mice that several years ago invaded our upstairs bedrooms. As with the ants, mice came with the house and remained scarcely more than a phantom presence for most of their tenure here, not becoming a force to be reckoned with until word leaked out that we run a twenty-four-hour diner where food and water are available at an all-you-can-eat smorgasbord. Since our birds run exclusively to house sparrows, finches, and canaries, I'm denied whatever small compensation I'd derive from titling this section "Of Mice and Wren."

The couple from whom I bought this incipient pesthole had a nine-year-old daughter who kept rats, gerbils, hamsters, and guinea pigs caged in the cellar. A lingering smell of rodent urine bonding with cedar shavings persisted for months. Wild mice attracted by the scent found their way inside and lived well by raiding the supply of food pellets the kid kept on hand to feed her pets. Pickings grew slim after I moved in, the mouse population dwindling to what I thought of as a band of postapocalyptic city dwellers that nested behind my lath and plaster, surviving on whatever food they could scavenge outside the house. We'd hear scurrying in the walls occasionally, find nibbled aluminum foil inside a drawer where that sort of thing is kept; we discovered a dead mouse at the bottom of a spare coffee mug on one of our upper cupboard shelves. Tolerable.

The first sign that our nonaggression pact had ended came midway through the six weeks I spent in Pennsylvania settling my father's estate. Rebecca telecommuted most days while I was gone, her then current project requiring very little face time at her office—a circumstance that saved us the anxiety of worrying about leaving B without company for eight or nine hours at a stretch. I could have phoned most any time and reached Rebecca at home, but generally saved that luxury for the evenings after I'd completed one more grim day stripping George's house, returning it to the vacant resonance it had before my parents and I moved in. One of my conversations with Rebecca contained the following exchange:

"You know in front of the hutch by the basement door where we feed the cats?" Rebecca asked with what seemed to me was excessive precision regarding the *locus in quo*—as if she thought it likely I'd be suffering from some kind of domestic amnesia brought on by protracted absences from home that year.

"What about it?"

"I saw a mouse over there eating kibble out of one of the cats' bowls. It was *so* cute. Now I know why Thea's been staring behind the hutch. I've never seen her work before."

"Did she *catch* the mouse?"

"No, it ran down the basement steps when it saw me. Thea was asleep on the couch."

"Of course she was. God forbid she'd show enough persistence to follow through on good intentions. But I doubt it makes any difference. Mice in *our* kitchen probably carry letters of transit."

"Carry what?"

"Letters of transit, like in *Casablanca*."

"I've no idea what you're talking about; I've never seen *Casablanca*."

Despite the obvious inducements our lifestyle provides them, I can say in our defense that house mice (along with raccoons living under people's decks) are a common problem in Portland, afflicting even those strange people I know who have dust-free furniture, gleaming porcelain, and polished floors. Shelves in local hardware stores fairly bristle with poisons arrayed alongside any number of cunning devices designed to trap, kill, or repel mice—business is steady. Rebecca and I take solace in the fact that we're not a pair of isolated nutters suffering the consequences of self-imposed and avoidable squalor. We're cannon fodder in the unending rodent wars that human beings are condemned to fight.

Rebecca mentioned during our next conversation that she'd sighted her mouse friend again as it dined alfresco on cat food in our kitchen. Vague as to why she thought it was the same mouse, she insisted that it really didn't matter because, one way or the other, it was definitely "cute." Here's the crux of that surreal exchange:

"I worked out a solution," Rebecca informed me after I suggested that we were on the verge of another infestation, that if she thought ants were a problem, she was going to find living with rodents far less congenial. Where there's one mouse, there are usually many, and if they were already making so bold as to steal cat food from cat bowls, the existence of which implied the presence of cats, then it seemed to me we had mice in our house that were fully prepared to seize the day. "I fixed it," she elaborated, "so they can't slip under the basement door. I mean, do we really care if they just live in the cellar? They're so cute the way they sit up and nibble."

"I guess not," I replied, pretending I felt at home in Rebecca's sunny universe. Knowing that mice had been an unobtrusive part of home life for many years didn't alter my belief that they were preparing to mount a pestilential blitzkrieg. I assumed they'd probably talked strategy with their colleagues, the ants. An idea naturally sprang to mind of bugs and rodents establishing a Reich.

"But that's not the best part," Rebecca continued, in reference to her work on the basement door. "Guess what else."

"I couldn't possibly."

"Guess."

"You locked Thea in the basement and told her we now have a 'catch mice or starve' policy."

"No, she *would* starve. Remember how we had several pounds of Marlowe's `Prescription Diet' left over after he died? I'm leaving it out in the basement for the mice—I don't think they're picky about what they eat. The food won't go to waste, and the mice won't have a reason to come upstairs."

I assure you the latter is a nearly verbatim rendering of what is one of the more memorable verbal exchanges I've had in my life. Rebecca admits to having been temporarily insane, beguiled into madness by her instinctive desire to do the right thing and by the undeniable cuteness of mice. By way of further mitigation, I feel I should mention a snapshot taken by Rebecca's father when she was about two years old. The setting is the middle of nowhere in Yellowstone Park, and the future mouse partisan rests on her mother's left hip as Beverly feeds grapes to a bear cub. This kind of sporadic goofiness is rampant in my wife's family, a tendency to banish Reason from her throne and approach certain aspects of existence as if real life couldn't possibly come true. I very much doubt I'd be married to Rebecca had that cub's mother appeared on the scene and jumped to conclusions. After assuming that here was a trio of tourists feeding poisoned marbles to her offspring, she'd have disemboweled them all.

When Rebecca outlined her plan for corralling mice in our basement and turning it into a rodent preserve, I couldn't bring myself to object. I didn't applaud her efforts, but I didn't ridicule. Malaise alters one's priorities, and as I rattled around George's house trying to reason my way free of an intermittent delusion that the past could be made as practical as the present, I noticed how tractable I'd become. If fate had dealt me a spouse given to farming wild mice, how much difference could it make in my life?

As it turned out, not much. By the time I returned home, Rebecca had discontinued her Feed-a-Mouse Program because, as she put it, "They shit all over the laundry room." I found old books I'd stored in the cellar shredded into nesting material. Thankless guests, mice. Catered dinners a thing of the past, they returned to the walls and bided their time until our upstairs—especially the back bedroom— grew ripe for plucking. The war has entered its fourth year. Rebecca now "hates mice."

I'm curled in a fetal position on B's couch as he stands on my sweaty shoulder trying to shriek me into getting up. Or maybe he's ordering me to turn down the heat, doesn't understand why I'm willing to lie here and baste. We need a window air conditioner, and every year a day comes when I curse myself for not having bought one—usually around four o'clock when it's as if I'm sitting in a sauna that smells like damp birds. A couple of fans circulating the same hot air cook us by convection. Rebecca believes that this room has its own weather system, that it absorbs and reemits heat, triples humidity.

All five finches are drowsing; Kess nods rhythmically on his perch, droops forward before catching himself with a start, eyes popping open at invisible hands working to unseat him. B peppers me with comments, while Seven, who's using strips of newspaper to customize the box I hung for him in the hallway, chimes in half an octave higher. House sparrow antiphony—call and response between two birds who have never met. I expect Baby to stick in his oar, but so far he hasn't commented on what his rivals are discussing. The last time I checked, he was busy ferrying pairs of Rebecca's earrings up to his shelf where he'll carefully arrange them. Baby will watch in silence as Rebecca retrieves items he's pinched, but complain like a burgled miser if he returns from the canary room to find anything missing or out of place.

"Canary room." I'm overwhelmed by the enormous challenge those words represent. I can't help juxtaposing a picture in my mind of the space as it appeared when it served as my study versus how it looks now under, as it were, the imperialist, extractive thumb of the mice. It's a rodent raj over there. Were it not that they've no interest in the trappings of power, the males would wear pith helmets and equip themselves with swagger sticks.

Most people are unaware that it's a violation of international law to write about mice in English without quoting Robert Burns—"Wee, sleekit, cow'rin, tim'rous beastie . . ." and, of course, the poem's most famous line, "The best laid schemes o' mice an' men / Gang' aft a-gley."

Too bad Burns couldn't have consulted me before he went shooting his mouth off about mice. Perhaps members of the Scottish variety were less brazen and clever two hundred years ago than the ones Rebecca and I contend with here. If I'm going to cite poetry in an effort to explain our rodent situation, I'll go with Robert Browning's "And what is our failure here but a triumph's evidence for the fullness of the days?"

"Our failure" is that I refuse to kill the mice. This is not to say I don't fantasize about murdering them, muse how satisfying it would be to haul them in tumbrils to a miniature guillotine. Rebecca and I sometimes drift over to the aforementioned shelves in hardware stores where lethal traps and poisons are stocked—so reasonably priced, so easy to own. We actually have a box of d-Con, but neither of us can summon up the Borgia frame of mind we'd need to deploy it. Aside from the aesthetic drawback of reeking carcasses in inaccessible places, there seems to me something shamefully underhanded (I had inklings of this when I deployed Terro against the ants) about using poison to solve a problem by exploiting a creature's understandable compulsion to feed itself. Rebecca bought the stuff three years ago after finding holes chewed in her favorite skirt.

That happened right after the initial wave of mice arrived in the canary room as if overnight, when, to use Rebecca's phrase, "We had mice swinging from the chandeliers." Except that we lack chandeliers, the description is accurate. It's not an exaggeration to say that hundreds of hungry rodents lived back there during the time of which I speak. There'd been hints that something, literally, was afoot—bread crusts dragged into corners, a couple of inconclusive sightings Rebecca reported as, "I thought I saw something duck into the closet, might have been a mouse." We heard noises in the canary room—enterprising noises—that ceased when we kicked baseboards or pounded on walls. Digging, gnawing, partying sounds emanating from deep within the house are still common even though I've driven most of the mice from the upstairs. For eight consecutive nights last month (I counted), an indeterminate number of mice clocked in about midnight to work on a project they had going above the kitchen ceiling. It was clear to me from the location of the sounds they made relative to the upstairs floor plan that they aimed to cut alternate routes into the canary room. As of now our ramparts are holding; historically they have not.

As with ants, the ability of mice to infiltrate is one of their most outstanding characteristics. Legions of them settled in the canary room after climbing up water pipes from the basement. This got them as far as the upstairs bathroom, from which it was an easy scoot under the door into the hallway followed by a short left turn into paradise. The puzzling thing is that we had no mounting evidence over a period of weeks to suggest an invasion. All of a sudden there were mice running errands in broad daylight. They strolled as though shopping on a sunny promenade; the females had parasols. I would not have believed in the existence of untamed mice so little interested in keeping up pretenses. If you walked in on them, they sauntered (fat ones waddled) off whatever they were on—bed, chest of drawers, settee—and disappeared into the closet where it was fashionable to chew up clothing and relieve themselves.

I disconnected the bathroom sink, pulled the vanity, cut and fitted a piece of Formica over the gap in the wall where the mice were coming through. This stanched the flow for several months until they discovered a somewhat more circuitous passageway leading out from under the tub—a claw-footed antique around which a former owner had wrapped a thin sheet of painted plywood. Mice scrambled through a gap in this questionable enhancement where the wood curves at the rear of the tub and meets the wall. Getting shed of every hungry, breeding, luxury-loving, impertinent freeloader has become my white whale.

We're stuck with a band of intelligent stragglers possessing an uncanny ability to avoid getting trapped. These ninety-ninth-percentile mice are rarely seen, something that cannot be said for the turds and spots of noisome pee we're constantly vacuuming up and swabbing out from the canary room closet. Granted, we could starve them to death by placing the birds' food and water on a high place inaccessible to mice. We've resisted this tempting option mainly because we don't want to make Timmy's life harder than it needs to be—precision landings aren't his forte. There's also the fact that it doesn't make sense to condemn a creature to a lingering death by starvation that we refuse to kill quickly in a trap. "It's kind of funny," Rebecca said to me one morning as she placed more of our possessions inside plastic bins with snap-on lids, "that we'd probably be able to kill the mice we wouldn't even have if we'd never gotten birds." Because I'm used to Rebecca speaking in riddles, I'm almost certain I know what she meant.

I remember how excited I was (how deluded that our problems were solved) when a pair of live-catch traps Rebecca ordered from PETA arrived in the mail—each one a six-by-three-by-three-inch rectangle made of transparent green plastic and shaped like a miniature tract house. Their operating principle is simple: Mouse enters trap via a ramp held down by a catch that releases after mouse has moved far enough inside to eat bait; ramp snaps into the vertical and seals entrance. A removable panel at the other end slides out when it's time to either release the mouse immediately or allow it to eat its way to freedom by gnawing through a cracker you have the option of installing as an intermediate barrier. The idea, apparently, is to reward departing pests with a farewell meal.

The only flaw in this otherwise admirable device comes from the designer's mistaken belief that mice are made of Einsteinium or some other absurdly dense element. After my first two outings with the traps resulted in stolen bait (peanut butter daubed on bread is my preference) and no prisoners, I inspected the mechanism and determined that it could be tripped only by something a good bit heavier than a standard mouse. I got around the problem by taping five pennies together as a counterbalance and placing them at an experimentally determined point inside the trap. This created a hair trigger that shut the door with virtually no additional pressure. Over the following months, I caught and released well over one hundred mice from my modified trap. Rebecca postulates the existence of a "magic escalator" that carries them back into the house within minutes of their release.

It's a delightful thing to wake each morning with renewed hope of finding a plump mouse cooling its heels in a trap you've set. Amazing to me how calmly they'd sit there, captives of their own desire, betraying no outward fear as they waited for fate to overtake them. I caught two at once on one occasion. After I released them, they ambled away together around the side of the house. Those days, it seems, are gone forever.

The remaining colonists are geniuses that won't go near traps or, as their predecessors did, hie themselves up into garbage bags searching for stale bread and other discarded bird comestibles. I've carted more mice outside in brown paper grocery sacks than I have in traps. I grew hypersensitive to the subtle rustlings of mice backstroking their way through fathoms of perfectly good food—good, that is, from a rodent point of view. They seldom chewed in from the bottom, preferring to work down from the top after leaping inside from the floor. Whenever I heard shifting debris, I'd grab the bag and beat feet outside to upend it by the backyard fence. Rebecca did the same, often cautioning the invisible spectators she apparently believes loiter in our hallway to "Stand clear! Bag-o-mice coming through." It's a year or more since I've had these pleasures.

I now accept that the canary room isn't a place where we could, in good conscience, accommodate guests. The odds against waking unnibbled really aren't good. I've suggested to Rebecca that we dedicate an afternoon's labor to stripping the room of all boxes, bins, furniture, and clothing. In theory, this will expose every furbearing son of a bitch living in there, allow us to drive them downstairs and out the front door. Unfortunately, other than an image of myself swinging a lasso while I sit on a quarter horse, I've no idea how one herds mice. But if (and this is a very big if) my plan succeeds, I'm buying a card table that I'll fit with a thick piece of foam so Timmy will have a soft place to land when he belly flops in for his meals. And as if furnishing épées with hilts, I'll slide a piece of cardboard onto each skinny leg—pieces too broad for mice to get past after their inevitable return and ensuing attempt to shinny up to what will be the only source of food and water in the room.

It's long after midnight, and B's chattering away in what seems to me a special vintage language he's saved for the occasion. Some of his "words" are familiar to me; most of them are not. An unusual syntax complements the quivering jubilation transmitted through his body as he turns circles in my hand. I'm certain he woke when he heard me greet Rebecca and fuss with the cats before I arrived in here a few moments ago, flashlight at the ready. When I illumined his perch, he hopped into my palm without hesitation. Rebecca would say he "B-lined" to me. Had I not been gone the past eight days on a road trip to Utah, I'd likely be on the receiving end of The Look—sleepy version. Or, he'd be giving me the bum's rush with a series of dismissive pecks on his mirror.

Except for the lack of barking and slobber, there's a canine aspect to this reception he's giving me. I suppose he'd find the comparison demeaning— dogs being such plodding, obsequious things when set beside creatures of the air. Nevertheless, I insist on the point in the privacy of my thoughts and wonder how many birds would roust themselves at night to rejoice in a home-coming. It'll be interesting to see if he gives me the "cold beak" about seven hours from now when I reappear with his breakfast. Wouldn't be the first time I've received a warm welcome followed by a cool breeze meant to remind me that he's never approved of my taking vacations. It's fascinating to watch him struggle between competing desires: "Although," I imagine him thinking, "I'd kill for a sliver of hazelnut right now, better play hard to get; can't have my so-called best friend thinking bad behavior won't go unpunished."

He lies in my hand very much awake, rays from a streetlamp framing him in profile. The curved tip of his beak pointing down offsets a wild feather on top of his head that sticks up. I'm exhausted physically, could easily fall asleep where I sit were it not that my mind constructs roads and furnishes traffic—an endless procession of oncoming headlights shooting past when I close my eyes, phantoms I'm stuck with until I'm able to shake the sense of inert motion that defines eleven hours riding in a car. I see hundreds of dead rodents, too. Marmots, actually. Some squished in the middle of the highway, the majority dead on the shoulder where, it seems to me, they must sit minding their own business until drivers swerve to the right and hit them. Life's just one damn thing after another for marmots near an interstate in southeastern Idaho.

"HE DIDN'T GET IT FROM MY SIDE OF THE FAMILY" IS WHAT MY FATHER likely thought to himself the day he inquired, in so many words, if B relieved himself anywhere he felt like it and I said that about summed it up. "Even on you?" he asked with the piping note of incredulity people adopt whose relationship with the excrement of their pets is comparatively distanced.

"Frequently."

"Let me get this straight," he warmed to his theme. "This bird . . ."

"House sparrow, Dad."

"This house sparrow flies around your upstairs and goes to the bathroom wherever it wants?"

Note the euphemism, "goes to the bathroom." While I'm not one of those people who believes their father invented swearing, I admired George's mastery of the art. He could weave expletives into a deserving topic in a way that emphasized content, improved scansion, and made otherwise prosaic statements ring with conviction. His repertoire of profanity certainly contained the verb form of "shit."

I bring this up not because it bears on the fact that birds produce large amounts of the latter commodity, but because I'd never noticed before that people seldom use cuss words in a literal sense. I took credit for this, as I believed, original insight until reading about a year later an informative ten-page dissertation on the word "fuck" in Hugh Rawson's improving book, *Wicked Words.* By way of illustrating my point for me, Rawson recounts an old story about a sailor telling a pal back on ship what a great "fucking" time he had while on shore leave. Went to a "fucking bar," had some "fucking drinks," met a gorgeous "fucking" lady, and ended up going with her to a "fucking" motel room where "we had sex." It seems even the crudest speaker will attempt to elevate certain details of his personal life by avoiding the use of perceived vulgarities when describing them.

Rebecca and I don't indulge ourselves in this way. There's bird shit over vast expanses of our upstairs, and we acknowledge the fact. I told George as much (since we had only B at that time, supplies were comparatively limited), stating that, in my opinion, the situation here was far preferable to that of a mutual acquaintance whose pet spider monkey routinely emptied his bladder while hanging from ceiling lights or standing on curtain rods. Even I'd draw the line at an animal exercising that much artistic license.

I estimate the combined output of our four sparrows, five finches, and three canaries to be 65,700 turds per year. This assumes (conservatively) fifteen contributions per bird per day. That's a lot of shit going down, but probably not enough to fill the average wastepaper can. In sheer volume, it pales beside the output of our cats.

Incomplete digestion wouldn't exist in a tidier world. Our bodies would transform chili, sauerkraut, and hard-boiled eggs washed down with beer into useful, nonpolluting energy, do so with absolute efficiency and no by-products. Birds, having already lapped the competition in the superior development of at least three essential systems (respiration, ocular, and nervous), will undoubtedly be the first creatures to evolve digestive systems as near to perfection as the laws of physics will permit. Kind of an apples-and-oranges comparison, but it's worth noting that while human infants shift only a tiny fraction of the food they eat into body weight, nestlings convert almost half.

It would make more sense to say that birds with poor appetites eat like humans rather than the reverse. Small birds such as chickadees and some species of fruit eaters consume anywhere from a third to three times their body weight in food per day. Digestion is rapid and remarkably complete; as a percentage of input, fecal production is low. Large mammals with similarly extravagant appetites would require their own sewage treatment plants. I knew guys in college teetering on the verge.

A multipurpose receptacle known as the cloaca (a synonym for sewer) is, digestively speaking, the end of the line in birds. This feature, also found in amphibians and reptiles, is a tripartite chamber that serves as the common terminus for a bird's reproductive, urinary, and intestinal tracts. One part receives urine from the kidneys along with, depending on gender, eggs from the oviduct or sperm from the vas deferens. Solid waste from the lower intestine is diverted into a second area. A third section forms a holding tank for excrement (feces and urine together at last) waiting to be ejected from the body. As far as I can tell, it doesn't wait long. B has tinted samples ready for shipment within half an hour of eating fruit.

An answer to my father's "Where does the bird go to the bathroom?" question is the essential bit of information most everyone craves once they grasp the rudiments of how Rebecca and I live. They, just as I would in their place, want to reason through the implications, it being virtually self-evident there's an unhinged aspect of our situation that bears looking into. The thought forms in their eyes as they add food and subtract cages from their mental image of X number of birds living freely in the upstairs of our house. Because it seemed to be asked rhetorically—an affirmative assumed, however ridiculous the concept—my favorite variant of the question is, "Can't you train your birds to go in a litter box?" I suppose, in a manner of speaking, we could. I have it on reliable authority that an elderly uncle of Rebecca's friend Susie taught uncaged zebra finches to confine their cloaca-moving activities to a fresh sheet of newspaper the old gentleman provided them each day. If said finches performed as advertised, I dare say I could teach house sparrows to use a commode, flush after doing so, and jiggle the handle when the valve doesn't shut off.

For most of my life, I'd have agreed with George's dictum that "Shit is shit," an opinion he clung to as if it expressed an indisputable fact of existence like *Cogito, ergo sum*. I'd been trying to explain that house sparrow droppings weren't all that bad once you gave them a chance. But since George never spent time with our birds, his reluctance to revise a belief supported by almost eighty years of empirical data is perfectly understandable. When he envisioned conditions in our upstairs, I imagine he had something pretty whiffy in mind, something along the lines of a poorly run chicken farm.

Rebecca and I were squeamish at the outset. B's fecal sacs commanded interest as amusing curiosities, were endearing in the way unlikely things connected with infants often are, but this isn't to say we had the slightest desire to handle his excrement without an insulating tissue in hand. We were, after all, sophisticated people. The idea of touching the gelatinous mounds B delivered after every third or fourth feeding was positively revolting. Neither our dignity nor the purity of our skin was threatened, however, as long as B continued living in a box. Confinement imposes territorial limits on birds, but cages are really shit-containment structures with a strong appeal to the human superego. Ironically, my hands are cleaner, overall, than they were before we had sparrows. I disinfect them frequently—my hands, not the birds—because I worry about importing into the upstairs any avian-attacking microbes I may have picked up outside.

Typical house sparrow turds are slightly moist cylinders half an inch long that have no discernible scent unless sizzling on a lightbulb—a process that smells like rancid liver frying in a skillet. Although these proportions are often reversed, one-third the cylinder's length is usually composed of fecal material ranging in color from ecru to black, the balance a pasty uric acid compound of such gleaming whiteness that you might consider painting a dispensary to match it. Naturally, there are some variations in size, texture, and composition—lack of odor remains invariable. B's first turds of the day contain very little urine. Large, dark, and relatively greasy, they leave yellowish stains on cloth, but most end up on the plastic tray at the bottom of his house. After I've fed him grape in the afternoons, output is usually tan and watery. I could have made a tidy fortune in the patent medicine trade during the nineteenth century by selling dissolved sparrow shit as the active ingredient in a gout remedy or baldness cure. Not an outrageous notion when you consider that people back then thought powdered mummy an effective treatment for a host of ailments, paid top dollar to get it, too.

Zebra finches leave sticky piles wherever they go, piles that resemble servings of two-toned frozen yogurt complete with curlicue swirls topping them off as a festive note. Although I've ceased being amazed by their habit of crapping in seed and water dishes (two places house sparrows won't drop a load), I still can't touch finch shit without a momentary sense of contamination. Same goes for my run-ins with canary dung—wettest of the three varieties we keep in stock. It's a measure of my particular fondness for B, Baby, Pee Wee, and Seven that their shit seems no more appalling to me now than a fingernail clipping or a strand of hair in the sink. Had Rebecca and I remained delicate, the dynamic in this house would be vastly different. Whatever relationship we'd have with our birds would be circumscribed by efforts to insulate ourselves from an aspect of their metabolism that's proved to be more amusing than vile.

You learn to make allowances. We rely on a loopy fatalism to help us enjoy lives in which we're literally shat on every day. Rebecca's laughter while declaring, "I'm probably the only person this has ever happened to" demonstrated the requisite esprit de corps. She'd been telling me about white flecks dropping off her towel as she dried herself after a shower at her spa. "At first," she said, "I thought they were grains of wild rice. The floor was littered with them. Thank God no one else was around. The people there already think I'm strange because I don't wear anything with a logo on it." She described what rehydrated sparrow turds looked like when smeared on her arms and across her chest. These light and dark streaks are what suggested to her that the stuff on the floor tiles wasn't wild rice. "I started back to the shower when I remembered I didn't have a clean towel. I used up half a roll of toilet paper before I could get dressed."

Rebecca has marvelous powers of concentration (absolutely first-rate when she's with our birds) but is usually preoccupied with something other than what she's doing. I've watched her spend forty-five minutes looking for car keys that turned out to be in her pocket. It's completely within character for her to have absentmindedly thrown a bird shit–encrusted towel into her carryall when she packed for the gym. I'd guess she was mentally working on a new belly dance routine when her brain issued a "Get towel" order without specifying "linen closet" as the source of choice. Plain bad luck that she happened to be passing a pile of dirty laundry when the directive came through. Worse luck that the towel she grabbed had seen a week's worth of action draped over a floor lamp in Baby's room—his favorite en suite defecation center. Debate continues over whether Rebecca's postshower adventure qualifies as a "stealth turd" incident.

I'm inclined to think it does not. Stealth turds, by definition, are deposited on people without their knowledge. The case here meets neither condition. The turds in question were deposited on a towel and done so openly. Rebecca considers my analysis legalistic, says I err by relying on the letter rather than the spirit of the law. The nub of her argument is that a stealth turd's essence lies in its ability to surprise. In her opinion, "stealth" designation is merited because she was taken unawares when the substance in question fell off a towel she was using in a relatively public place. Something in this, of course, but I'm not convinced. Sloppy attitudes like that will only hasten our little society's descent into chaos.

God knows how many times Rebecca and I have been "stealthed" only to go outside with bird shit in our hair or mashed on our pants. I once sat through a business meeting with one of B's best adhering to the Windsor knot of my dark blue tie. B introduced the stealth turd concept, perfected its delivery. Each of our other three sparrows has reinvented it in turn but without ever mastering B's incomparable technique. His ability to surreptitiously drop freshly minted stools inside a V-neck shirt borders on the miraculous. I've found samples as far south as my navel. Rebecca's favorite example of his work lay in the middle of my forehead like a third eyebrow waiting for a corresponding eye to appear underneath it.

B leaves the bulk of his droppings on my knees and arms when I'm with him, while perched on his sword when I'm not. Index fingers applying the right combination of lateral and downward pressure are the most effective tools for lifting fresh sparrow dung from clothing or skin without leaving a trace; a well-executed fillip flicks it into a garbage bag. A difficult trick with projectiles not uniformly moist from one specimen to the next. This makes for a "stickiness variable" that can affect the trajectory enough to create fecal boomerangs that return to your hand. B has left turds on my nose, my ear, and on that part of my beard growing out from my lower lip. Although done without my knowledge, these very creative efforts all failed the stealth test. I was napping each time and didn't, as it were, have a sporting chance to observe his movements.

A person's worldview shifts after this kind of thing. You either develop a more expansive philosophy or you forgo a close association with very small birds—clearly the attractive option if they wielded the firepower most mammals do. I'm not suggesting, please understand, that any of this makes me a better person. But trying to maintain a sense of self-importance is tricky under the circumstances—mirrors are quick to remind me from time to time that I'm just a guy with bird shit on his cheek.

"I love you," Rebecca says to me, emphasizing "love" and stretching out the "you." It's a good thing she does and that the feeling is mutual. The way we live, we're well-nigh unmarketable. For some reason, she's moved emotionally by seeing me scrubbing B's floor on my hands and knees. He clings to my forearm, changes sides when I switch the cloth I'm using from hand to hand.

This is a weekend devoted to eliminating bird shit from our upstairs rooms, a daunting task not quite on par with Hercules cleansing the Augean stables. The principal difference being that Hercules diverted a river to wash away an accumulation of ox manure that had reached, I gather, mythic proportions. I've got a bucket and a rag against what the uninitiated might think were hundreds of toothpaste smears dabbed across the floor. Lots of finch shit on the windowsills, varying amounts everywhere else; sparrow turds break the monotony but are concentrated for the most part in two or three spots. The finches are far more profligate than B is in distributing bounty. I removed a six-inch stalagmite of Bert's accreted droppings from a branch on the dead ficus directly below his customary roost—hated to do it, felt as if I'd lopped off Pikes Peak. Listing badly, this natural wonder would have soon gone over of its own accord or because Bert's tail feathers toppled it overnight, the thing having grown nearly tall enough to poke him in the ass. I valued it as a topographical feature, the same as I would any other eminence risen from flatland.

Rebecca's on break from laboring in the canary room and hallway. In theory, she's entertaining B while I scrub. Our house cleaner's recent work on the downstairs has inspired us to do bird rooms a week ahead of schedule. Two floors of the house burnished at the same time: what an appealing idea. Apart from daily maintenance, we deep-clean bird zones about once a month whether, as the saying goes, they need it or not. As the day approaches, gallows humor prevails but gives way to a satisfying sense of having served the common weal once the task is completed. Of course, history begins repeating itself.

I've finished step one. This involves using a paint scraper to loosen every dried turd I can find, a process B interprets as a game in which his part is to attack the scraper while voicing a version of the house sparrow danger call—a cross between scat singing and playing the spoons. Today, he stayed on Rebecca's shoulder and fussed with her hair. Stage two would go faster if he'd return to her now. I can't scrub vigorously with him glued to whichever hand is holding the rag; I fear whiplash even if he doesn't. I've never known a creature so intensely curious. What a pleasure it was to watch him examine the new flashlight I placed on his bookshelf this morning—the way he circled it on foot, touching the switch and lens with his beak. And the way he stays on my hand as I swab, the constant glancing at my face, the eye contact that belies the presumed vacuity of the nonhuman mind.

I hold B high above my head as I stand from my crouch. Stage two is complete, wood drying into a milky blur. We'll sit with Rebecca for a game of Cap before I get fresh water and rinse the floor. I've got a good view of his undercarriage, of the tiny fawn-colored feathers tapering up to meet his tail. Each part of his body looks to me as if it could fly independently of the whole, every structure sleek enough to confound gravity into releasing its grip.

Preceded by a distinctive bounce like a small cannon recoiling, B's feet tighten on my finger as he releases a plummeting load. "Butt flaps flapping?" Rebecca asks, watching sparrow shit mar my almost clean floor. "Butt flaps flapping," I hasten to assure her. She doesn't trot out "B-fouled" for a change, or one of our other apropos tropes.

Situated on either side of his southern aperture, B's "flaps" blend seamlessly with the rest of his feathers. They appear to ventilate the machinery by whiffling open and closed for five or six seconds following each launch. Something, incidentally, I'm half-convinced he does at will as a kind of commentary on things I've said that deserve a riposte. God *knows how much eloquence he's directed my way when he thinks I've been blathering. That he's crapped on a floor I've just risen from cleaning is apparently the most hilarious thing Rebecca's ever seen. I hope she inhales a moth while she cackles. "Laugh," I say, "but digestion marches on." Cycles are involved here, and B has pulled a koan from his butt— "What is the meaning, my son, of one turd splatting?" Nothing I can do but heft my rag, ponder inevitability. Say, "Thank you, sir. May I have another?"*

11

ALL OF A PIECE

Life is not enough, in my opinion, *per se*. It's the quality of life
that matters, and a fellow has to have something to live *for*. Some
fine, ennobling, enriching experience.
—John Mortimer, *Rumpole and the Age of Miracles*

Who knoweth the spirit of man that goeth upward, and the spirit
of the beast that goeth downward to the earth? (Ecclesiastes)

Elizabeth's attention was riveted on the antics of a sparrow on the
flagstones outside, as if in its small person it was about to provide
an answer to the mysteries of the universe.
—Minette Walters, *The Ice House*

*H*AD THIS BEEN A TYPICAL SUNDAY MORNING, I'D HAVE SPENT A SOLID HOUR
with B in between delivering his breakfast and going out for espresso.
*But Baby disappeared without a trace for two and a half hours, and
Rebecca and I spent the time combing the upstairs in an effort to find him.
B stopped calling for me after about forty-five minutes, milled around on
the floor in front of his heating grate, looking through the slats into the
middle room and watching our feet move past as we paced in and out
more and more baffled over where to search next. I pressed my face
against the vent and spoke to B twice, but he showed me his back and*

stepped away. If he understood my hasty explanation about trying to find Baby, I imagine he thought, "Why would anyone bother?"

I'm currently peeling a grape while B dances a kind of jig inside Hugh's house, hopping in place like a finalist in a urine-holding contest. Bert, Lisa, and Kess are blocking his exit as they preen one another on the stubby branch that's bolted beneath the cage's door. B would ordinarily blow through them without preamble or at most a couple of quick feints with his beak to signal intent. His deference to them reflects my own benevolent mood that's risen with my relief over a tragedy averted. For a while, at least, I'm living in the best of all possible worlds.

I thought at one time in my darkest moods that God, assuming, of course, that such a being is more than a desperate construct of the human mind, should in the spirit of fair play and reconciliation ask our forgiveness. A form letter with a rubber-stamped signature would have sufficed: "Dear Creatures, Please accept my apologies for having brought you forth without first seeking your permission (no way around that, I'm afraid) and for plaguing you with stuff you apparently don't like. I see now that pain is real to you—an eventuality I failed to anticipate the day I exploded into everything that is. I felt my sanity slipping out here by myself, lonely in the way only a First Cause can be. You can't imagine how close I came to folding beneath the weight of my own not-quite-infinite potential, bound in a vacuum that even divinity is powerless to escape. Small wonder I bollixed details of the world I created to keep me company. I was fright-ened of myself and in a terrible hurry to get reality on the table. Made most of it up as I went along, could have planned better. I blush to think of the platypus. Amusing to look at, but the poor animal doesn't know if it's reptile or mammal. Shows what happens when I blurt things out. Anyway, just wanted to prove to everyone that I'm big enough to admit my mistakes. All best wishes for the future. Yours for Eternity, By Whatever Name You Know Me By . . . P.S. Life forms too dim to grasp their own existence should disregard this communication—as if you could do anything but. Ha, ha!

Take it as read that I accept Baby's deliverance as proof that cautious optimism has a place in the world. We're all screwed in the end but are cut some slack in the interim. When Rebecca called from next door saying she couldn't find Baby, I hustled over not particularly worried. He hides in the bookshelves or sequesters himself in closets as part of the chase-and-be-chased workouts he has with Seven and Pee Wee—or oftentimes because he appears, as with B, to enjoy a game of hide-and-seek. Ten minutes is about the longest he'll contain himself before losing patience with our hapless attempts to find where he's hiding. He'll emerge from an obvious spot that we've passed five or six times.

So you can imagine how distraught we felt after spending half an hour with no Baby to show for our efforts. Another odd thing was that he hadn't had breakfast. Rebecca told me he and The Kids had been zooming in and out of his fort when she went downstairs to get their food, but by the time she returned, only Pee Wee and Seven presented themselves to be fed. In and of itself, this wasn't unusual since Baby sometimes tanks up on seed before breakfast is served, waiting until the others have had their bread, corn, or whatever before winging over to get his share. Even so, too much time had elapsed for us to go on believing we were still safely within the bell-shaped part of the curve.

We forget how physically tiny house sparrows are because, I guess, they're otherwise such an enormous presence in our lives. Thus, two good-size bedrooms with large closets plus a bathroom and hallway represented an impressive amount of acreage to cover. And the task of searching soon became fraught with the conviction that finding Baby would be to find his corpse. Every time we looked behind a book or box or under the bed or pulled furniture away from the wall, a squirt of adrenaline (and the thought that now is when our sorrow begins) punctuated our movements.

We even searched downstairs. It seemed unlikely he'd have made it past the screen door without our noticing, but after two fruitless hours of ransacking bedrooms, we were running out of ideas. Desperation sets in when you find yourself going back over the same territory for the second or third time. Now and then we'd stop what we were doing and listen for rustling or chirps or for anything we could construe as a trapped or hidden sparrow. We asked The Kids if they knew where he'd gone. Initially, they followed us around like referees in some strange sport in which it's easy to foul your opponent, poking their beaks into the middle of the action as we moved this or undid that. I think actually that Baby's absence troubled them, that they understood on some level we were trying to find him. After a while, though, they flew into the canary room and sat for the duration huddled together on the ceiling fan, having either lost interest in the project or become wary of Rebecca and me upending their space.

The chest of drawers in the middle bedroom is 150 years old if it's a day and lacks the runners you find on modern bureaus that allow drawers to slide easily in and out. We have kind of a screwy arrangement here, but suffice it to say that Rebecca uses the upper three drawers for her stuff; I get the bottom one for underwear and socks. The drawers are like heavy boxes that you're in effect raising or lowering into slightly larger boxes whenever you open or close them. Sometimes they angle and catch as you move them, and so we tend to leave them ajar or even open a sparrow's width or more, especially mine, which is the largest and crankiest of the four.

Because it occurred to me midway through the hunt that Baby might be in with my socks for some reason, I sifted through them with care and then haphazardly closed the drawer again, leaving perhaps a half-inch gap on the left-hand side. About every fifteen minutes, Rebecca and I parlayed amidst the dislodged junk that was piling up as we searched. We'd restate the obvious fact that we were running out of places to look, brood together over what was fast becoming a nearly unfathomable turn of events. By the end of the second hour, hope had vanished that we'd see Baby again without finding him dead. I'd look at Rebecca's face and see the effort of maintaining her composure pulling the skin taut around her eyes. It was agony trying to reconcile our memories of a cheerful, playful, affectionate Baby with the small, limp body we'd become determined to find.

Of course, based on his intelligence-gathering activities at the vent, B probably knew the exact moment when I found Baby in the bureau. I'd just finished giving Rebecca a pep talk, asserting that we were perhaps, after all, being too pessimistic. I pointed out that if Baby had taken ill or injured himself, we'd have found him by then, it being unlikely he'd have had the desire or ability to disappear without a trace. He's a bird that complains to Rebecca when Seven is mean to him. I reasoned that he'd gotten stuck in some out-of-the-way place and was too frightened to answer our calls. Or that he'd slipped into that quiescent state of shock I'd twice seen with B.

Rebecca shrugged when I finished speaking and turned to searching the middle-room closet, a task I'd already completed twice. For no other reason than that I'd been leaning against the chest while I delivered my analysis, I knelt down and pawed through my socks again. I was stalling, giving myself something to do with my hands while I waited for a scrap of inspiration to suggest a bird-size hiding place I'd so far overlooked. And it came to me fully thought out, a kind of unassailable equation that proved to me the existence of Baby an instant before I took out the drawer.

B gives up being polite to the finches, more or less elbows his way through them on his way to me. He's now on my shoulder eating grape, turning after taking each piece in his beak to listen to Rebecca next door cooing over Baby and the miracle, if you will, that he wasn't killed.

"Baby!" I exclaimed—I mean, really exclaimed—with an actual exclamation point that's still hovering in the other room like an escaped helium balloon. "He's okay, he's okay, he's okay," I added right away to let Rebecca know that the news was good. And indeed, you'd think that spending time inside a bureau in the path of a heavy drawer being shoved in and pulled out was a wholesome activity central to Baby's idea of a really good day.

By the time Rebecca emerged from the closet, Baby had greeted me with a chirp and flown to his bookcase. How he survived is unclear to me. When I removed the drawer, he was standing along the left-hand side of the chest, halfway back. If, at any point, I'd have shut the drawer flush with Baby standing behind it, he would have been crushed. If, instead of pulling it out straight, I'd have jerked the drawer open the way I usually do, I'd have smeared him in an instant.

I won't even speculate on what our mental state would be right now had Baby died today—let alone how I'd be feeling had I done him in with a drawer. I'm not even all that curious to know why he ended up in the bureau to begin with—let alone in a dangerous, recessed part of the thing. It violates what I thought I knew about the house sparrow's obsession with caution. Rebecca gave him a lecture about risky behavior and about the importance of responding to our calls if he ever again finds himself trapped. I've sworn a vow to keep all drawers closed.

Full of grape, B stands on my wrist; his tail marks time as if he's remembering a tune. It occurs to me that the tiny white feathers accenting the sides of his eyes are but one of a score of distinctions I know on his face. I'll never get over the importance of his life—or Baby's, or Pee Wee's or Seven's. We've been shown a tender mercy today, and I'm thankful.

The words "Our sparrows" form in my mouth as a completed sentence, hundreds of verbs implied by the noun. I watch B watching me *and see, as I sometimes do, a place where thought and reality slip past one another. In the normal course of my life, I miss it completely.*

≡

JEAN-PAUL SARTRE COMMENTED ON WHAT HE CALLED "THE MONOTO-nous disorder of everyday life." A case could be made that disorder preys on monotony, but I'm willing to accept the old existentialist at face value. That an observer could find deadening regularity in the ran-domness of Parisian street life wouldn't seem to bode well for someone who sits around with a sparrow as much as I do. Sartre's real problem was how to squeeze meaning out of an impersonal universe in which each human being awakes frightened and isolated into a consciousness that eventually dies in the emptiness that spawned it. We're compen-sated metaphysically with the absolute freedom to define and pursue whatever it is we believe will make our lives worthwhile—a dubious birthright that imparts a wearisome burden of its own. Rather like choosing one all-important meal from an infinite menu.

It may be so. I'd guess that Sartre was probably as fundamentally wrong about these things as everyone else who's ever given thought, passing or otherwise, to all the deep questions. Philosophical systems have a habit of collapsing under the scrutiny of the next malcontent to come along. It's like a casino: the House always wins. The most I've ac-complished philosophically is to make myself all that much more un-happy by fretting over this stuff whenever I'm depressed to begin with. Beyond a firm belief that many things aren't as they appear (perhaps the biggest lesson I've learned from B), I haven't the foggiest notion what goes on behind the scenes—or why. I'm simply not qualified to under-stand the universe. Reason, it seems to me, is useless in these matters, becomes either an apologist for faith or its persecutor. Catch me tomor-row; I may change my mind. Today, I'm happy deferring to the muddle.

Rebecca and I revel for the most part in the "monotonous disorder" of the life we have chosen or, depending on how you wish to look at it, the life that has chosen us. When I first met Rebecca, she was spending the summer in Portland and hoping to somehow use her impending in-ternational-relations degree as a means of entering a journalism career. She saw herself in foxholes with a notebook and a portable tape

recorder. I assumed I'd travel, write novels eventually that would redefine the form. Had either of us had a premonition that we'd wind up as
fanatical sparrow tenders as a consequence of our marrying one another, I for one would have backpedaled.

Rebecca returned to school in southern California, entered a radical
feminist phase, got her degree, settled in San Francisco, landed a well-
paying corporate job. Her more famine-resistant friends accused her of
selling out. All news to me by the time I received the chatty letter she
sent me shortly before I went to San Francisco in August 1990 for my
nephew Marc's wedding. I hadn't seen Rebecca in almost four years
when we met for dinner my second night in town. Apparently, I was
charming. A month later, she visited Portland, moved in with me the
following summer.

She was informative about belly dancing, a topic she'd mentioned
in her letter and subsequently enlarged upon during our meal. If someone had given me a long list of activities and asked me to choose a few
I thought Rebecca likely to pursue, belly dancing, which, it seemed to
me, had something to do with stripping, would not have been one of
them. She isn't prudish by any means, but she is shy. I found it hard to
imagine a costumed Rebecca dancing for an audience of would-be
sheiks. I didn't understand at the time that belly dance performances
occupy about the same niche on the lewdness scale as PTA bake sales.
None of which has anything to do with our birds except that our sparrows have never cared for this facet of Rebecca's life.

They aren't comfortable with her costumes and disapprove of a
time commitment that takes her out of the house in the evenings before
they've gone to bed. Her Friday-night gig at a nearby Moroccan restaurant that requires her presence about seven-thirty is a weekly thorn in
their sides. Baby, especially, sees no reason she should leave him and
dance for twenty or thirty minutes so diners eating lamb kabobs and
couscous will have something to look at besides their masticating
spouses. I, however, benefit because she treats me to a late dinner out
as compensation for the extra work she thinks devolves to me in her absence. When she asks how things went, I varnish the truth so she'll
think she's getting her money's worth, "Whenever *you're* gone, dear,
the birds are always in a dither." Rebecca, by comparison, is scrupu-
lously honest if I've been away: "B wasn't happy but went right to bed

when I turned off the lights. The finches wouldn't settle; you know how they are. I really didn't have much trouble at all."

Baby and The Kids note changes in Rebecca's routine that signal her intention to bail out early. There's her late-afternoon shower, curling-iron wielding in front of her mirror, the application of makeup. If you can imagine how someone might react to a trusted friend showing them a homemade collection of shrunken heads, you've got a good idea of Pee Wee and Seven's response to Rebecca donning a belly dance costume. B doesn't fear her outfits but seems to find them repulsive, gives her a wide berth whenever she's wearing one. Baby views them as omens.

If it's a Friday around seven o'clock on a summer's evening and Rebecca has on a shimmering purple bra, or is strapping on a glass-beaded belt, or is stepping into a gauzy skirt with little mirrors embedded in it, or arraying herself in some other ensemble from her sizable collection, Baby understands that he's about to get shafted. He tries bribing her into changing her plans. All he's got to barter with, of course, is swag he's stolen from her and stashed in the bookcase. He recently offered her a one-dollar bill—oddly appropriate since belly dancers get most of their tips in the form of small currency stuffed in their belts. He'll play Get the Bird as flamboyantly as possible, break into a passionate display of Love Baby. The long version with all the trimmings—"Eh-eh-eh" seduction calls, struts, bows, flutters, nips to Rebecca's nose. I can't say whether he'd be more pleased or frustrated to know how close he comes to getting his way.

"Baby's such a love," Rebecca announces when she rattles into B's room to tell us she's leaving. "I'm tempted to call the restaurant and cancel. It's so hard to leave Baby. Listen to those shrieks—he's really upset. Remember to give him millet and another piece of corn." Same instructions every week. At this point, she's usually wearing a black and orange dashiki-like article over her dance costume—an attempt to avoid riling B who expresses contempt for her getups by looping the room. The garment in question functions outside the house as a coverall that prevents Rebecca from looking like a belly dancer while she's in transit, something, evidently, that's just not done. It also obviates the necessity of changing in and out of her costumes at gigs. Accented with black stripes, it gives the illusion that Rebecca is not only two hundred pounds heavier than she is but a miniature zebra that can drive a car. She claims it's made her the envy of all the other dancers, who find it hard to believe she got such a wonderful thing at such a reasonable price. My feeling, which I kept to myself the night she debuted it, was that any rational person would marvel that anyone anywhere paid anything at all.

That Baby's a crafty manipulator, highly skilled at playing the martyr, is another thought I refrain from airing. I'm scarcely in a position to be snide when it comes to commenting on other people's concerns over what a bird does or does not want. I admire Rebecca's dedication to a thing that's important enough to her that she'll inconvenience Baby once a week to pursue it. I've never been entirely clear about the reasons behind her belly-dance mania, knowing only that she took it up as an anodyne to the anxiety she felt after graduating college and moving into a job she loathed. Her stated intent has always been to dance professionally.

It's neither here nor there, but the halcyon days of the 1970s when belly dancers could comfortably support themselves performing in restaurants are over. There are too many superb dancers competing for too few engagements—at least in the United States. That's why Rebecca documents software as her primary source of income. But she's beaten the odds: restaurant owners pay her to dance; she wins local contests. Over the past few years she's found faint lines around her eyes, one or two gray hairs in her sea of brown. She tells me that belly dancing, although performed by women of all ages (and some men), is a young woman's game when it's down to a question of who gets hired. I tell her she's young and beautiful, but I don't know if she takes me at my word.

Rebecca's beaten the odds because she views belly dance as the art form it is and has worked hard to perfect her technique. She says she's fortunate that birds and dance are the twin passions in her life. I'm gratified to know I've squeaked in at the bottom of her priorities list. In the event our house catches fire and I'm unconscious, she promises to return for me after getting birds and costumes to safety first.

About half an hour after Rebecca heads off to perform, I usually begin getting Baby and The Kids situated for the night. B doesn't like deviation from an evening routine in which he feels a proprietary interest. He's accustomed to my running in and out during the day, but expects our time together in the evenings to be uninterrupted. He generally hangs on the screen door until I return, calls for me the way a wild sparrow might who'd misplaced his mate. Seven answers B's chirps in a peevish voice, as if he's lost patience with a caller who's repeatedly dialed the same wrong number.

Last week I sat in the rocking chair in Baby's room after he'd finished playing in my hair. He'd eaten two pieces of corn and scattered most of a handful of millet on the floor. He flew to his house, drank a few sips of water, hopped into his nest, and settled with his beak resting on the edge. Diminishing sunlight mottled by moving leaves outside the windows worked all objects in the room into quaking things nearly rinsed of color. Very pretty, but animated with nervous energy, filled with motion as if a scene were changing and I were being hurried along in some broad sense regardless of how much I dragged my heels. There's a poster on the wall behind Baby's house, a black-and-white photograph taken by Edouard Boubat of two little French girls side by side on a Paris street in 1952—the year I was born.

The Kids called for service; B chirped at the heating grate, issued bulletins on his rising frustration. I sat looking at that poster until the girls' faces became indistinct. For all I could see, one child may have been the other. I wondered how many people there were with whom I was establishing an anonymous, inadvertent connection by yoking my thoughts to the same shift into darkness they may have watched from their own chairs during the bulk of a century this house has stood. Like me, passersby working to preserve themselves and whatever it was they loved from vanishing in a succession of instants superimposed on one another, an infinite regression of layers forever closed to inspection. If, however, the light cooperates, you can sometimes riffle the edges.

Seven sounded like a bird that would, if he had them, be on the phone with his lawyers demanding all he had coming to him. I recalled how upset Baby had been the day Rebecca grew tired of the poster under consideration, rolled it up, and put it away in a tube. We've never understood why, as a result, Baby refused to enter his house. I like to think he was making a statement about the value of art in our lives. Rebecca had to rehang it before Baby would go to bed that night.

There are few, if any, degrees of separation between our birds and most everything else in my daily life. A fact emphasized a few minutes later as, watching Pee Wee eat millet from my hand, I remembered Rebecca dressed in stretch pants and tank top in front of a full-length mirror practicing hip movements with Pee Wee riding on her shoulder—big movements in which a belly dancer's left and right hips heave alternately up and down, the trick being to do so while keeping every other part of the body still. Rebecca tells me she knows when she's doing it perfectly because Pee Wee doesn't wobble, isn't forced to cling, change her footing, or flick open a wing to stay balanced. Birds, poster, dance, light—they're really all of a piece.

IN AS FINE A DEMONSTRATION OF MULTITASKING AS I'VE EVER SEEN, B PREENS chest and belly feathers while he plays a moderately paced game of Hit the Cap. He's in excellent fettle on his special day, met me at the screen door with the dark blue cap he's hit so many times there's a hole punched through its center. Rebecca and I always think of June 10 as B's birthday even though it's actually the date we found him in the yard. Today, he turns eight. Rebecca will bake vanilla cupcakes this afternoon—chocolate is out of the question; it's poisonous to birds, as are rhubarb leaves and avocado. (Kudos to Rebecca for the way she's handled the chocolate prohibition. When the fever is upon her, she wallows in chocolate, certainly has the same kind of personal relationship with it as a four-year-old has with a Fudgsicle. Knowing, however, that our sparrows very much like grooming our fingernails, she washes thoroughly after dispatching anything with chocolate in it—cake, ice cream, brownies, or candy.) I'll get a kick out of watching B evaluate his cupcake. I've always felt he'd like to employ a court taster the way paranoid kings used to do. There won't be candles, but we'll sing "Happy Birthday." If there's anything sillier than a human being, I have yet to hear about it.

A few years ago, I attended a twentieth-birthday celebration for Scott and Linda's cat, Woody. Twelve or fifteen human guests showed up, a gathering of friends on a warm evening in July. It would be difficult to convince me that Woody remained oblivious to his role in the proceedings. You understood intellectually that he'd once been a young cat—a kitten even, but it was hard most of the time to summon up the requisite image from what your eyes were given to work with. He slept more of most of the time than younger cats do and had a pronounced totter when circumstance compelled him to get on his feet. Maybe it's me, but I've often thought that age, apart from the physical deterioration it brings, alters a cat's convictions, disarms it of whatever outlook is necessary in a creature that by nature kills for a living. Hard to tell with Woody—he'd always been such a gentle cat.

He was certainly at his best for the party, made an effort to mingle. I can see him eating his portion of birthday fish, Linda blowing out his candle for him. The strange thing was that he appeared in no hurry to retreat outside to his spot on the deck for a nap. You'd look down, and there he'd be at your feet staring up, either giving a benediction, it seemed, or hoping to receive one. His grave is marked with small stones beneath a stand of aspens in front of Scott and Linda's house.

"Wow, that bird of yours is still alive," people I haven't spoken with in years say to me. "Christ, how long do sparrows live, anyway?" It's fortunate my parents taught me to always be civil.

I fear B's death as much as I fear anything. I will grieve as deeply when he dies as I have over the loss of any person—an attitude many people understand, others find disturbing, a kind of blasphemy they seem to believe I'm guilty of that devalues human beings generally and threatens them personally. Why should there be improper objects of grief, despair apportioned to no avail, as if birds are of dust inferior to our own? As a young man, British writer Laurie Lee spent a year walking through Spain in the 1930s. In As I Walked Out One Midsummer's Morning, Lee's beautifully written memoir of his travels, he describes "Jorge, who'd trained a sparrow to sip other men's drinks and then carry them to his mouth by the beakful. When the bird died, said Jorge, he would weep, weep, weep." One is left wondering which he'd mourn more: the loss of the bird or the loss of stolen liquor. But it's clear to me. Assuming, that is, that Jorge was my brother under the skin despite whatever differences we may have had over the propriety of expecting our birds to provide us with alcohol.

Looking like a restaurant patron evaluating lobsters in a tank, B examines bits of hazelnut I've placed on his saucer. He circles the rim with the spirit of honest inquiry animating his face, stops periodically, taps his front toes as if impatient with his own inability to make a decision. I suppose when I dice nuts with my fingernail I must inadvertently facet them into angles and planes that B's eyes resolve into details worth seeing. He rearranges a few slivers with his beak, picks one up and spits it out, flies to the self-serve area on top of the television to have a go at the spinach. I'd like to know why B, Baby, and Pee Wee all eat spinach by pulling pieces from the leaf in a direct frontal attack, whereas Seven shears off portions using his beak as a scissors. Why, for that matter, have I never grown tired of the sound B's wings make when he lands on my shoulder? I can't say it's the same incomparable thrill it was the first time he flew to me, but, as repeat experiences go, it's paled very little.

Rebecca enters wearing a blue pullover shirt with a colorful butterfly silk-screened on the front. She parks herself next to me on the couch, and B zooms from my hand. He has no ax to grind with moths in the flesh but has a problem with psychedelic butterflies on the clothing of his servants. He isn't mollified by Rebecca's "Good morning, B. Happy Birthday, big guy." He stands on his house giving her The Look, flicks his tail, mutters oaths. They've argued this point before. "B, why do you hate this butterfly?" she asks. "It's a lovely butterfly." I've timed these feuds, and three minutes is the longest Rebecca holds out. Their eyes lock—she removes the shirt and then replaces it inside out. B lands on my knee with a respectable thud (birds can be surprisingly heavy-footed), galumphs from there up to my chest. He regards Rebecca sideways, his head tilted forty-five degrees to port. Rebecca says she feels "like an employee who's had two written warnings and is about to be fired."

B turns eight today. I've heard of house sparrows living to be thirteen or fourteen, that the oldest on record was twenty-three. Eight years already spent, an upper limit fixed in biology, chance, or the mind of God. Most days I trust the timelessness we have in this room to keep us locked in a circle that veers back on itself in an infinity of arcs, an illusion that works best on days when milestones don't intrude with their intimations of immutable tenses. I don't suppose birthdays hold meaning for B, busy as he is with more immediate concerns such as pulling Rebecca's hair and glancing at me to see if I'm watching. But I believe he knows, in his way, that humans didn't convene eternity. That we neither control it nor own it.

KBPS plays Papageno's aria from Mozart's Magic Flute, "I am the birdcatcher, always merry, tra, la, la!" I'm curled on the love seat, my legs drawn up, B napping on my neck. I've had a kind of reverie, the music molding reality as long as I remained balanced on the edge of sleep. For a while I was Papageno, exhilarated to be in the woods—dressed in feathers, a big cage strapped to my back, panpipes in my hand. I woke remembering a day when I was twelve and early at St. Matthew's for catechism class. I found Father Phillipson in the nave taking potshots at two frantic birds flapping near the ceiling at the approximate longitude of the communion rail. An armed priest in a cassock is especially distinctive if he's striding past the stations of the cross, wending between pews, and firing bird shot in the air at a pair of doomed pigeons.

B stands up from my neck, puffs out his feathers, and stretches. I'm acutely aware of the warm spot his body leaves on my skin, more so when it's touched by the breeze from his wings flitting him up to the finger I offer. A bird's eyes supposedly become less lustrous as it ages. Since running across this disturbing factoid, I occasionally stare at B's eyes in a clinical way. Exactly the kind of thing I could become systematic (and obsessed) about checking. The reason I haven't is because I can't rely on what would necessarily be a subjective interpretation of what I was seeing. Imagination would soon dominate the procedure, needlessly upping my anxiety level. As it is, my temples throb with the thought of life and brightness linked in B's face, the latter diminishing as the former is spent. When looking to see in B's eyes the same gleaming points of reflected light so prominent in, for example, two-year-old Seven's pitch-black orbs, I have to admit that B's twin beams are dimmer by comparison. I recognize, as well, that his activity level has decreased somewhat over the past year or so. Less sustained is how I'd put it. He now takes breaks after fifteen minutes of intense exertion; earlier in his career he'd play games by the hour.

I've given Birthday Boy a teal-colored cap as a present. He pulled it from my pocket, flicked it to the floor, pecked it to death next to my foot. Strange to associate the clicking of plastic on wood with the sound of contentment. One tap at a time, B nudges his gift upward on my thigh, hinting broadly that I take some initiative. He pauses for a count of three between each hit. He nods his head, fans his tail, opens his beak slightly, and does something with his tongue that might be possible to describe if English had at least one more verb. I hook my finger over the rim and tug, and B yanks back with a vengeance, his feet dug in as if there's an immediate possibility of being dragged off a cliff. Rebecca is next door handing out grape to Baby and The Kids; I catch the words "birthday," "eight today," and "you'll get cake too." She's as certifiable as I am.

It's now nearly ten o'clock, and I've only just killed the overhead light. B has been fighting sleep, mad to continue playing with his cap. Loud pops coming sporadically from outside have made him edgy. The part of

Fourth of July that involves gunpowder begins earlier every year. As holidays go, this is the one tailored to the sensibilities of teenage boys or, for that matter, the lumpen of all ages. It used to be that Rebecca and I could expect a few preliminary volleys on July 3, combat conditions on the Fourth itself, an impotent reprise on the night of the fifth. Fireworks season now begins in June. The sticking point is that it's hard on our birds; on most animals, I suspect. The stray cat we feed every night makes himself scarce.

There appears to be a segment of the population that equates sublime entertainment with creating and/or listening to an ongoing series of explosions. My twenty-something brother-in-law's infatuation with mindless noise is a perfect example of what I mean. His concept of an afterlife must involve merging not with the godhead but with an inexhaustible supply of firecrackers and bottle rockets. Although no longer an adolescent (chronologically, at any rate), he's addicted to shattering the peace of rural Montana by going into the woods after dark and blowing something up. Rebecca has tried reasoning with him to no avail. Our suggestion that he's destroying the sleep, if not the health, of countless birds and other woodland creatures strikes him as risible. Should a cherry bomb go off some night within thirty feet of his bed while he sleeps, Rebecca says she'll vouch for my whereabouts.

Except for a kid dribbling a basketball down the street, it's quiet outside. Rebecca collects her debris, says goodnight to B, describes in set terms what she'll do for him come morning. He punctuates each word that interests him—Cheerio, War Bird, kisses, games—by tossing or inclining his head as she speaks. He watches her exit, returns his attention to me when the outer door to his room clicks shut. I cross to the table lamp; B plumps in my hand, nestles himself against the sudden darkness that comes every night at the flick of a switch. He greets it, as is his custom, with four barely audible clucks.

This scene, played out at least two thousand times, is as regular and tranquil as evensong in a monastery. "May we play it thousands more," I whisper to an eight-year-old bird whose trust in me is boundless. Against my shortcomings must be balanced the fact that I've never broken faith with this creature—a thought B might take exception to, seeing as how I haven't honored his wish that I drop anchor permanently in this room. Of course, it's possible I'm flattering myself. Better to say I've never broken faith as far as it's been within my power to give B a good (if unusual) life for a house sparrow. Without the luxury of sitting down and discussing these things, or an exchange of position papers, all I can do is hope that he knows I've worked hard to further his interests. And it may well be he's happy to get rid of me for part of the day, wouldn't be the first time a sentient being has taken that view. Could be he spends his alone time riddling over what lies beyond this house—a world I appear to dip in and out of at will, a world symbolized by the sky and trees he sees from these windows. Maybe it's my flightlessness or my otherness or the mystery of our connection that sometimes occupies his thoughts; I wish I knew. But if, as Rebecca suggests, B is my familiar, my totem, my spirit animal, he concedes through his actions that I, equally, am his.

Reaction to an exploding firecracker ripples through B's body into my skin—his neurons ignite for an instant, light up pathways unsealed from sleep; sentry calls to sentry and back again with the message, "You're safe in the hand that has never harmed you." He untucks his beak from the right shoulder, retucks it in the left. I lift him to my face, kiss his head, inhale his scent—a subtle musk noticeable during mating season, again when he molts. It's as if I'm sniffing a nosegay of feathers. And into these feathers I pray an agnostic's half-assed prayer, asking whatever in the universe is good and kind to "Please watch over and protect this bird."

NEWS THAT HOUSE SPARROW NUMBERS ARE DECLINING IN ENGLAND IS partially offset by the bumper crop at our feeding area this year. A mated pair I call Big Bib and Stumpy (when I first made her acquaintance, she was growing new tail feathers) function as titular leaders of a group of about fifty birds that hangs around or near our house. Big Bib and Stumpy watch me. They know I'm the one who usually provides fresh seed, the one who tosses out bread—a popular commodity during months when ravenous hatchlings are shrieking to be fed. It took weeks, dullard that I am, until I sorted out how these two birds manage to be waiting on the porch banister or fence gate every other time I walk outside. Or often enough, at any rate, to preclude coincidence as an explanation.

At first, I thought they'd hit on the idea of ensuring themselves first place in the breadline by simply waiting on hand for bread to appear. Since people desperate to snag concert tickets are inane enough to camp on sidewalks overnight, I figured house sparrows were smart enough to adapt the technique for procuring food. Eventually, I noticed that the chances of finding Big Bib and Stumpy in attendance were decidedly better if I'd recently come down from upstairs, far slimmer if I hadn't. Turns out they monitor the window on the stairway landing overlooking the patio. They laze in the photinia bushes until they see me pass by on my way downstairs—their cue to fly out front and await developments.

Stumpy flits back and forth across the porch when I open the front door; sometimes she'll hover there to make certain I've seen her. My bona fides are such that she'll land for the dime-size piece of bread I've placed on the banister, land with me only inches away. Meanwhile, Big Bib sits on the fence railing with members of the entourage that trailed behind when he and Stumpy made their appearance. Although nothing about this operation involves dead fish in a bucket, I now know what it's like to feed a group of hungry seals.

I'll have about fifteen sparrows lined up on the railing, poised in readiness for the shower of bread to begin. One or two grab their piece before it hits the ground. The rest dive for the sidewalk, scramble for what they can get; others chase bits of runaway hazelnut, which, considering how well hazelnuts bounce, may as well be constructed of rubber. More sparrows drop in as word of the bounty spreads. Stumpy avoids the fray by returning to the banister for additional helpings. Big Bib waits for the crowd to disperse. In a gesture of noblesse oblige, he takes nothing for himself until the other birds have gotten their share.

We have house sparrows in our trees, in our bushes, peering at us from the edges of the roof. They arrive singly, in pairs, with fledglings in tow. I listen in admiration as their alarm calls sound when the neighbor's cat is on the prowl, appreciate their fine discrimination in ignoring the gentle stray that often camps on our porch, a cat they've accurately pegged as a confirmed nonhunter. A female I recognize rises from the sidewalk with bread in her beak. She heads four houses away to her brood—vocal but obscured behind a gap in the flashing. It's worth the effort to keep the birdbath scrubbed and filled with fresh water; it's worth what we spend on bread and seed.

I sometimes stand on the porch feeling as if it's the border between two worlds. I can see B on his window perch if I crane my neck. Fifteen feet to my left is the spot where he fell to earth; above it, his eave. It's been vacant the past couple of years, but on the theory that you never can tell, I regularly monitor the ground below. I hear Seven and Baby swearing at each other beneath Clive's boisterous song that blasts out from the side of the house and mixes with the chatter of the wild sparrows perched in the bushes. They are the broader reality against which I measure what B and his fellow lodgers have lost and gained.

Three days after the equinox and the first storm of autumn is here. All five finches are together on a windowsill watching big drops of rain splat against the glass. With the shortening days, B now goes to bed early enough in the evenings that Rebecca and I are able to once again step into the social whirl of eating dinner in restaurants that don't have the words "Open All Night" on their signs.

This is fine as far as it goes. We emerge for part of the year as more fully engaged members of the human community. "Vampires," Rebecca calls us, that rise in the dark months. I look forward to this time, but regret that the price I pay is fewer hours with B. The day will arrive when one more moment with him will be the only thing I truly want. I try willing these instants to a spurious halt by watching, as intently as I can, B's respiration as he sleeps in my hand. He's almost completed his molt (early for a change), and again I'm taken with how exquisite he is, how perfected and beautiful without mangled tail feathers marring his sleekness.

I was thinking recently about my fifth-grade teacher, a severe, angular woman who had no patience for the fact that children didn't behave like miniature adults. She frightened me into learning how to diagram sentences and inadvertently set my aesthetic expectations vis-à-vis house sparrows— referring to them that moving as "dingy little birds," "dingy" being an adjective she'd already applied to the snow in the gutters through which she herded us on a field trip over to Neidig's Dairy. I'd love a word with her now. Grant her point about the snow but explain that because things have turned out strangely for me, I can't subscribe to her house sparrow stance. "Miss Kepner," I'd say, "let me tell you about B."

EPILOGUE

REBECCA'S NOTE ON THE CALENDAR READS, "TODAY OUR SORROW BEGINS."
The date marked is November 26, 2002—two days before Thanksgiving.
B is in the past, and I am broken, and Rebecca is broken, and we sag
through these days as if our bones have deserted us. Only now, three
months after his death, can I bring myself to sit in his room.

Our relatives and friends were more than kind. Some brought food;
some sent flowers; others "In Memoriam" tendered donations to wildlife groups. Establishing a House Sparrow Anti-Defamation League is,
I'm certain, how B would want this money spent, but Rebecca and I are
grateful for these gestures, nonetheless. Cards arrived; messages blinked
on our answering machine.

Letters from strangers continue trickling in. These people tell me
about themselves, about aspects of their lives B's story apparently
touches on: One woman freed her parakeets from their cage. A daughter nursing her handicapped parents is no longer certain she is the victim. A couple who've lost a child want me to know how thoroughly
they believe we understand one another. Whenever a beloved life
winks out, distinctions, they say, are irrelevant.

It wasn't a good death. There was unused time on B's meter we
failed to redeem. Of course, birds are notorious for hiding symptoms
when they're sick, a fact that does little to ease the remorse I carry for
not realizing sooner that B was ill. He died of a treatable condition mis-

diagnosed as a virus—a more or less benign complaint the vet assured us would run its course without danger to the patient. Unfortunately, she overlooked a minute cut on B's right foot with a cavalier attitude to detail that's never a virtue in medical personnel. By the time we took him to an avian specialist several days later, antibiotics were useless. Blood vessels networking through a bird's feet meander through its kidneys, the place where a strain of staphylococcus settled in B. Uremic poisoning resulted—the kind of auto-toxicity that may have killed Mozart.

Steam rises from the street during the second sun break we've had in an hour. Wisps of vapor scuttle over the base of our maple tree out front—B's tree as I've come to regard it. For a week or so in October, its leaves flood this room in an aureate glow; in spring, house sparrows and other birds dine in the mornings on the pale green buds. For almost ten years, B and I watched these changes as they cycled through our temperate season. What wouldn't I give to sense him on my shoulder, if only in that way amputees reclaim severed limbs via spurious itching or phantom pain? The mind recoils from loss, fills in gaps as best it can. And if B should materialize, what proof would I accept I haven't sewn his form from the whole cloth of my missing him? And where is he now if he still exists? I imagine acreage that discourages trespass, a place where B is happy, if not already in charge. Because I'm unprepared to visit him there, I beckon his shade to visit me here—defying the logic of what I really believe. I hope Beddoes erred when he wrote,

> There are no ghosts to raise;
> Out of death lead no ways;
> Vain is the call.

We recently paired Monday and Bert with two zebra finch females, Abby and Anne. The boys, thrilled to have girlfriends, fill the room with sexual chatter—a welcome sound that tempers the dirges that have palled our thoughts since last November. Rebecca brought the sisters home from a bird show, named them after the advice columnists and told me not to be startled should they ask us in finch-speak to get counseling for our grief, an option I'd consider if I found myself obsessed with maintaining a shrine. Not that the thought didn't appeal to me during those first weeks after B closed his eyes and died in my hand. For days I pondered Absolute Zero—the perfect absence of heat and an unavailing metaphor to describe what I felt. I craved more and better words, ways to negotiate a loss I'd pre-grieved for years.

There wasn't any point in leaving B at the vet's. Other than keeping him on oxygen, there was little they could do. By early afternoon it became evident he was dying, and we wanted to take him home. He was uncomfortable, I think, but not in pain, his vent tender from urine burn caused by his growing inability to eliminate waste. Rebecca and I sat with him on the couch I'm sitting on now, the site of so many good years during which the three of us became an unlikely trinity—"Husband, Wife and Holy Beast," someone once called us. As the hours passed, B grew weaker, his appetite fading, the poisons in his system shutting him down. We struggled for a while to clean him out using special Q-Tips the vet had given us. But you know when you're beaten and heroics are misplaced. Around five o'clock, I left the room for a few minutes, stepped outside to clear my head. B had given up flying an hour beforehand, nestled in my hand, desperate to nap. He was very weak. I shifted him to Rebecca who cupped him in her palm, holding him beneath her chin, tears welling in her eyes. Upon my return, sick as he was, B struggled from her hands to get to me. A few minutes before six, he quivered, gasped and was gone. My dearest friend was gone.

Although it's impossible for me to imagine any scenario under which B's death would have been propitious, the timing of it was particularly bad. The hardback edition of *Providence of a Sparrow* had come out two months before (I regret not taking pictures of B atop a copy of the book), and I had numerous promotional commitments in Washington state, a block of them scheduled for the first weeks of December. The prospect of hitting the road to do bookstore readings was not an attractive one. "I'll call and cancel for you," Rebecca said. She looked like hell; I looked worse. We anesthetized ourselves with videos and awoke in the morning exhausted by sleep. November is a goblin here even in the best of times; it tinkers with your mind and does something to hinges. Thanksgiving Day we filled plastic containers with bird food, drove downtown to feed hungry sparrows—pissed-off groups of them that hung around the deserted light rail tracks waiting for their customary patrons who were at home eating turkey. Rain fell off and on, and everything had that preserved-ruins aspect that cities assume when the tribe is elsewhere. We drifted through the streets until we ran out of seed.

Late in the afternoon, we stumbled across a tiny Russian restaurant that was inexplicably open. The owner (Boris, naturally) was cheerful and couldn't have seemed happier had we dropped by to rob him. Muttering to himself in his native tongue, he prepared our order—two bowls of borsch, pirogues stuffed with potatoes and cabbage. Seated beneath a glossy poster of the Manhattan skyline lit up by fireworks, we ate our Thanksgiving dinner, no B to go home to.

I decided I'd do the readings. Chalk it up to the restorative properties of Russian food on an empty stomach. B was gone, but Rebecca and I needed to eat, the directive to survive rising from the guts as it always does. In that odd little restaurant that may have darted into existence because we required the distraction as well as the nourishment, we downed our first substantial meal in almost two days. I reckoned my grief in Rebecca's face and she, doubtless, saw her own pain in mine, our redirected fortune knitting us together as we pondered in silence the loss of our anchor. "Having B was such a privilege," she said at last, "such a privilege." Vouchsafed a small mystery of infinite proportions, we'd been fortunate, indeed. The least I could do for B was present his biography to those who would listen.

Too upset to do otherwise, Rebecca took time off work and accompanied me on this leg of the tour. All went according to form. I'd show up early, find a place to have coffee and sit marking passages I intended to read. Event coordinators asked me if I needed anything, pointed out the lectern and divulged the location of my free glass of water. Before going on, I checked my watch, my glasses, and my zipper. Rebecca brushed lint from my jacket and fussed with my hair in a losing battle to make me presentable. I felt gaunt. B-reft.

Ten minutes past the hour is when these things typically begin—after stragglers take their seats and once whoever's emceeing has run through a list of upcoming events. As a rule, facing an audience doesn't unnerve me, but these appearances were different, and I shifted into performance mode with diminished faith in the script, its defects rendering it scant consolation for the loss of the creature it attempts to describe. And I knew—knew absolutely—that during the question and answer session following the reading that someone would ask, "And how's B doing, I'll bet he misses you when you're away like this?" Not even Rebecca noticed me glancing at my shoulder when I replied that B was fine and that I was reasonably certain he missed me very much.

B's door remains open now. The finches won't venture past the threshold, but the canaries visit, as do Baby, Pee Wee and Seven. Whatever agenda they have doesn't include colonizing this space—whether out of deference to B or satisfaction with what they already have, I cannot say. For the first time in years, a pair of house sparrows is building a nest in the eaves. I glimpse them through the window, coming and going with dried grass in their beaks. We wish them many strong children in return for reminding us of the redemptive quality of continuity—a necessary concept for Rebecca and me to remember as we contemplate changes to this room and teach ourselves to live here once again.

Printed in the United States
by Baker & Taylor Publisher Services